John --

for
sug

over

years now!

RUPERT BROOKE IN THE FIRST WORLD WAR

Alisa Miller

RUPERT BROOKE IN THE FIRST WORLD WAR

Alisa Miller

CLEMSON
UNIVERSITY
PRESS

First Edition, 2017

ISBN: 978-1-942954-34-7 (print)
eISBN: 978-1-942954-35-4 (e-book)

Published by Clemson University Press
in association with Liverpool University Press

For information about Clemson University Press,
please visit our website at www.clemson.edu/press.

Library of Congress Cataloging-in-Publication Data
Names: Miller, Alisa, 1980- author.
Title: Rupert Brooke in the First World War / Alisa Miller.
Description: First edition. | Clemson : Clemson University Press, 2017. |
Includes bibliographical references and index.
Identifiers: LCCN 2017023597 (print) | LCCN 2017035737 (ebook) | ISBN
978-1-942954-35-4 (e-book) | ISBN 978-1-942954-34-7 (print)
Subjects: LCSH: Brooke, Rupert, 1887-1915. | Poets, English--20th
century--Biography. | Soldiers--Great Britain--Biography.
Classification: LCC PR6003.R4 (ebook) | LCC PR6003.R4 Z715 2017 (print)
| DDC 821/.912 [B] --dc23
LC record available at https://lccn.loc.gov/2017023597

Typeset in Minion Pro by Carnegie Book Production.
Printed and bound in Poland by BooksFactory.co.uk

Contents

Acknowledgements

This book has had a long, intermittent gestation, resulting in a large number of people to whom I owe acknowledgements and thanks. This also means that there is a great likelihood that I will leave people off, accidentally. So to all who have contributed to the book over the years, in any number of ways, thank you.

I would like to thank Professor David Stevenson, who first discussed the project with me when I was an MA student at the London School of Economics. Dr Alexander Sedlmaier and Professor Hew Strachan agreed to supervise the Oxford thesis that provided the bones for this book, initially comprised of some very long, rather obscure and convoluted sentences (hopefully mostly clarified in this version): their patience, expert advice, and support were and are very much appreciated. Thanks also to Dr Adrian Gregory and my examiners Professor Roy Foster and Professor Jay Winter, who gave me a tough but considered viva that helped enormously – even years later – in reshaping the text for publication. The late Professor Jon Stallworthy was incredibly kind and generous in offering not only his personal advice and perspective on poetry and publishing, but also in offering the full support of the Brooke Estate for the project.

I should also mention the American Friends at Christ Church for their generosity in providing three years of invaluable funding. Thank you also to the Hartley family for offering free accommodation during many extended archival visits to Cambridge. Work on the First World War Poetry Digital Archive enabled me to undertake research in the United Kingdom and at the Berg Collection in New York, providing me with a broader awareness of the literature and archives relating to the war poets of the period: many thanks to Professor Stuart Lee and Kate Lindsay for enabling me to be part of that wonderful project.

Moving to the years when I put the draft to one side to work on research policy, only to return to ponder it from time to time, I would like to thank my colleagues at GuildHE and CREST, the University of Chichester and Norwich University of the Arts for their perspectives. Many thanks also to colleagues at King's College London, including those working on the European Research Council-funded projects 'Beyond Enemy Lines' and 'Ego-Media': particularly Dr Lara Feigel, Professor Max Saunders, Professor Clare Brant, Professor Bill Philpott, Dr Santana Das, and Ania Stawarska for their insightful comments and patient ears as I prepared the final draft.

Acknowledgement and thanks are owed to Patricia McGuire and Peter Monteith who were so welcoming and knowledgeable over the course of the many years I spent visiting the rich archives at King's College, Cambridge, and who helped with the images. I am grateful that the Trustees of the Duncan Grant Estate allowed me to use the artist's portrait of Brooke for the cover of this volume.

The list of friends and colleagues who have offered advice and support is very long indeed, but I would like to single out (in no particular order): Professor Marcia Pointon, Dr James Kitchen, Dr Paul Stock, Dr Monica Steinel, Dr Miranda Kaufmann, Anne Tovatt, John Springford, Dr Daniel Steinbach, Dr Thomas Morton, Dr Scarlet Baron, Dr Eleanor Thompson, Dr Pierre Purseigle, Professor Suzie Hanna, Victoria Mitchell, and John and Veronica Porter. Jonathan Conway deserves a special mention for taking so much time in discussing earlier drafts of the manuscript, and in helping me to conceive of it as a proper book. Professor Jonathan Marwil, who supervised my first tentative efforts at cultural historical writing in the guise of my undergraduate thesis at the University of Michigan, has been a stalwart, tough yet encouraging voice for many years now.

I am eternally grateful to Dr John Morgenstern, who as editor provided both encouragement and critical advice, and to his colleagues at Clemson University Press and Liverpool University Press for their work on the book. I think this is the point to say: any mistakes contained within are my own.

Finally it is only left to thank my immediate and extended family, and in particular my wonderful, ever-supportive and generous parents and their partners, as well the Weeks and Geddes families. I wanted to mention three especial bibliophiles – my Aunt Kathy Kissman, Amelia Moore, and my late Grandma Nina Miller – for instilling in me a love of reading and writing (more the former, less the latter, perhaps, but the two go hand in hand).

And, finally, much gratitude is owed to my husband James Weeks, for his patience, sense of humour, love, and support.

Introduction

As afternoon descended aboard the deck of the *Duguay-Trouin*, a French hospital ship anchored in Trebuki Bay near the Greek island of Scyros, Arthur Asquith and Denis Browne faced a decision. Their good friend and fellow officer Rupert Brooke had just died of a blood infection, the only patient aboard an eerily quiet French hospital ship awaiting casualties from what everyone agreed was sure to be a great battle, set to commence the following day. Asquith's and Browne's division was under orders to set sail for Gallipoli at 6 a.m.: 'Our escorting battleships open fire on the Turks at 5 a.m.'[1]

Both agreed that Brooke would not have wanted to be buried at sea, and decided to take him to the island of Scyros. They had support from on high; Winston Churchill, then First Lord of the Admiralty, had followed Brooke's deterioration from London. He sent a telegram to Major John Churchill to encourage him to attend the funeral as his representative. He was too late, but Major Churchill wrote back, reassuring him that 'poor Rupert Brooke' had had a 'most romantic funeral'.[2] Even General Sir Ian Hamilton, responsible for overseeing the Gallipoli landings, paused to reflect: 'Alas, what a misfortune! ... He was bound, he said, to see this first fight through with his fellows.'[3]

1

Churchill's private secretary and Brooke's close friend, Edward Marsh, had already contacted Brooke's mother, Mary, to inform her of the situation. In Rugby, she grieved the death of her second son; Richard, the eldest, had died of pneumonia in 1907, followed by his father a few years later. Mary's tragedy would soon be compounded when her youngest son, Alfred, was killed in action near Loos in June 1915, less than two months after the death of his by then famous brother.

Browne went ahead with another fellow officer and friend, Charles Lister, to Scyros with the digging party comprised of men from the Hood Battalion, Royal Naval Division. They set to work on an inland grave nestled picturesquely in a grove of olive trees; ironically, Brooke had sketched sections of the hill where he was buried just a few days before his death.[4] Back aboard the *Duguay-Trouin*, the French sailors constructed a makeshift plinth for the coffin out of small palm trees. As the sky darkened, Asquith burnt Brooke's name and the date of his death into the wood, and the sailors draped the coffin with the British flag. On Scyros, Browne and the men lined the grave with sprigs of olive and flowering sage, hammered out two simple crosses in white wood, and recorded Brooke's name in black paint.

Meanwhile, aboard the Battalion's transport ship, the *Grantully Castle*, a party of officers set off to collect the coffin. They were towed in to the shallows by a steam pinnace supplied by a ship anchored nearby with the rest of the fleet. By now the sky was black, the moon clouded over, and only the gently bobbing lights were visible to Browne and his men as they waited onshore. Once the coffin was unloaded onto the island, it took the twelve bearers more than an hour to reach the gravesite. Asquith had to lengthen the hole with a spade to make the coffin fit. The Battalion's colonel threw in an olive wreath, and the Chaplain read the burial service of the Church of England. Volleys were fired, and arms presented; the Last Post rang out. As the group made their way back to the ship to prepare for the morning, a few of Brooke's fellow officers stayed behind to build a cairn from the stones of pink and white marble that littered the site. On the smaller cross, the Battalion's interpreter inscribed an epitaph in Greek:

Here lies
the servant of God,
sub-lieutenant in the English Navy,
who died for the deliverance of Constantinople from the
Turks

The men agreed that whoever survived the coming battle would return to the grave to build a wall around it.[5] All in all it was considered by those present to be a timeless – even mythical – farewell: 'no one could wish him a burial place of more beauty or glamour'.

*

Most readers know that Rupert Brooke died from an infected mosquito bite without ever having experienced battle. It was not a death that the most famous of English poet-soldiers of the First World War would have chosen. Arthur Asquith noted the anticlimax in a letter to Marsh: 'If he had to die, how one wished it could have been by a bullet.'[6]

The conventional biographical tropes prefiguring that fateful day in April 1914 – Rugby, Cambridge, Grantchester, poetry, and death – are well known, and can be easily summed up in a quick and neat paragraph. One can be forgiven for thinking that they speak of a privileged, if not exceptional, existence and, had it come to pass, a promising future. Certainly, the publication of the famous 'War Sonnets', as they came to be known, might, in other times and under different circumstances, have passed unnoticed. 'The Soldier' provided some very quotable lines: 'If I should die, think only this of me: / That there's some corner of a foreign field / That is for ever England.'[7] Yet the First World War inspired plenty of war poetry – and provided plenty of young martyrs – for readers to draw inspiration from. The question persists, what made Brooke exceptional? Why – and how – did he achieve a mythical status during the war? From 1914 to 1920 Brooke's poetry and prose sold more than 100,000 copies in Britain alone.[8] He was translated into numerous languages and was extremely popular in the United States, where he was considered to be one of Britain's great exports. At home and abroad he became simply 'England's Poet-Soldier';[9] a fated exemplar of patriotic sacrifice feeding a growing celebrity.

Brooke caught only the edge of the maelstrom that others experienced head-on. While in his most famous poems Wilfred Owen dissects the war's violence and degradations within a rigorous formal poetic structure and achieves a kind of timeless transcendence rooted in specific experiences, in 1914, Brooke, also a gifted formalist, inspired by and looking to distil the general sentiments of the first months of the war, turned away from the realistic style he had begun to develop in earlier verses. Since he worked with limited material, he ended up projecting his expectations of what was to come onto an unknown future. His poetry imagined what he thought this modern war would – or at least should – be like, but stopped well short of illuminating its horrors. His friend E. J. Dent noted the exceptional nature of the War Sonnets: 'In the first shock of the moment that romanticism he so hated came uppermost'.[10]

In the end, Brooke's hazy poetic impressions would prove sufficient to feed a myth about the poet-soldier that persists to this day. His tragic and glamorous image – his very 'English' life, his connections, and his timely death – form the basis for an archetype that still resonates, even as the poetry that appealed to readers from 1914 to 1918 has been downgraded in the canon. Scarcely a war drama does not contain its requisite scribe. Sometimes the approach to the character is comic. F. J. Robert's *The Wipers Times*, published in the trenches around Ypres from February 1916 to December 1918, was already parodying the poet-soldier that Richard Curtis and Ben Elton returned to in *Blackadder Goes Forth* (1989). Tom Sharpe's *Porterhouse Blue* (1974) and *Grantchester Grind* (1994) make full use of the Brooke figure; the television series, adapted by Malcolm Bradbury for Channel 4 in 1987, includes a vignette of a crusty Fellow of the fictitious Cambridge college advising a young undergraduate to take inspiration from the closing lines of 'The Soldier' while working out his sexual energies with au pairs and language students.

Further literary examples abound. Ernest Raymond named the narrator of *Tell England* (1922) Rupert Ray; the typified Brooke reappears throughout the novel in various guises as well as in the film adaptation, released in 1931. He reappears again as the tragically absent brother hovering over Dorothy Whipple's popular family drama *The Priory* (1939). His most serious (indirect) literary reincarnation was undertaken by Brooke's friend Virginia Woolf in her modernist novel *Jacob's Room* (1922), in which – critically – the portrait of the vague, beautiful young man even prior to his death in the war is drawn almost solely from the impressions of those around him.[11] Alan Hollinghurst's *The Stranger's Child* (2011) recasts the poet-soldier in the person of the aristocratic (which Brooke was not) Cecil Valance. Seducer of both men and women, he is another victim of the First World War who writes a poem that is promoted by Churchill, and subsequently secures a place in the common consciousness. These are just a few examples of 'Rupert Brooke', reborn in various popular forms.

It helped in 1915, and ever after, that Brooke was beautiful. He was fair and rumpled, with floppy, bright hair and striking colouring: literally and figuratively the 'golden boy'. In widely accessible photographs he always appeared younger than he actually was. In terms of popularity, throughout Brooke's life his charm and good looks increased his immediate appeal to friends and potential champions. In Henry James's words, reading Brooke's poems, 'which one had first to read while he was still there to be exquisitely at stake in them … is a sort of refinement both of admiration & of anguish'.[12] During the war his looks made him more marketable and more compelling to readers. He looked the part of the romantic hero, and when he died the aesthetic sacrifice – the loss of not just any poet but, like Byron, a *beautiful* poet – added to the sense of a perfect tragedy. His perfect image became so ubiquitous during the war that Pat Barker, in a chilling sequence in her novel *Toby's Room* (2012), uses his face for the mask worn by the disfigured protagonist when he ventures out drinking in London: 'Gradually, uncertainly, people began to respond, raising their glasses, smiling ghost smiles at what must have seemed, to most of them, a ghost'.[13]

Many wartime readers, feeling their way through a horrible war, responded fervently to the death of the poet-soldier. The scale of the tragedy unfolding in the bucolic Belgian and French countryside, in the gritty desserts of Mesopotamia and on the blazing beaches of Galli-poli, must have seemed incomprehensible. People needed figures like Brooke to humanise the experience, and to focus public and private grief. They also needed, and in many cases preferred, entertainment, distraction, and beauty.

After his death Brooke appeared to offer a blank canvas on which to project the sentiments and ideals of the war's survivors. He also offered them a vision of death that was poignant as opposed to jarring: the notion that the dead would live on, as Brooke put it in 'The Soldier', as a 'pulse in the eternal mind',[14] was both a comfort and shield against dark thoughts for many readers. Not every soldier, let alone all of the civilians who participated in the war and are examined in this account of it wished to face its stark terrors directly. Many wanted nothing more than to look beyond its ugly surface and be reassured that, in the end, all of the suffering and death meant something more than the sum of its parts.

Rupert Brooke was not a blank canvas. He was first a young man bounded by particular circumstances and experiences. The world that existed from 1914 to 1918, ironically, killed *and* created the poet-soldier: a world that, despite all attempts at literary and cinematic reconstructions, remains cloaked, ghostly, and strangely inacces-sible. It may be common territory, but it is not familiar. To borrow the memoirist, poet, and soldier Edmund Blunden's haunted sentiment as he attempted to convey the true 'image and horror of it', we 'must go over the ground again'[15] to gain a sense of both the romance and disgust the war inspired in its perpetrators, witnesses, and victims.

Brooke is likewise both familiar and unknown. Biographically, he has received plenty of coverage, which has led to a greater under-standing of the man: of his moodiness, his prejudices, his complicated relationships with women and his homosexual experiences.[16] What has received less careful attention is the process by which – and in what forms – the ideals and texts associated with the myth 'reached the hands, and therefore potentially the minds, of different constituencies of readers … of how knowledge was constituted and diffused, how opinions were formed and consolidated' and how 'group identities were constructed'.[17] How and why was this one young man distilled down to become the ultimate incarnation of an ideal, *the* poet-soldier, dead for England's sake: in his own words, 'If I should die, think *only* this of me'?[18] By deconstructing and examining the language, the overlapping political and literary networks and the media mechanisms – some of which are recognisable in their purposes, forms, and methods today – that promoted the syndication of the myth, it becomes possible to pin down his particular celebrity. We can better comprehend the prevailing attitudes towards war, celebrity, and sacrifice, and move closer to reconstructing the frame of mind that made the First World War possible and – whether or not you consider this a good or a bad thing – endurable.

I

Life

1

Youth

Rupert Brooke grew up in an age when, to an extent, the Victorian order held. Loosening but resolute class structures and respect if not devotion to the monarchy still influenced the lives of people living and dying in Great Britain, holding together a system that sometimes buckled but refused to fracture completely. In Europe, as in Britain, the old system was far from harmonious: localised wars in the Balkans, the pressures and exploitations of empires, and the blusterings of the Great Powers did from time to time threaten the collective peace. Closer to home, labour unrest, Irish nationalists, and suffragettes ensured that political violence remained familiar to Brooke and the polity.

This was also a period when, particularly for the secure middle classes, decorous, considered social progress and reform seemed possible – and indeed preferable – to fractured and violent alternatives. The Brookes were a solidly middle-class, conservatively progressive, educated family, having sent their sons to Cambridge for two generations. In the eighteenth century, they had risen from tenant farmers to established gentlemen: Rupert's grandfather Richard England became Rector of Bath Abbey and Chairman of the School Board, a pillar of provincial Victorian society. Brooke's father, William Parker, was the second of five children. Dependable and studious, small of stature, he excelled at Latin and Greek, winning the school prize for these subjects at Haileybury, followed by a scholarship to Trinity College, Cambridge. He ended up moving to King's College, which had previously only accepted students from Eton, quietly and without fanfare making college history.

His ambition was to be a schoolteacher. He moved directly from Cambridge to Fettes College in Edinburgh, where he became acquainted with the sister of a colleague, Ruth Mary Cotterill, who was serving as matron at neighbouring Glencourse. She also came from a family with ties to the Anglican Church; her uncle was bishop of Grahamstown. In other ways the pair suited one another: 'He could safely get on with his routine of Latin and Greek while she managed the business of life'.[1] They were married in December 1879 at St Mary's Cathedral in Edinburgh, and set off in January 1880 for Rugby, where William had been offered a position as tutor with the promise of a promotion to the post of Housemaster as soon as one opened up.

*

The second of three sons, Rupert Chawner Brooke was born at 5 Hillmorton Road on 3 August 1887. Richard England – named after his grandfather – had been born in 1881, and the baby, Alfred, arrived in 1891; an older sister had died in infancy, and his mother desperately wished that Rupert might have been born a girl. In a family that valued language and history, the rather fanciful 'Rupert' was suggested by his father, and 'Chawner' was selected by his mother, a reference to a dashing Cotterill relative rumoured to have been involved in a regicide.

The Brooke family's first home in Rugby had been built in the 1850s to provide accommodation for married tutors, and it was on the compact side, more a large cottage than a substantial family home. Mary was lucky in that she had a small legacy to contribute to her husband's salary, which allowed them to employ a maid and a governess for the boys. In 1891, the family moved up in school staff terms when William was, as had been promised, made Housemaster of School Field. This was an imposing late-Victorian building with apartments for the family, including a drawing room for Mary and a study for William, along with all of the trappings of a large dormitory for the boys in their charge. Although School Field employed a number of staff, along with a matron, Mary took a very active role in its running. William's primary – albeit benevolent – contact with his sons took place over Greek and Latin grammars.

Rugby was a provincial red-brick market town: a sleepy, ordered place. In addition to its factories and station (an impressive junction), the town boasted pretty trees, a bandstand, a bookshop, and a café, as well as a grimmer workhouse, which pushed the sharp reminders of Victorian and Edwardian poverty to the edges of the town. Founded in 1567 as a Free Grammar School for local boys, Rugby School was its own strictly ordered world in miniature, its Gothic and pseudo-Gothic front and gates discouraging unwarranted and uninvited access, and once inside its doors the green of the Close, comprising 17 acres in 1890, rolled out graciously, providing plenty of room for sport, play, and controlled exploration. School days ran to 11 hours, beginning with daily chapel at 7 a.m. Roll was called three times a day and studies included Latin, Greek, French, Scripture, History, English, Geography, and Mathematics. Newcomers to its endlessly renewing hierarchies found themselves making toast for the senior boys, or receiving a whack (or worse, in some cases, if the degradations and abuses recounted in many memoirs of public school life are accurate).

Having his family so close at hand, Brooke was relatively insulated from the lonelier and nastier sides of boarding school life, where boys were often left to 'formulate their own ethics and to construct their own conduct' at the behest of ever-renewing gangs of bullies.[2] He first went to school just down the road at Hillbrow; Richard, or 'Dick' as he was known, saw him safely there every morning. He began a collection of friends (and stamps – he was a keen collector when he was young) including Duncan Grant and James Strachey. At Hillbrow he excelled at Latin and French, but his English results were poor; he eventually improved. Family holidays were spent at the seaside or at his grandfather's house in Bournemouth. At St Ives he played on the beach with a young Virginia Woolf; at Brighton he met James's older brother Lytton. He became good friends with Geoffrey Keynes – 'the young and credulous Geoffrey'[3] – and Hugh Russell-Smith; later at Grantchester he would pursue (and describe) a brief sexual encounter with the latter.[4] These emerging networks of friends – always personally and professionally important to Brooke – would also prove instrumental to ensuring his wartime literary fame, attesting to both his literary promise and to his great personal charm.

Upon his return from one family holiday, with the aim of practising for his preferred profession, journalism, he started a one-off single-author magazine – the 'School Field Magazine' – that included a bit of travel writing as well as a story called 'The Final War', about a group of brave young seamen of the Royal Navy and the adjacent political drama of Whitehall embroiled in a 'war for the world'. The story bares the imprint of children's novels about the heroics of imperial conflict with all its 'thunder and flame, its glories and sorrows'; the three ships bound for glory proudly sail with the Channel fleet under the banners of the 'Terrible', the 'Caesar' and the 'Orlando'. These images of naval heroics Brooke combined with what he must have overheard from his tutors, parents, and their friends, and what he read in the newspapers about lesser conflicts: 'By evening posters were put up all over London announcing the declaration'. As the century turned, martial heroics and national reputation were, as ever, something to think about, even in safe and ordered Rugby. In 1900, his mother joined, out of interest and some conviction, a local Liberal meeting against the Boer War and found her somewhat baffled middle son staring out at her from the stage amongst the speakers. He had come along to see what the fuss was about, and been brought up on stage to be commended as the conflict's youngest protester. In Brooke's youth, actual, violent war was still a remote idea; the young schoolboy balanced out his tense and serious story in 'School Field Magazine' with a poem about the weather.[5]

At Rugby, Brooke excelled at cricket (and, in particular, bowling), joined the Officers' Training Corp and edited a literary supplement to the school's magazine that merrily pushed at the boundaries of propriety. He spent a fair amount of time in the Temple Library reading newspapers as well as ancient and modern literature and poetry. Although he started without one, he eventually secured an entrance scholarship. He was never a great scholar – tutors complained that his work was imprecise – but he was popular; he wrote long, often slightly ridiculous but decidedly amusing and literate letters to his ever-growing body of friends. He worked hard to be naughty in clever ways; at one point, Rugby's Master wrote to William Parker to complain that Rupert had bribed a young musician to serenade the class – loudly – during a particularly dull lesson.[6] In looks he was striking, praised for his golden features and translucent skin, lovely almost to the point of delicacy.

*

As Brooke grew up, Rugby began to grate. Extended stretches spent quietly at home with his family often drove him to distraction, leading him to write to friends to pose more glamorous and exciting alter-natives. He favoured languid poetry centred on the great romantic themes of nature, youth, and death. Later he would mock the senti-ments expressed in poems like 'The Path of Dreams', but at the time they struck the appropriate note:

> Strange blossoms faint upon that odorous air,
> Vision, and wistful Memory; and there
> Love twofold with the purple bloom of Triumph
> And the wan leaf of Despair.[7]

'Evening', written in 1905, offers another willowy, wistful example of
his early verse:

> Not as the glory of day found us,
>> In the dreams and folly of youth's delight:
> But only the silent sleep remaineth
>> Now, and the infinite starless night
>>> Lies coldly around us.[8]

He would never completely abandon these sentiments, metaphors and
tropes. The War Sonnets, with their references to the 'Sweet swine of
youth'[9] set against the 'worst friend and enemy' that is 'but Death',[10]
bear traces of these melancholy musings, even as they capture and
condense a particular public moment and mood.

Relatively speaking Brooke was, of course, living a fortunate existence. He benefited from young, literary tutors eager to open their
pupils' eyes to modern literature, including Baudelaire, Wilde, and
Swinburne, as well as learned men willing to discuss Chaucer, Byron,
and Milton at length with their charges. Even at Rugby, his cultural
horizons were expanding. As the Brooke boys grew, the family
ventured further afield, regularly travelling to Italy, France, Belgium,
and Germany.

In the winter of 1904, following a bought of flu, his mother agreed
to send Rupert for a two-month holiday to Italy with his cousins to
recuperate. He thoroughly appreciated the glamour and comparative
informality of the Continent, visited historical sites and museums, and
generally enjoyed himself. As part of the holiday he was even allowed a
few days in Milan alone, and returned home via London, where he met
up with his older brother and had a night out at the theatre. (This may
have been when he went to see J. M. Barrie's *Peter Pan*, which was then
the most successful show in London: he found it excellent, the best play
he had ever seen.)[11] For his eighteenth birthday, he attended the Marl-
borough v. Rugby cricket match at Lords. In an age when many people
remained, throughout their lives, almost exactly where they were born,

or only moved out of economic necessity, Brooke enjoyed a substantial amount of freedom and access to European culture. If not financially, in educational terms, he numbered amongst the privileged elite.

As part of his convalescence, in 1904, Brooke was also allowed two weeks in France, where he was inspired to write his prize-winning poem 'The Bastille'. It described the old prison, 'Huge over Paris, grey and motionless', brooding as the people inside and beneath it toil and sweat and suffer. He imagined the inspiring revolutionary storming of the fortress but, upon reflection, drew the lesson that the memory of 'Liberty, young and fair' with the 'glory of sunrise on his hair' was not sufficient unto itself. The 'bright glory of that early faith / Is faded now, and tarnished'; 'peace and freedom' were not won by a 'single blow' but by a sustained effort. He was hopeful enough to imagine a day 'Somewhere beyond our dreams' when the old would be made new, 'the quest over, sin and bondage past, / Men shall be Gods, and every vision true, / And Time Eternity.'[12] This was the sort of articulate and idealist poetry – very much in vogue – that Brooke excelled at in his teenage years.

In 1905, he set off to sit his Cambridge entrance exams. Despite his inconsistent academic performance over the years, the preparations paid off in the end. He won a Classics scholarship to King's, his father's college; his good friend Geoffrey Keynes would go along as well, having received a scholarship to Pembroke College. Now a senior boy at Rugby, and afforded additional freedoms at school, Brooke grew his hair out to a fashionable, if controversial, floppiness, and started to sport a blue ribbon on his straw cap to indicate his place in the cricket first XI. On Speech Day, he was awarded the King's Medal for Prose in recognition of the fair amount of critical writing – particularly writing about theatre – he had produced while at the school.

Cambridge beckoned, but Brooke was conscious of new challenges. His life at Rugby, despite its tacit links to the wider intellectual and the political world afforded by the school, had been limited, orchestrated to a large degree by his tutors and parents and, in particular, his mother. At university, he would have to make his own way. Despite his natural popularity, he was not particularly rich or particularly clever. The Rugby Head Master's report provides an interesting summary of his weaknesses and his potential:

> His work is more uneven than that of any boy in his form; he either dislikes details or has no capacity for them. But when he is good – on the purely literary side of his work and scholarship he is capable of very brilliant results, and in English composition he *must* make a name. Always a delightful boy to work with. I am very sorry to lose him.[13]

Wanting to cut a good figure, and conscious of social inferiority and the potential to be relegated to the ranks of a provincial second-rater amongst the Etonians, he wrote to Keynes for him, to please 'help curb my fantastic family's taste for suburban furniture and puce wallpaper',[14] when the two went off to choose furnishings for their rooms. Although light-hearted, this comment hints at more serious insecurities; at King's he would have to perform and impress, socially and academically, and there was no guarantee that he would be a particular success in life.

In the transition to Cambridge and an independent future, he could first, and fortunately, rely on his network of school friends. Hugh Dalton helped to reinvigorate Brooke's interest in Fabian socialism; this was the period of the review of and wider debate about the Poor Laws, and the rise of Beatrice and Sidney Webb as influential social commentators. James Strachey also helped pave the way, suggesting to his brother Lytton that Brooke be considered, on the strength of his literary writings, his cultural curiosity, and his general charm, for the influential secret society 'The Apostles'. In the pre-war years the society developed into a close, mutually beneficial network for budding writers; it also became a place where 'talk about philosophy and the good life was combined with compulsive flirtation' between established men and potential 'embryos'.[15] Intrigued, Lytton wrote to Brooke – the noted beauty – from Trinity College, Cambridge, constructing a questionnaire around what he considered to be some of life's more important questions:

> Do you approve of the Royal Academy?
> What are your view on Wagner, Mr. Chamberlain, and Christ?
> Are you in favour of war at any price?
> Why are you going to Oxford? [Brooke still hoped to at this point]
> Does Jackson play such a good game as Fry?

Brooke replied sharply, amusingly, and ironically, displaying an awareness of the points to pick up on if one was to adopt a conventionally bohemian, reactionary pose:

> Certainly I approve of war at any price. It kills off the unnecessary. As for Mr. Chamberlain I detest him. He is a modern politician, and I hate modern politicians; he comes from Birmingham, and I abhor Birmingham; he makes noise, and I loathe noises; he is utterly materialistic, and …! About Wagner I have no views. I am very sorry, but I can't help it. I have tried hard for years, but I *cannot* appreciate music. I recognise that it is a fault in me, and I am duly ashamed. In Literature, and a little even in Painting, I humbly believe I can feel the Beautiful, but I am born deaf. This is a Tragedy. For Christ – I am so obsessed by *De Profundis* that I have no other views on this subject than those expressed therein. The Perfect Artistic Temperament.[16]

He did his best to appear worldly and disdaining, despising red-brick Birmingham, all commerce and politics, preferring Oscar Wilde's interpretation of organised religion to anything he had been exposed to in daily chapel.

His cousin Erica Cotterill, also relegated to the drudgeries of the schoolroom and with more limited options than Brooke, was a comfort to him throughout his teenage years; the two loved to discuss poetry, culture, and their mutual yearnings for excitement. From Rugby in January 1907 he expressed his annoyance with all things dull, dreary, and conventional. He hated the tedium of memorising to rote, as well as a focus on dry 'facts': 'How delightful it is knowing no facts. I flee knowledge as others seek it. The more one knows the less likely one is to find the Light. In consequence I shall take a bad degree'. He dreamed of a more hedonistic and cosmopolitan existence:

> I shall go to London or Paris & live for one year a life like a great red flame. As I know nothing, I shall fear nothing. As I seek for nothing, all things will flock to me. I shall wreathe scarlet roses of passion round my smooth brow & drink the purple wine of beauty from the polished skull of some dead Archbishop. I shall write subtle tribrachs & strange anapaests that shall have more delicate melody than all the lilies swaying in the wind of Dawn.

And, coming back to the reality of the flu, a further feature of a rather dull holiday, he concluded: 'I shall never have a cold in my head'.[17]

2

The Idyll

Brooke was often ill, and sometimes very; the entire family was always getting over something or other. As a child he was particularly prone to pink-eye and chronic sore throats. Cut off from his friends, isolated in the sick room, alongside his passion for literature this accounts for the fact that, even at a young age, he produced so many letters and poems. His writing must have entertained him as much as it did others, lest they forget about him. His fragility also allowed him space for fantasy, even as he bemoaned the fact that this was 'the most exciting part of my existence at present'. At one point he recorded a particularly compelling instance:

> A vivid dream this morning. I dreamt that I had a fierce dagger-fight with some stranger, was stabbed by him thrice under the left shoulder blade and knew no more, – presumably dying. Afterwards I came back and haunted the house, causing much terror at a dinner-party. The feeling of haunting is rather pleasing: I think I shall take it up – if it is allowed – afterwards.[1]

Actual death was less romantic. Suddenly, only days after his fanciful letter to Erica Cotterill, wherein he dramatically proposed to

21

drink wine from polished skulls,[2] his elder brother Dick was dead from pneumonia. Shocked, Brooke quickly returned to Cambridge. Of 'our trouble', as he called it, he wrote; 'I could not face everybody. The only thing was if I could help Father and Mother by staying, but they say not, and I do not think so. And if I stayed I know that I should break down'. He worried about his remote but gentle father in particular, who 'is very tired and broken by it'.[3]

*

Although the loss of his brother was a blow, Brooke did begin to find his social feet at Cambridge. His friendship with Hugh Dalton helped; in addition to their political activities, they decided to set up a semi-literary, mildly political group called the 'Carbonari'. This provided an opportunity to read poems and discuss the state of the world with a group of like-minded and, it must be said, carefully selected and screened undergraduates: Brooke was ever a keen controller of his company. Brooke did complete a lengthy, impassioned examination of a topic close to his heart – 'Democracy and the Arts' – which he delivered to the Cambridge University Fabian Society in November 2010. After his death, his friends discovered a box left behind at Grantchester containing lecture notes from the Fabian Summer School in Harlech, as well as writings on topics including socialism, unemployment, and poverty, and sociological and political tracts by Thomas Davidson and Franklin Henry Giddings.[4] Brooke did find these topics compelling. However, enjoyment and fun were as important: the writings he produced for the Apostles and the Carbonari included, 'Are the playing of cards and the attendance at theatre amusements consistent with the character of a clergyman?' – again poking fun at the hypocrisy of the established Church – to 'A conversation with an embryo (unfinished)'.[5]

More profound for his self-confidence as well as his growing visibility was his involvement in university theatricals. He joined a Greek Play Committee, and made friends with Justin Brooke, who encouraged

Brooke to re-read the Elizabethan dramatists. Brooke would later write his dissertation on John Webster. He joined the Marlowe Society and, showing an appreciation for modern as well as period drama, took on the role of Algernon in a production of Oscar Wilde's *The Importance of Being Earnest*. His mother was underwhelmed: she worried about his health, as well as the potential for her unfocused, fanciful son to set his mind permanently to pursuing a career as a bohemian actor. Brooke wrote to reassure her – he kept up a constant and lively correspondence with Mary whenever he was away – about preparations for one performance: 'Comus will only take two or three hours a day; there will be hardly anyone in Cambridge; so I shall get through quite as much reading as I could at home. So my work will not suffer, only my pocket!'[6] Practically speaking the theatre helped Brooke to make quite advantageous connections. It was in the role of a page in *Eumenides* that Edward Marsh, then a civil servant in the Colonial Office, first met Brooke, becoming a friend and lifelong – and posthumous – champion of Brooke and his writings.

*

In literary as in social terms, Brooke did well at Cambridge. He published poems in various literary magazines, and continued to write reviews of the theatre; he found himself the only undergraduate on the board of *The Cambridge Review*. He spent a fair amount of time in between abbreviated periods of study enjoying college life with friends, including women from Girton and beyond: Katherine ('Ka') Cox and the aristocratic Olivier sisters, Margery and Noel, numbered amongst his acquaintances and sometime romantic interests.

He discovered the picture-postcard village of Grantchester after following the three-mile riverside 'Grind' as it was known. It offered the possibility of a country idyll away from College eyes, with tea served at the cottage by the Granta, a rambling, ramshackle house with lawns in which to live and work, and a deep swimming pond by the mill. It was a lovely place. In his ode to Grantchester, and the moments

he would spend there over the course of the next few years, he would
write of 'the chestnuts' that

> Beside the river make for you
> A tunnel of green gloom, and sleep
> Deeply above; and green and deep
> The stream mysterious glides beneath,
> Green as a dream and deep as death.[7]

Brooke decided to take rooms and proceeded to play host to numerous
acquaintances. He walked about eccentrically clothed – barefoot while
wearing a jacket and tie – and bathed naked in the river, all the while
charming his landlords and the neighbours. He did not get much work
done, and did badly on his Tripos.

Then, on 24 January 1910, following a period of decline, Brooke's
father died at the age of 59. Moved, Brooke wrote to Raverat: 'Death's
horrible. I've never seen it before. But death's kind'.[8] Materially, the
loss of his father meant a change in the Brookes circumstances. He
was hardly impoverished, but the safety net of familial support was
reduced. For a time, he took over William's long-held post of Housemaster, allowing his mother to continue to serve as matron at School
House. After the relative glamour and freedom of Cambridge and
Grantchester, this was not a happy or hopeful time; Brooke emphati-
cally did not want to repeat his father's quiet life at Rugby. The family
eventually moved to a small house on Bilton Road, and the pressure for
Rupert and Alfred to secure a financial future for the family increased;
tellingly, 'Democracy and the Arts' was largely concerned with how
poets, writers, and artists would earn a living if the age-old structures
of private patronage disappeared.[9] Luckily for Brooke, despite his
poor exam performance, he received £70 in prize money after being
awarded the Harness Essay Prize. These sorts of sums helped, but he
also relied on his friends for unofficial support. Marsh, living largely
off a substantial inheritance, was particularly generous: Brooke often
stayed and was entertained by him when he visited London.

Thus Brooke was able to keep attending Lady Ottoline Morrell's literary salons, to hear speeches by H. G. Wells on reforms to the Poor Laws, to meet would-be publishers like Henry Nevinson, the influential editor of the *Nation*, and to discuss poetry with poets and critics like Edward Thomas and William Butler Yeats, who called him 'the handsomest man in England'.[10] He resolved to work harder, to return to Grantchester, to write his dissertation and to win a fellowship (he had tried once already and failed) to King's. This would allow him to secure for himself at least some financial stability and independence, while at the same time provide him time and space to continue his literary and social pursuits, whenever possible, including sailing with the Olivier sisters, visits to see the Russian Ballet at Covent Garden, and camping trips with Cox and friends.

He relished the 'peace and holy quiet'[11] of Grantchester, but the dissertation proved a challenge. He worked very hard, and afterwards went to his mother's new house to rest. He had fallen in love with Cox, who provided a sometimes passionately existential, sometimes calming and domestic influence: when Yeats commented on Brooke's beauty, he also noted that he 'wears the most beautiful shirts' (sewn by Cox). The relationship was not a smooth one; she had an ongoing, unresolved relationship with Brooke's good friend Jacques Raverat. In periods he wrote almost exclusively to her for weeks and even months: 'I'm lying in bed now in this funny room ... When I shut my eyes and whisper your name over, I can feel your hands and face and hair above and about me'.[12] The sexual tension destabilised Brooke, a 'self-divided puritan', who never truly came to grips with his physical and emotional impulses.[13] In a letter written in the opening months of the war Brooke would reflect that 'I am – how shall I put it – carried along on the tides of my body, rather helplessly. At intervals I realise this, and feel rather aghast'.[14]

Throughout 1911 and 1912, Brooke's friends were concerned about his health and mental state; exhaustion, coupled with his worries about the situation with Cox, led to another trip abroad. After a brief visit to Munich, Mary and Alfred Brooke joined him in Cannes. Hoping to convince Cox to meet up with him in Verona and travel on with him for an extended conjugal stay in Munich, Brooke wrote updating her on his status, which changed daily: 'I'm really getting on very well: my body ("nerves"). But I wish you were here to look after my soul'. His mother's presence oppressed him: 'Half the day she spends in reproducing to me verbally her conversations of the other half'. She criticised his flamboyant dress, and in particular a very bright yellow tie: 'so conspicuous!'.[15]

With Cox he promised to control his more extreme dependencies: 'I *won't* be a bother to you this time, a whining baby on your hands. Please look forward to it only with happiness – and not a sigh too, that you've the great load of me to carry'.[16] Cox reluctantly agreed to meet him in Germany, but Brooke was increasingly unhappy. Later, reflecting on the period, he wrote: 'Love is a breach in the walls, a broken gate, / Where that comes in that shall not go again; ... / They have known shame, who love unloved.'[17]

Sex, friendship, and poetry intertwined to produce a hothouse environment for which Brooke was not entirely ill-suited; it is not incidental that he started to make some literary progress within the small world of literary London in the pre-war years. In 1911, Lytton Strachey introduced Brooke to the publisher Frank Sidgwick, who decided to take a chance on the young poet. The publishers worried about the potential for Brooke's *Poems* to make money, but felt that the work was interesting and would get a fair amount of coverage in the press. Sidgwick agreed to a print run of 500 copies, which sold well, if not spectacularly. The publishers had to wait a little longer for their investment in Brooke to pay off. Benefiting from the wild popularity of the War Sonnets, the sale of *Poems* picked up significantly after Brooke's death; the volume would go through 37 impressions by May 1933.

It is interesting to note how prudish many of Brooke's critics and readers were: he received a fair amount of criticism as well as teasing for one particular poem in the volume entitled 'A Channel Crossing'. This included a 'shocking' description of sea sickness: 'Do I forget you? Retchings twist and tie me, / Old meat, good meals, brown gobbets, up

I throw'. Literary tastes were very polite indeed, and not used to bodily functions and fluids being given serious treatment in verse. Even Marsh, keen to do all that he could to establish his friend as a serious and successful poet, could not help voicing his disapproval in a review of *Poems* that he wrote for the *Poetry Review* in April 1912.[18] Others, however, were more positive. Edward Thomas, another poet-soldier who would die in the war, wrote in the *Daily Chronicle* that 'copies should be bought by everyone over forty who has ever been under forty. It will be a revelation'. Brooke was speaking for youth, and doing so very well in Thomas's opinion. His future, he predicted, would be a strong one, for 'If they live yet a little longer, they may see Mr. Brooke a poet. He will not be a little one'.[19]

*

Long before he came to embody the lost youth of the war years, Brooke became skilled at deploying images and ideals that played to common sentiments about cultural security and continuity. Increasing in literary – if not personal – self-confidence after the generally positive reception of *Poems*, Brooke continued to write, publishing poetry and prose in a variety of newspapers in the years leading up to the war. It was to an England entranced by its own pastoral glory that he unofficially dedicated 'The Old Vicarage, Grantchester', which was to become one of his best-known poems during and after the war.

He originally called the poem 'The Sentimental Exile'; Marsh helped him to settle on the eventual title. Written in Berlin in 1912, it fits well alongside the idealised vision of England offered in the War Sonnets. (Some readers from 1914 to 1918 would come to believe that the poem was something of a prophesy, crafted specifically to conjure up an ideal of what the nation was fighting for.) With its sing-song rhymes and patterns, 'Grantchester' reads as a kind of a schoolroom ballad, and could apply – and indeed appeal – just as strongly to the homesick English soldier or official stationed on the fringes Empire as to the melancholy, emotionally fragile Cambridge graduate living 'sweaty, sick and hot' amongst strangers in 1912. In 'Grantchester' these were specifically identified by Brooke as urbane '*Temperament-voll* German Jews'; his admiration for Hilaire Belloc as well as the casual prejudices of many of his friends and acquaintances led him to absorb and, more frequently in the years leading up to the war, to invoke anti-Semitic rhetoric. The poem also makes conscious reference to a number of stars of the English literary canon, including Chaucer, who 'hears his river still / Chatter beneath a phantom mill', Tennyson, with his 'studious eyes' regarding the flowing waters, and Byron, whose 'ghostly Lordship swims his pool / And tries the strokes, essays the tricks, / Long learnt on Hellespont, or Styx'. From 1915 to 1918, appreciative critics and readers, willing Brooke to immediate elevation to canonical heights, would return to these lines as invocations of the nation's literary heritage.

At its heart the poem turned on a contrast between the controlled and contrived world of the city where 'tulips bloom as they are told' and the gorgeous chaos of the natural world that grew around the Granta, where 'the May fields all golden show, / And when the day is young and sweet, / Gild gloriously the bare feet / that run to bathe …'. England in the poem is only semi-official, more loose and informal than conventional: an 'unofficial rose' under an 'unregulated sun'. Its pastoralism is also highly local; its gaze focuses down and down again on to a smaller and smaller world, distinguishing the hamlet from adjacent Cambridge, where 'people rarely smile / Being urban, squat, and packed with guile'. Brooke consciously overstated and simplified his memory of the provisional bohemian society that congregated around him to create an almost comic ideal of purity and youthful disdain of age, disappointment, and middle-class morality:

> In Grantchester their skins are white;
> They bathe by day, they bathe by night;
> The women there do all they ought;
> The men observe the Rules of Thought.
> They love the Good; they worship Truth;

They laugh uproariously in youth;
(And when they get to feeling old,
They up and shoot themselves, I'm told) ...

The poem invokes a number of themes idealised in Edwardian popular culture as sacred elements of the English pastoral countryside, often by people across the country and the Empire who had only a theoretical understanding of that landscape; of a village grown up in the shadows of the learned Cambridge colleges, and of the pleasurable idleness of a life spent under 'Great clouds along pacific skies', with honeyed tea waiting to be enjoyed. Brooke probably meant it to be read straight in some moods. He personally felt a great and genuine affection for his memory of the time spent with friends at Grantchester in the little world he created and enjoyed there, for a time, before life and friends moved on; all this he put in to the soon to be famous poem.

Yet his world and his personal life remained under strain in the years leading up to the war. English, British, and, of course, Imperial society was not all 'Beauty', 'Certainty', and 'Quiet'[20] in 1912 any more than it would be in 1915 or 1918. Nor was Berlin such a horrid place; it inspired some good writing and created a positive impression on Brooke that lingered even in the heady summer and autumn of 1914 when all things German became targets of collective hate and fury. The following passage taken from Brooke's diary at the time offers a different impression from that advanced by 'Grantchester':

This afternoon, on Karlstrasse, under a railway bridge, I saw flakes of gold and of colour – like confetti – blowing down the street. There was a fresh wind, and a bit of noise from the trains, and an afternoon sun. They were scraps of bran from the tin bucket that served a nose bag for a horse standing there. As he ate they flew and the sun caught them.'[21]

These and other brief passages from the period reveal Brooke as making progress with his prose. But 'Grantchester' would become his most recognisable pre-war poem, offering what was to become an extremely persuasive vision of the 'holy quiet'[22] land of happy English memories, and one into which the handsome idealised vision of the pre-war poet-soldier – melancholy or not – fit very nicely.

*

Brooke's literary career continued to develop. He was awarded his Fellowship to King's for *John Webster and the Elizabethan Drama*, an impressionistic academic work that would be reprinted, like much of Brooke's writing – optimistically, in this case, considering its relative limitations as a popular piece of writing – after his death. He continued his friendship with Marsh, helping him to edit the first volume of *Georgian Poetry, 1911–1912*, conceived of by the former as being issued 'in the belief that English poetry is now once again putting on a new strength and beauty'.[23] This appeared in 1912 (Brooke contributed five poems).[24] In the same year, the *Poetry Review* selected 'The Old Vicarage, Grantchester' as its 'best poem' for the year on the recommendations of a committee comprised of a number of Brooke's friends and literary colleagues, including Marsh, T. E. Hulme, Edward Thomas, Harold Monro, Henry Newbolt, and Ernest Rhys. *Georgian Poetry* also provides a catalogue of Brooke's expanding network: Lascelles Abercrombie, Walter de la Mare, John Drinkwater, and Wilfrid Wilson Gibson would publish their poems alongside his in the first printing of the War Sonnets for the literary journal *New Numbers* in 1915, and others, including Gordon Bottomley, G. K. Chesterton, D. H. Lawrence, and John Masefield would all become prominent writers and critics and, in some instances, direct champions of Brooke's poetry and shapers of the myth of the poet-soldier during the war.

Personally, the emotionally taxing situation with Cox continued to play on Brooke's nerves. He had started to see something of a young actress, Cathleen Nesbitt, but their relationship did not appear to be too serious. Despite his love of friends, in 1913, Brooke decided to escape from interlinking circles of acquaintances and their expectations for him. In 1907, he had written to Geoffrey Keynes of his perpetual sense of displacement: 'what I chiefly loathe & try to escape is not Cambridge nor Rugby nor London but – Rupert Brooke. And I can only do this by rushing suddenly to places for a few days'.[25] The literary editor of the *Westminster Gazette* provided the professional and financial means for Brooke temporarily to disengage. He would travel to the United States and Canada, and provide accounts of his impressions of modern life there; the newspaper would pay him for each of his articles. (These would be collected and published together as *Letters from America* after Brooke's death.) His adventures also provided a convenient excuse not to write too much poetry: to Harold Monro from Honolulu in 1913 he wrote that 'I *cannot* write when I'm travelling'.[26] He did produce a few sonnets, including 'Clouds', written during his travels in the Pacific. In this poem he returned to familiar – and future – themes:

> They say that the Dead die not, but remain
> 	Near to the rich heirs of their grief and mirth.
> 	I think they ride the calm mid-heaven, as these,
> In wise majestic melancholy train,
> 	And watch the moon, and the still-raging seas,
> 	And men, coming and going on the earth.[27]

Over the course of his travels Brooke ended up covering a fair portion of the North American continent, from the great bustling cities to rural encampments nestled in vast forests on the edges of black lakes and remote rivers. He began in New York, where he wrote to Cox that they must, for good this time, draw a line under their affair, also taking time to convey his first impressions of the new world: 'The American race seems to have developed two classes, and only two: the upper-middle and the lower middle'.[28] He loved Fifth Avenue, 'the handsomest street imaginable',[29] but was repulsed by the overt commercialism: 'America has a childlike faith in advertising. They advertise here, everywhere, and in all ways. They shout your most private and sacred wants at you. Nothing is untouched'.[30]

He moved to Boston, where he attended the Harvard v. Yale base-ball match: he did not think it measured up to cricket, being 'merely glorified rounders ... There is excitement in the game, but little beauty'.[31] He went on from Boston to Montreal, Ottawa, Sarnia (where the upper Great Lakes empty into the St Claire River), Winnipeg (he was impressed by the 'public spirit'[32] of western Canadians), Edmonton, Calgary, Lake Louise, and Vancouver. The seemingly untouched vistas and clear air inspired a certain calm reflection: 'It is the feeling of fresh loneliness that impresses itself before any detail of the wild. The soul – or the personality – seems to have indefinite room to expand'.[33] He was keen to encounter 'Indians', but concluded, sadly, that 'Civilisa-tion, disease, alcohol, and vice have reduced them to a few scattered communities and some stragglers, and a legend, the admiration of boyhood'.[34]

From Canada he travelled to Seattle and San Francisco. There he caught the SS Sierra to the islands of Hawaii, and afterwards visited Samoa, Fiji – where he wrote to his mother of the 'great time' he was having, how nice everyone had been to him, and that he had attended the funeral of a Fijian princess who had died from pneumonia at the age of twenty[35] – and to New Zealand. In Tahiti, he ran short of money, and is alleged to have had an affair with a local woman. In March, he wrote to Marsh of an accident that further weakened his immune system:

> I got some beastly coral-poisoning into my legs, & a local microbe on the top of that, & made the places bad by neglecting them and sea-bathing all day (which turns out to be the worst possible thing). I was in country when it came on bad, & tried native remedies, which took all the skin off & produced such a ghastly appearance that I hurried into town. I've been lying on my back for eight or nine days suffering intensely while I swab my skinless flesh with boiling disinfectant. However, I've got over it now, & have started hobbling about. At first I had a bit of fever: but I feel very spry now.

This was, it turned out, an ominous letter for a young man who would later die of a blood infection on a ship bound for Gallipoli. Feeling better, he determined that he had had enough of travel: 'I shall be glad to be back among you all, & tied to somewhere in England. I'll never never go to sea again. All I want in life is a cottage & the leisure to write supreme poems & plays'.[36] He made his return east via Arizona, Chicago, and New York, and was back in England in time to catch the final months of the peace.

3

Self-Mobilisation

During July and August 1914, people around the world watched apprehensively as the global crisis that would become the First World War took shape. While to some it was clear almost immediately that the assassinations of the Archduke Franz Ferdinand and his wife Sophie in Sarajevo would provide the spark in the tinderbox that many observers had been expecting for years, it took weeks for the framework to emerge, for alliances to settle, and for the war to become a fact.

More than most, Brooke had access to well-placed individuals – Edward Marsh, and Violet and Cynthia Asquith – with some insights: 'Everyone in the governing classes seems to think we shall be at war'. Friends with any real political responsibility were run off their feet, meaning that Brooke saw out the final days of July in a state of heightened and semi-ignorant anticipation. Rumours spread quickly and were consumed voraciously by a tense citizenry. In cities, towns, and villages nervous crowds gathered, waiting to hear the news as telegrams flashed between European ministries. Marsh, who was virtually sleeping at his desk, was too busy even to write. He eventually stole a moment to send a message to Brooke, noting wryly that this silence 'must have brought the reality of war home to you more than anything else'.[1]

On 1 August, Germany declared war on Russia, and the mood shifted. On the same day Brooke wrote to Jacques Raverat, wondering 'what can one *do* if there's war?' On 4 August, Britain declared war. He later described the moment he, and fellow Londoners, found out for certain that the period of speculation was over:

> I've just been to a music-hall. I feed with Eddie every night from 9 to 10. Then he goes back to the Admiralty. Tonight I turned into the Coliseum. It was pretty full. Miss Cecilia Loftus was imitating somebody I saw infinite years ago – Elsie Janis – in her imitation of a prehistoric figure called Frank Tinney. God! How far away it all seemed. Then Alfred Lester. Then a dreadful cinematography reproduction of hand-drawing patriotic things – Harry Furniss it was – funny pictures of a soldier and a sailor (at the time, I suppose, dying in Belgium); a caricature of the Kaiser, greeted with a few perfunctory faint hisses. Nearly everyone sat silent. Then a scribbled message was thrown; 'War declared with Austria. 11.9.' There was a volley of quick low handclapping – more a signal of recognition than anything else. Then we dispersed into Trafalgar Square, and bought midnight war editions, special.

Brooke was touched by the communal nature of what he experienced as the crowd exited together into the new reality: 'All these days I have not been so near tears. There was such tragedy, and such dignity, in the people.[2]

*

Mobilisation was not immediate, be it individual or collective; England's policy of volunteerism opened up the space for contemplation and self-reflection. In *Memoirs of a Fox-Hunting Man*, Siegfried Sassoon's protagonist recalled his dismay at the possibility of lost time: 'I had sometimes thought with horror of countries where they had conscription and young men like myself were forced to serve two years in the army whether they liked it or not. Two years in the army!'[3] Everywhere small but momentous personal decisions fed the rising tide of mobilisation.

For Brooke, this process was also not entirely straightforward. He carefully weighed up the political and moral ramifications of war for his country and for himself before volunteering. He might be frustrated with his life to date, but he was not keen to throw it away. On the one hand, international treaties caused Brooke some pause as belligerent nations defined their allegiances. He was not convinced that he approved of the emerging situation; England's allies were not all that he wished them to be. For years Liberals, including Brooke, had criticised the despotism of, in particular, Imperial Russia. Germany, with its strong socialist parties, parliamentary democracy, and the stirrings of a welfare state, did not initially appear as a natural enemy for many in Britain, or for Brooke.

In the War Sonnet 'Peace', Brooke would write of swimmers leaping into a new, clean future, leaving the 'world grown old and cold and weary'.[4] This was a neat, attractive idea, but if this was not to be a progressive war, offering up some evidence of fulfilment and honour for the allies as well as individual soldiers, what was the point of offering up his body as a sacrifice? Fretting, he wrote that 'Everything's just the wrong way round. *I* want Germany to smash Russia to fragments, & for France to break Germany!'[5] Trying to explain his as yet unresolved position, Brooke turned to a literary source to contextualise his lack of resolve: 'Have you ever read *Sanine*?' The novel, written by Mikhail Petrovich Artsybashev and published in 1907, was a highly naturalistic story centred on Sanin and his encounters with village neighbours after he returns to his hometown following a long absence. Its depiction of Russian life caused something of a scandal. Having read the book in its English translation, Brooke determined that 'That's what Russia is like'. (Brooke, although well-travelled, had never actually visited Russia.) Fighting alongside the Tsar's armies meant a tacit endorsement of a singularly 'backward', despotic, and vicious order.

Gloomily, he concluded that 'the future is a Slav Empire, world-wide, despotic, and insane'. He found himself – counter to the image of the resolute, clear-eyed volunteer and 'legendary war enthusiast'[6] – irritated, fretful, and 'depressed'.[7]

Brooke's restlessness in the opening days of war stemmed from the need to negotiate a new identity as a man of action, freed from the uncertainties replete in his 'anchorless'[8] life over the previous few years. Having returned home to spend a few days with his mother and brother, he reflected on the general mood of anxious anticipation. He fixed on national reputation as the linchpin, writing to Marsh: 'I'm anxious that England may act rightly. I can't bear it if she does wrong'.[9] He took the political situation personally, and was equally concerned that he might find a way to 'act rightly'.

Much of the poetry and prose Brooke produced in the early weeks and months of the war showed that when contemplating the situation and how he should respond to it he set upon a formula. He might doubt or rebel to a point, but ultimately he would measure his resolve against an imagined barometer of national sentiment and honour. As a result, from August 1914 on, in his own mind, there was very little differentiation between 'Rupert Brooke' and 'England'. Just what it meant in finite terms to 'act rightly' he left unspecified for the moment, but almost immediately he began to project himself – contemplative and exhilarated in equal parts – onto the war's stage.

In early August, Brooke began searching for ways to get involved in the conflict, on his own terms. This set him apart from many of his fellow British and Imperial recruits and, eventually, conscripts. As a member of the upper-middle classes (by connection and education if not, strictly speaking, in terms of actual wealth) he expected to be treated as an individual, and for his preferences to be taken into account. His immediate instinct was not to become a soldier; he did not think that the life would suit him. While living in Berlin in November 1912 he had confided in the philosopher T. E. Hulme that he would link himself to the much-anticipated European war in some capacity, but most likely through his writing.[10] He liked the idea of becoming a war correspondent,[11] thinking that his record with the *Westminster Gazette*, and in particular his published 'Letters from America' from 1913 might provide a sufficient résumé. He wanted room to observe and consider the war, but was not sure he wanted to involve himself directly in the fighting of it.

Enlistment for Brooke was not only a public political act; it was also a state of mind. In England in 1914 (and indeed throughout the war), where conscription was a major political controversy, much was made of the volunteer; less so of the intense mental deliberation that in many cases informed the decision to join up. Brooke was not particularly inclined towards militarism or violence, but he was looking for ways to fit his own sentiments into a popular as well as a moral context. As a writer, he was highly attuned to the nation's sentimental pulse, and as such utilised newspapers and pamphlets written by admired, established figures in order to inform his decisions and frame his actions. As he worked this position out through his writing, he joined, early, an ongoing conversation about the meaning of the war. Even in 1914 he had a great deal of material to work with.

*

For all that has been written in the wake of the First World War, very little that was produced and read during the period survives in the public consciousness. Perhaps this is due to the sheer scale of material; so many official documents, so many leaders in newspapers, so many poems, so many pamphlets, so many songs, to say nothing of the personal material produced: the diaries, letters, journals, art, ephemera. At the time in England all classes consumed narratives of the war voraciously. This was one of the first 'big' wars in which the emergence of a more uniformly literate population played its part. It was also *the* topic of conversation, and everyone had an opinion about it. And most of those opinions bore the traces of other opinions. Such was the case with Brooke, and what he read at the time helped to determine his fate in the war as well as his writing on it, including the famous War Sonnets, which he first began work on in August 1914.[12]

The great minds of the day weighed in, and their opinions were taken seriously, at home and abroad. In Germany and in Britain, scientists, authors, philosophers, and artists published statements testifying to the moral righteousness of their respective homelands. Their justifications of and commitment to mobilisation were reported with interest in neutral nations as well as combatant ones. They made the First World War, even in its infancy, one of the most discussed conflicts in history. Inadvertently, much of what they wrote would also provide ammunition for those who later argued that the 'old men' (and virtually all women) of the home front – in their enthusiasm – were responsible for sending the young out to be slaughtered.

Brooke, for one, wanted to hear what these old men had to say. One whom he came to admire greatly for his intellectual clarity with respect to the war was the Oxford classicist and public intellectual Professor Gilbert Murray. Murray was the author of *How Can War Ever Be Right?*, published as part of the Oxford Pamphlet Series in 1914. This set out to justify, in moral and political terms, the nation's entry into war. Brooke had stayed with the Murray family in Norfolk in August 1912,[13] establishing a direct connection to the author. In November, he wrote to Rosalind Murray, Gilbert's daughter:

> I'd like to thank him for it. In all the bad stuff written or said *a propos* of the war, it was so good. And it said, so finely, many things I'd been feeling – or feeling towards – perplexedly in this welter. Oh, I *knew* them, I boast, but couldn't express them. Now they are clear.[14]

In 1914, Murray was for Brooke what Brooke became for many others posthumously: someone who could condense emotional and political reactions to the war, and offer ways to 'express' them as well.

Murray's credentials on the topic were well-established; Brooke's were limited to his brief celebrity as an 11-year-old war protester at a local Rugby political meeting. Murray had been a harsh critic of the nation's handling of the Boer wars; he was almost ousted from the

Liberal Party for his public opposition to it. In September 1899, he had written to his friend Lady Carlisle, expressing his distaste for vociferous patriotism: 'As I read the cries of 'Rule Britannia' in answer to every appeal for reason and fairness, it seemed to me like the real cry of the nation in its madness; the people shouting seemed to express the one thing the Jingoes care for – to go on conquering, rule more and more till the crash comes and the world will not tolerate such a nation any more'.[15] Recalling this position in 1914, as another Imperial conflict loomed, Murray was careful to reassure readers that his conscientious resolve remained steadfast: 'I have all my life been an advocate of Peace'.[16]

Murray was acutely aware, as were many political observers at the time, that British entry into the war was not fated; it was a choice. As Garrett Mattingly, the great historian of the Renaissance would write in 1955, the nation's detachment was a cherished principle of world diplomacy. Since the Hundred Years War and the loss of the French possessions, 'Secure behind its seas', England could 'take as much or as little of any war as it liked'.[17] Technology and, in particular, aeroplanes were now threatening this long-held assumption, but the nation was not compelled to commit its armies and navies to war across the Channel. Various complex treaties and, in particular, Germany's more straightforward invasion of neutral Belgium provided the grounds, but politicians could have fixed on other statutes and arguments to counter involvement. While in retrospect it seems unlikely that Britain could stand to the side of a relatively large European conflict, at the time a parallel process of deliberation mirroring the one undertaken by Brooke went on in national political discourses as well.

Murray's pamphlet outlined the argument for neutrality, wondering why Britain could not have stayed an observer, like the United States, working to 'help refugees and sufferers, anxious to heal wounds and not make them, [and] watchful for the first chance of putting an end to this time of horror'.[18] Yet he determined that this was the wrong way to go about it. He did not believe that the Germans were inherently evil; he pointed out that there are 'militarists and jingoes in every country; our own have often been bad enough'. That said, he noted that the current German approach seemed 'unusually blatant'.[19] Given what was emerging at the time (much of it verified, some exaggerated)[20] about the atrocities committed by the German army in Belgium and northern France, this would have appeared to many readers to be a very reasoned and understated assessment of the situation.

Taking another line of argument, Murray pointed out that the concerned citizen could also make a case for 'honour, pure and simple'. For him the sentimental appeal of the Belgian case did not in itself provide sufficient grounds for British involvement. At issue were the legal and subsequently the moral precedents that would be set by not interceding. Murray believed that these ultimately justified the nation's entry into the war as a fully fledged partner.[21] He concluded that the risks associated with neutrality were too great; the consequences of abandoning standing treaties would forever alter international relations in Europe. There was no way that Britain, 'a very strong Power', could stand by while 'here, under our eyes and within range of our guns, a thing was being done which menaced every living creature in Europe'.[22] Murray remained conscious of the danger of being carried away by wartime emotions, which lent themselves to 'foolish bombast'; it was important to avoid becoming one of the 'jingoes'.[23] Everyone must realise the likely costs: of life, property, animals as well as 'brutaliz[ation] by hardship and filth'. Nonetheless, Murray determined hopefully that 'we may venture to see in this wilderness of evil some oases of extraordinary good'.[24]

*

Around the same time Brooke constructed a piece of prose for the *New Statesman*. He gave the essay the semi-serious, semi-ironic title, 'An Unusual Young Man'. It would be republished as an addendum to his collected *Letters from America* in 1916. Like Murray's pamphlet, the essay tried to reconcile a mindset resistant to violence to support for the war – in his case physical as well as philosophical – by providing a pretext for a singular, considered patriotism. Brooke respected Murray's form of expression, and in the end both reached the same conclusion, even if the latter followed more cerebral avenues. Writing in the third person, Brooke acknowledges the facts of the case, but clarifies that for him the process of justification and mobilisation could not be explained in academic terms. He had a direct stake in war and mobilisation, and as such traced an evolving 'feeling'. The essay offers a singular portrait of Brooke's state of mind in the late summer and early autumn of 1914.

The individual in question is 'a normal, even ordinary young man, wholly English',[25] who maintains an awareness of 'that air of comfortable kindliness which Germany had always signified for him'. Like Murray, Brooke was conscious of war's tendency to inspire patriots to a sort of blind suspension of reason, and even to a menacing hysteria. This he hoped to avoid, if possible, in his own case. He mulled over and acknowledged pleasant memories of Germany; for him, not the 'barbaric Huns' but – a civilised nation of quiet parks, cafés and earnest discourse. Despite the contrast between urban Berlin and the idyllic 'Old Vicarage, Grantchester' he had created in the eponymous poem, Brooke concluded that, like Murray, he could not locate any irrational and patriotically motivated dislike, although 'England demanded' that he 'must hate these things, find evil in them'.[26] For Brooke this was too extreme a position to assume in August 1914. It involved a split not only from the past but from German friends and the nation's hefty social and cultural legacy; 'that half-conscious agony of breaking a mental habit, painting out a mass of associations, which he had felt in ceasing to believe in a religion, or, more acutely, after quarrelling with a friend'.[27]

Brooke personalised the theoretical processes driving the European crisis and, in his case, eventual enlistment. His ultimate conclusion is based not on a rationale, but on a feeling, as a sudden recognition of 'England' and all that the nation meant to him 'seemed to flash like a line of foam'[28] across his consciousness. 'England', both as a physical and theoretical entity, became the inspiration. This was 'a new feeling', and he 'didn't know whether he was glad or sad'.[29] The security of his homeland and all this represented – the beauty of the English countryside, London,

Cambridge, and Grantchester, the heritage of literature and thought and above all friends – *was* important to him. The thought of 'enemies and warfare on English soil … sickened him',[30] filling him with what he shamefully admitted was a feeling almost of '"holiness" … the triumphant helplessness of a lover'.[31] This might be a conventional sentiment, but Brooke was coming to see its centrality to his literary philosophy as well as to his moral and civic resolve. The 'thoughts by England given' that he would shortly explore in 'The Soldier' – which he originally considered entitling 'The Recruit'[32] – were beginning to take shape.

With the War Sonnets Brooke would also detail his journey from poet to 'England's Poet-Soldier', utilising the genre most associated with sentiment and feeling. The poems would achieve a wider and more lasting fame than was afforded either Murray's pamphlet or 'An Unusual Young Man'. Although his young man was an unusual one, Brooke acknowledged, albeit at times 'to his disgust', that the 'most commonplace sentiments found utterance in him'.[33] He was also capable, unlike Murray, of being flippant. 'An Unusual Young Man' contains one of Brooke's glibbest, oft-quoted declarations: he 'kept saying to himself – for he felt vaguely jealous of the young men in Germany and France – "Well, if Armageddon's *on*, I suppose one should be there"'.[34]

Central to Brooke's mindset, to his war poetry and ultimately to the success of the idealised myth of the poet-soldier was the fact that, in August 1914, he determined that the increasing conventionality of his patriotic sentiments did not undermine their value. Instead, he determined to raise them above less sincere and considered propaganda. Jingoism, Brooke concluded, was not jingoism if it was recognised as such by its author. The War Sonnets must offer clear evidence of reason, beauty, and passion. To borrow Murray's words, they must reveal 'the extraordinary good' hidden in the 'wilderness of evil'[35] that was war. Viewed thus, the sentimentality and high emotion of the War Sonnets – 'God be thanked Who has matched us with His hour';[36] 'bugles' bringing 'Holiness, lacked so long, and Love, and Pain';[37] and 'our hid security, / Assured in the dark tides of the world that rest'[38] – become more understandable.

4

Enlistment

B rooke might be increasingly sure of his moral resolve, but he still had to find a way into the war. His path to becoming an officer would meander for a little while longer. Brooke, like many readers in England and around the world, was impressed by the romantic accounts of Belgian and French heroism in the war's opening weeks. He would have read of the gallant (and desperate) halting of the German Army at the Battle of the Marne. This was grim and heady stuff: Paris menaced, and the famous taxis ferrying troops up the line to defend the city. The war, for all the horror of the appalling casualty figures of its opening weeks, seemed romantic, desperate, *and* modern, particularly as it was presented in the Allied press, which painted a picture of men willing to go all out – *à outrance* – to defend their homes, families, and civilisation.

Less gloriously, but no less bravely, the professional British Expeditionary Force (BEF) faced the numerically superior Germans as it made its long, dusty, and bloody-footed retreat from Mons; newspapers – and in particular *The Times* dispatch on 30 August – detailing the retreat aided in the great push for volunteers that ultimately fed Kitchener's new army.[1] Meanwhile, in the East, the Russians, rag-tag but voluminous, advanced into Germany. Across Europe the armies left behind them the swelling bodies of dead comrades and dazed masses of refugees. Brooke thought of accompanying his friend Jacques Raverat to France under the pretence of helping to garner crops; he reasoned that he might join up with some sort of informal military expedition there. Like many potential volunteers in August and September 1914, he increasingly feared that he might miss his chance to see direct action, and that all the best stories, even the tragic ones, might already have been told.

Although it remained appealing, Brooke quickly turned from his first preference of becoming a journalist. Given their limited access to battlefields, which professional armies initially intended to be kept free of civilian observers, war correspondents were well supplied. While experienced and already deployed correspondents were clamouring to cover the war in whatever capacity they could, Brooke was not already in convenient residence abroad with access to first-hand accounts, and possessed no particularly exceptional language skills or familiarity with the places under fire. The idea of obtaining a commission to an attractive regiment now moved to the forefront. Adapting to the limitations of his situation as well as its opportunities, he wrote to Raverat that, 'There's plenty to fight for' with regard to Belgium and English honour. He added, solicitously, that there was also 'the pleasure of fighting on the side of France'.[2]

Privately, to his friend Eileen Wellesley, Brooke explained the evolution of his outlook to the point where he definitively decided that he must volunteer for active service. The tone of the letter was particularly self-aware, and provides another example of Brooke's tendency to align his personal path to mobilisation with a mythical notion of England's resolve: 'I find in myself two natures ... There's half my heart which is normal and English – what's the word, not quite "good" or "Honourable" – "*straight*", I think ... Half my heart is of England'. This was the part of him that identified with the community of the nation and its conventional expectations of what he should do. Brooke also acknowledged that the other half of his nature had been that of 'a wanderer and a solitary, selfish, unbound, and doubtful'. This was the side that, when the war broke out, led him to think, 'Let me alone. What's all this bother? I want to work .:. If I'd wanted to be a soldier I should have been one'.

Presciently, he also weighed up the fact that a mass, modern war risked the danger of degenerating into a tyranny of bureaucracy and banality, with the individual reduced to 'a mere part of a machine'. This was a real concern, given his belief – not always consistent, but present – in his self-worth and particular capabilities: 'I can't help feeling I've got a brain. I thought there *must* be some organising work that demanded intelligence. But, on investigation, there isn't'. Having resolved to enlist, he predicted that the war was 'the biggest thing in your seventy years', a collective experience of enormous proportion that no one of his generation could avoid.

So the wandering poet resolved to becoming the poet-soldier. The war as Brooke perceived it offered a chance to move forward, to recast his identity and to test his assumptions about personal honour, bravery, friendship and what it meant to be English. His was a conscious deci-sion; he had weighed up the situation, and determined to choose the 'straight' and 'decent' path and volunteer.[3] He would put on his uniform. Once Brooke's self-mobilisation was for the most part achieved and the final decision made, he immediately resolved to cast aside doubt and began to shed his civilian identity, self-fashioning[4] himself with the aim of becoming the perfect officer. When Frances Cornford, antici-pating a more limited, traditional conflict as opposed to the culturally consuming one that now faced their generation pointed out that *soldiers*, not poets (and Cambridge Fellows), fought battles, he replied, 'We shall *all* have to fight'.[5]

He also recognised that war offered him a new topic of universal interest to readers of his poetry. *Poems* was fine, but it had not played to the sensibilities of the majority of readers; the War Sonnets would speak to the consensus and to posterity about the great and storied themes of war, youth, friendship, and death. And he would be living these themes as a soldier in service of the nation. He would reinvent himself and his writings. In recasting his public image as a charming but rather unstable and unserious poet, critic, and scholar, Brook's itinerate and bohemian existence in the years leading up to the war had caused the wife of C. G. Steel, the new Housemaster at Rugby, to offer 'sympathy with poor Mrs. Brooke for the shame that Rupert had brought on her and the school'.[6]

Mrs Steel's was by no means the unanimous opinion of the young man, but the opportunity to adopt what was a universally respected and increasingly reverenced pose did appeal to him in 1914. No more ambivalence and middle-class disapproval: as he would write in 'The Soldier': 'If I should die, think *only* this of me'.[7] His life now had a definite purpose, with all roads leading to the honourable, universally applauded act of volunteering. Despite his internal dialogues, fears, and doubts, becoming a soldier was in the end the safest option for Rupert Brooke.

*

Personal resolve was only one facet of the process of mobilisation. Counter to what Brooke and his generation might have gleaned from the pages of pre-war boys' magazines and novels, the First World War did not allow keen English volunteers simply to decide that the cause was just, to pick up a gun and charge headlong into the enemy's ranks and on to glory. Actual enlistment turned out to be another matter, and one not so easily achieved, despite the consensus that this was to be a war of unprecedented scale, demanding hitherto unimagined commitment and resources. Brooke might have thought to volunteer as early as 1 August, but in the end he spent weeks trying to find the best route into uniform.

Early in the war the British Expeditionary Force was rather limited in numbers, lacking the means to mobilise additional men quickly and on the scale of the great Continental conscript armies. The skirmishes of Empire, and even the larger engagements in the Crimea and the Transvaal, had required tidy professional outfits; Kitchener's sprawling volunteer force was still just an emerging idea in the autumn of 1914 when the professional BEF first engaged in the fight. This meant that would-be volunteers, including Brooke and many others like him, were kept in a state of voyeuristic limbo, forced to read about the exploits and deaths of already-serving friends and European counterparts in the newspapers. When the French poet Charles Péguy was killed at Villeroy on 4 September on the eve of the Battle of the Marne, Brooke noted ruefully that 'I am envious of our good name!'[8] The American poet and soon to be French Legionnaire, Alan Seeger, watched as Paris emptied of his literary friends, leaving him behind. It was terribly frustrating … for some. Isaac Rosenberg, who was in South Africa when war was declared, reacted sombrely: 'Some spirit old / Hath turned with malign kiss / Our lives to mould'.[9] (Nevertheless he still returned to England to volunteer in 1915.) War was dramatic, tragic, and compelling, but it was also elusive; even if you wanted to, you could not get at it quickly.

Brooke made his initial application to receive a commission at Cambridge where M. R. James, the Provost at King's, provided him with a character reference. James found himself signing many such forms, as the colleges emptied and many scholars – most of them younger than Brooke, and some directly from the Officers' Training Corp – made their way into the army, many never to return. Brooke's application included evidence of his 'military' experience as a Rugby School Cadet Officer in 1906:[10] Brooke wrote to a friend that he had only a 'faint, almost prenatal remembrance of some khaki drilling'.[11] Limited as this might be, it was more than many eventual British servicemen could claim. The forms were sent off for processing, and the waiting continued.

Hoping to get things moving now that he had made up his mind to fight, all the while anticipating a commission, Brooke joined the Inns of Court Regiment. He described the company as being composed of 'groups of lawyers'.[12] He was not particularly impressed with his fellow volunteers, or with the semi-serious experience of drilling. This was not at all what he wanted; he felt that he was still playing at war. Impatient, he wrote to an acquaintance in charge of processing commissions at Cambridge: 'I'm volunteering for *active* service, if you've any way of noting that'.[13]

His connections were such that in the end he was afforded special treatment; the Cambridge application was never required. At a dinner at the Admiralty on 23 September Churchill offered to help the young poet to find his place.[14] Not surprisingly, behind the scenes it was Marsh who pulled the necessary strings to make sure that Brooke got what he wanted: he was not yet an important case for the busy First Lord of the Admiralty to spend too much time on. Brooke received his commission based on Marsh's recommendation, which was endorsed in the final week of September.[15] Ironically, Marsh hoped that his involvement would provide a means of exerting some control over Brooke's whereabouts. No doubt he felt a certain level of responsibility, as well as a palpable fear about what might happen to his much-loved young friend. He wanted, as much as he could, to protect Brooke, and probably thought that the elite Royal Naval Division was a relatively safe place for him (Arthur Asquith, the Prime Minister's son, was another well-connected officer assigned to the outfit).

Marsh was, of course, ultimately thwarted in this regard. Not only Brooke's, but the fate of the Division, like many units comprised of British elites that saw action in 1914 and 1915, was a tragic one. Over the course of the Gallipoli campaign alone, from 23 April through to December 1915, casualties would grow to 102 officers and 1,551 other ranks killed; total losses amounted to 332 officers and 7,198 other ranks. Another favourite of Marsh's as well as a close friend of Brooke's, the musician and fellow of All Souls College, Oxford, Denis Browne, died in the early stages of the assault.[16] Arthur Asquith would be wounded no fewer than four times while serving with the Division. Following fighting near Beaucamp in December 1917, he was finally evacuated to England for good. He lost a leg as the result of his injuries.

Yet in September, the Royal Naval Division must have seemed an ideal outfit. Brooke was aware of interventions made on his behalf; he was rather proud of his special case status. When Cox wrote asking how to obtain for a friend a commission in the Royal Naval Division,

Brooke advised them both not to expect much: 'I've been bothering to get [another friend] Alpers in for a long time, & given up. And Alpers an officer of experience. The only way now is to be a son of the P. M., which Mr. Keene could hardly manage, or to have some considerable PULL.' Brooke admitted that his assignment had benefited from connections with Marsh and with Churchill, who were unlikely to get involved on behalf of Cox's friend: 'E.' – meaning Marsh – 'doesn't have anything to do with it except in very exceptional cases like me and the Governing Classes'.[17] He might mock these, but he was enjoying the advantages of having powerful friends.

*

As a serving officer Brooke would do his best to avoid appearing precious at the risk of undermining his relationship with the men in his charge, but his overall desire to maintain some control over his situation – an understandable yet very civilian desire, despite his military posturing – and, to the extent that he could, choreograph his terms of service, meant that he was initially as unsettled in his new military existence as he had been in his civilian life. Marsh continued to monitor Brooke's experience as the Division moved to camp and commenced training exercises. Hoping to make Brooke's time as enjoyable as possible, he endeavoured to have several of their mutually approved acquaintances placed in the same battalion. Brooke was momentarily pleased, and later wrote as advice to another friend who was trying to decide what to do 'to join anything fairly good one can, but to do so with some friend or friends. It takes the edge off if you've somebody with the same sense of humour'.[18] For all that he had little idea of the realities of active military service, Brooke, who valued his friends above all else, did anticipate the importance of unit camaraderie.

Despite his relatively fortuitous experience of enlistment, Brooke soon proved capable, right from the outset, of adopting one of the favourite pastimes of soldiers: grousing. While briefly attached to the Nelson Battalion, he decided that he did not like one particular senior

RCB/Ph/259. Professional photograph (photographer unknown) of the Hood Battalion at Blandford, Dorset in 1914 or 1915. Brooke is second from left in the middle row, Denis Browne is fifth from the left, also in the middle row, and Arthur Asquith is on the left in the back row.

officer. He wrote to his mother, and to various others – as did Browne and Asquith – criticising the man's leadership. The three determined that he had annoyed them to the point that they would have to transfer to another battalion.[19] There was little that she could do, and he knew it, but Brooke took things a step further when he complained directly to Marsh about the situation while staying with him in London in late September.[20] He was reassigned along with his favourites.[21]

    Later he explained the change to his mother, not terribly concerned by his rather unmilitary behaviour in lodging complaints outside of the chain of command, and specifically naming the offending officer:

'Oc [Arthur] Asquith & Denis Browne & I & one or two others applied to be transferred from this battalion, because we couldn't stand Cornwallis West. We've succeeded, so we leave tonight'.[22] In November, now an officer with the Anson Battalion, he again found further cause to express his displeasure with the company.[23] He was subsequently moved a second time to the Hood Battalion. As a result, everything became rather confused. Writing to Katherine Cox to request a new set of gumboots (Cox, despite their painful history, continued to fill a domestic roll in Brooke's life), he explained that 'the explicit vagueness of my address is due to the fact that I don't know what battalion I belong to: I keep changing'.[24] The poet-soldier, risking all for England, did so much more on his own terms then could be said for many fellow officers, let alone enlisted men.

Overall, Brooke was pleased with his placement in the Royal Naval Division, even if he grumbled about the specifics. Recalling his schoolboy fantasies about the Royal Navy, he wrote to Raverat that he had not joined the Army, 'but I've joined the Navy – a more English thing to do, I think'.[25] The Navy was, to his mind, the romantic option. Although he would come to dislike life in camp, he appreciated being in uniform, and wrote of his immense pleasure at hearing himself referred to as 'lieutenant'.[26] He knew that he cut a fine figure, that his uniform increased his sexual appeal, and that his friends and, indeed, his rivals noted this, and followed his exploits with some interest. Happily, he wrote to one potential lover, deploying sentiments of soldiers the world over: 'We can have fun together, can't we? And supposing I go off and get blown to pieces – what fools we should feel if we hadn't had fun – if we'd forgone our opportunities – shouldn't we?'[27]

He was also keen to persuade others that the path he had chosen was the right and 'straight' path. Having successfully obtained his commission and, eventually, a satisfactory placement, Brooke resumed his letter writing with new vigour, spending a fair amount of his time in camp writing to friends with the aim of convincing them to join up. From the Royal Naval Barracks in Chatham he wrote to Dent, 'Love to everyone. Make everyone enlist, in some form. They'll be wanted'.[28] He questioned the patriotism of some; of Dudley Ward, who was working as a journalist in London, Brooke wrote that his resolution to stay out of uniform saddened him, but was quick to assure Raverat that Ward, despite his 'German wife' and 'anti-Russian' position, was not a pacifist.[29] He promised Raverat, who was still being denied access to the French Army due to his health, to intervene with Marsh and attempt to find him an interpreter's job (he was unable to).[30] At least Raverat, he wrote to Cox at the beginning of November, 'is very French. I hope he'll be able to fight'.[31]

Brooke now viewed enlistment and commitment to the war in some form as absolute, and feared what would become of friends whose access to the prime experience of their generation was denied. He felt that they would be subsequently isolated from their peers. Trying to convince John Drinkwater to join up he wrote, 'there's great health in the preparation. The theatre's no place now. If you stay there you'll not be able to start afresh with us all when we come back'.[32] This was the moment to draw a line and 'start afresh' in life, and to turn 'as swimmers into cleanness leaping'.[33] The real, meaningful dramas were now reserved for men in uniform.

*

Once committed, there was something of a frantic – not to say arrogant – edge to Brooke's recommendations. He half believed the rhetoric of a war that one could, if one were slow off the mark, or unlucky, miss. He was troubled by his own relatively cosseted existence in camp in England; the war was going on elsewhere, and needed to be experienced in the flesh. He, like many young men who enlisted in 1914 wanted to *move*. The complicated emotional process of self-mobilisation was eventually subsumed by a desire to achieve the status of the soldier-hero that, in the heady, early days of war, despite difficulties and drudgeries, attained for many an irresistible attraction.

Looking at his enlistment process from a distance, it also becomes clear that for Brooke it was not sufficient quietly and privately to resolve

to act, and leave it at that. A published poet and writer with influential friends, he viewed himself as an emerging public figure, or at least
a person of interest, and acted accordingly. He wanted to 'express'[34]
the importance of the historical moment and his place in it as well.
Reflecting on his period of contemplation and self-mobilisation in
August 1914, Brooke would later write a brief parody of a man with
many of the uncertain characteristics he displayed in the first weeks
of the war, before he convinced himself to take on the mantle of the
poet-soldier, and sorted out the practicalities of enlistment. In this he
became 'Mr. Ripe', a man of pacifist and intellectual sympathies, whose
purpose was neither to attack nor defend, 'only to relate'.[35] After August
1914, he would work – publicly at least, whatever his private musings
or contradictions – to dismantle this persona. Now, he was a soldier
with a cause, and (for the most part) like the nation he served, resolved
to do his duty, whatever this might entail.

5

War and Waiting

In terms of narrative expediency and proximity to the anticipated test, by joining the Royal Naval Division, Brooke initially got exactly what he wanted: immediate active service. He was scarcely trained when he was sent to Antwerp on 4 October as part of an expedition that later garnered for Winston Churchill, its architect and commander, a great deal of criticism. For Brooke, his early knowledge of the deployment represented the first in a line of '*dead* secrets'[1] shared with his friends Jacques Raverat, Cathleen Nesbitt, Katherine Cox, and his mother in the months leading up to the Division's departure for Gallipoli. This bit of knowledge was gleaned from a lunch at the Admiralty on 23 September.[2]

His relatively informed position again marked him out as not necessarily a singular, but a privileged case. Brooke's 'secrets' were in essence rumours, although better informed than most, helping him to make sense of his war. One insight that emerges from the study of letters, war diaries, and memoirs from the First World War, and probably any war, is that these writings impose a narrative structure on to situations that are, in actual experience, bewildering. Brooke's reading and writing about the war also served to raise his expectations of what was to come, and to heighten his sense of proximity to the war without physically drawing him nearer to it. In early October, he was impatient to cross the line, to experience a rite of passage wherein 'the initiate ultimately leaves the liminal state and is reintroduced to the community with an altered and superior status'.[3]

*

The overall aim of the Antwerp expedition centred on plans devised as early as 1905, with a purpose that was threefold: establish a base through which the navy could easily supply the army from Britain; attack a portion of the German flank that was vulnerable to harassment by a small force; and maintain autonomy from a rival command, something less likely if operating from a French, as opposed to a Belgian, port.[4] Both General Joffre in France and Lord Kitchener refused to send troops, while Churchill was keen on engaging directly in the fight. Brooke's Anson Battalion travelled across the Channel, landed, marched, and took up a position near the village of Vienne Dieu. The weather was warm and dry. Over the course of the one night Brooke spent holding the line, the Germans directed very little fire at the forts or trenches. When the Belgian army began to fall back, the Royal Naval Division retreated, walking or catching intermittent trains all night to Selzaete, ending up portside where they met their naval escorts, and headed off back home.[5]

This was hardly the transformative catharsis that Brooke had hoped for. A fellow officer of the Royal Naval Division characterised the experience as a 'dreary anti-climax':[6] Overall, the retreat's popular label of 'disaster' was mainly the result of confusion, of battalions being separated, ending with a large number of British personnel interned in Holland for the remainder of the war.[7] Churchill was himself personally blamed in the *Morning Post* and the *Daily Mail*,[8] but tried his best to contextualise the retreat in sympathetic terms. Upon their return, he addressed the Royal Naval Division, reassuring them that, 'The Belgian people will never forget that the men of the Royal Navy and Royal Marines were with them in their darkest hour of misery, as, please God, they may also be with them when Belgium is restored to her own by the Armies of the Allies'.[9] The episode was cast as part of the greater struggle, turned into a positive vision of the nation's honourable commitment to Belgium, and to all of the victims of the war. While this might have been of limited value for Churchill's political opponents, it does offer a model for how Brooke would present the experience to his (at this stage still) limited, but no less rapt, public.

*

The fact that Brooke's only front-line experience was of a confused retreat was something that he to an extent played down in discussion with friends and family when presenting himself as a seasoned soldier. Privately, he experienced the initial confusion of many raw recruits, but having volunteered to fight and gone on to experience the retreat at Antwerp afforded him the opportunity to offer direct testimony: to act, very briefly, but in his own view authentically, as a 'moral witness'.[10] He focused particularly on the plight of refugees, a key topic for the British as well as the international press and readership, and one that became increasingly important to Brooke emotionally as justification for his involvement in the war. Reflecting on the experience in November, Brooke wrote of 'the feeling of anger at a seen wrong ... whatever happens I'll be doing some good, fighting to prevent *that*'.[11]

Privately, he drafted an immediate and spare account of the retreat in his diary, concerned only with the bare details of the expedition:

> Sunday, October 4, Woken by Maxwell 5 am; Parade 9.30, Start 10.30, Dover 1.30–2, Embark, start 7 pm ... Wednesday 9–10, R.12 [numbered trench] gun bursts: confusion ... 4, fire on R.12 ... Thursday, German airplane overhead ... shelling in port ... Alarm, 5, 5.30 out of trenches ... retire to Hoboken ... through deserted mile ... march to station, in a medley of Belgians, transport, etc., detrain 7.45 am confusedly.[12]

These observations were as much description as he had time to include, and reveal how front-line service was not conducive to producing considered, literary portrayals or poetry (and make the achievements of poet-soldiers like Isaac Rosenberg, who drafted and revised his poems in often appalling circumstances, all the more moving and impressive). Writing about the war, even for individuals later grouped as 'trench poets', was best done some distance from it.[13]

Brooke's notes chime with other accounts of the retreat: unsure of what was happening, concerned merely with keeping track of his own men, and aware only in passing of the presence of the enemy. With time to reflect, his version to Gwen Raverat on Trafalgar Day became more elaborate and metaphorical: 'I've been in Antwerp, & seen a city on fire, & heard shells shrieking invisibly in a blue sky over my head, like evil spirits, & seen a city on fire, & saw half a million refugees with white faces moving away into darkness at the rate of half a mile an hour'.[14] These lines are tinged with, and even mimic, hyperbolic newspaper accounts of the retreat as well as of the great civilian tragedy (can one really see 'half a million refugees'?); they also demonstrate Brooke's penchant for dramatic description – 'shells shrieking invisibly in a blue sky over my head, like evil spirits'. Writing to Rosalind Murray on 20 November to inform her of both his commission and his presence on the retreat: 'I *tried* to notice the points of literary & psychological interest at the time. But actually I was thinking: "When will the men – and when shall I – get our next meal?"'.[15] All in all the experience lacked certain qualities that he might have expected and hoped for. He was not alone in this. Lieutenant H. P. Baylis of the Howe Battalion concurred, recalling the mundane and demoralising nature of the retreat: 'I felt too tired to take much notice of anything except the slowness of our progress'.[16]

Despite the material and emotional limitations imposed by the brevity of the Antwerp deployment, and the fact that it was not particularly glorious, many of Brooke's uninitiated friends and acquaintances were genuinely interested, not only in his safe return but in his general impressions. 'What of Antwerp?' inquired Drinkwater.[17] Even the writer and future pacifist Lytton Strachey was intrigued. His brother James, a former close friend of Brooke's from Cambridge, also waiting to see if the sight of battle had had an immediate effect, wrote to him that 'His [Brooke's] account of Antwerp was of interest, though nothing much seems to have happened there. The Horrors of War haven't in the least got inside *his* head yet, as far as I can make out'.[18] Brooke had hardly witnessed or directly experienced enough to be fundamentally altered by the 'Horrors of War': for others the psychological effects of combat were cumulative, contributing to a shift in political opinion or poetic sensibility only after extended exposure. At most Brooke would later use the experience as a point of personal honour when writing to friends about his time so far as an officer: 'I was in it'.[19] This was distinction enough, for the moment.

The improvisational nature of the retreat dominated Brooke's unresolved narrative of Antwerp. Writing to Drinkwater about Jacques Raverat's attempts to circumvent medical refusal into the army he concluded that: 'I think he could just join as one [an interpreter] unofficially. Campaigning's an odd thing. Anybody who gets there can do anything. If he bought a bicycle, he needn't walk'. War was still, on a personal basis, an eclectic exercise for the semi-civilian Brooke. He could really only hypothesise about more direct contact with the front lines from what was an incomplete 'baptism of fire'. In so doing he stretched the story to make himself appear more of an experienced soldier than he may actually have felt himself to be. To Cathleen Nesbitt, he observed, rather superciliously: 'It's queer to see the people who *do* break under the strain of danger and responsibility. It's always the rotten ones. Highly sensitive people don't, queerly enough'. Brooke had not fallen to bits under fire; he was reasonably pleased with his initial performance, at least as he wanted to present it to Nesbitt, whom he wished to impress. He went on to admit to the limited nature of the experience, that 'I don't know how I should behave if shrapnel was bursting on me and knocking the men round me to pieces. But for risks and nerves and fatigue I was all right. That's cheering'.[20] He was still essentially speculating and, with time to reflect on his initiation, performing another act of mental

mobilisation, even as the retreat represented a disappointing half-expo-
sure to his inherited, poetically construed version of the battlefield as
both physical and metaphysical, the dividing point in a Blakean binary
between innocence and experience. What he hoped would illuminate
something about himself and the state of the English soul at war would
have to remain, for the moment, presumed.

Brooke's jottings reflected more general attempts to historicise
and, to an extent, aestheticise the conflict as it was happening, something exhibited by individuals as well as institutions from the very
beginning of the war. Lord Northcliffe, proprietor of *The Times* and
the *Daily Mail*, proposed *The Times History of the War* series as early
as the middle of August 1914. Gilbert Murray would publish a history
of Grey's foreign policy in 1915,[21] and various propaganda pamphlets,
not the least the famous Bryce Report, were begun almost as events
unfolded. In December, Brooke wrote to Cox requesting a copy of
The Times History, the 'Fall of Antwerp [number], just out'.[22] He was
careful to point out that journalistic accounts of the war to date exhibited much of the jingoism that both he and Murray had attempted to
distance themselves from in their earlier writings: to Raverat in August
he wrote, 'I hope you'll believe only a quarter of what you read in any
paper, and an eighth of what you see in *The Times*'.[23] He considered the
newspaper to be politically incongruous with some of his own more
liberal, anti-establishment beliefs, but he was still curious about how
the 'newspaper of record' presented the retreat, and in how he might
contextualise his own small role in relation to the wider war. Later,
The Times in particular, and the press more generally, would play a
vital role in constructing and disseminating Brooke's own posthumous
reputation, as they were instrumental in influencing the legacy of military campaigns, even inglorious ones.

*

When he returned from Antwerp to camp at Chatham and moved on
to training camp at Blandford, Brooke tried to understand and master

military life as a very new officer. He spent a large amount of time attempting to keep track of his platoon, trying to identify them from memory (for example, by whether or not they were Irish). He was preoccupied with the more mundane aspects of life in uniform, and how these effected the morale of his men. His Anson Battalion officers' notebook contains pages of requests: '1 Rifle wanted for Cassidy, and 1 Bayonet; 4 Blankets, Gors, Kavanaugh … knives, forks, spoons, caps, boots, water bottles, haversacks, greatcoats'.[24] To Cox he wrote, 'I can't find a machine gun. Tell Dudley'.[25] He asked her to please tell 'these domestic ladies making socks, mufflers & belly bands … to send them to me. I can always use them for my platoon'.[26] Little luxuries were important: he asked for mince puddings from his mother, as many as she could make, and turkeys as well for the stokers at Christmas. He also requested that she get in touch with one of his men's wives who hadn't yet received her allotment, and also that she should do something for her while this was being sorted out. On another occasion, he asked Cox to get involved in supplying actual kit: 'We're getting eight rifles with telescopic sights, for our company's snipers … Each officer is getting the money for one or two, promised. I thought you and I might give 4 guineas each'.[27] Providing supplies was a responsibility expected of the wealthy officers of the Hood Battalion in 1914,[28] and despite the reduction in his family's financial circumstances, a product of the death of his father that made him even more dependent on the patronage of friends, Brooke needed to keep up appearances.[29] His characterisations of the Royal Naval Division at this stage makes it appear almost a semi-private enterprise, as the gears of the war bureaucracy creaked slowly into action in response to the scale of the conflict. He promised to pay back family and friends who helped out materially and financially, for he 'had it from Mrs. Churchill' that their kit allowance was to be £40.[30]

After the anti-climax of Antwerp, he now found himself occupying something between a kept and a Spartan existence, and providing for his own material comforts also occupied his time and writings. His mother supplied him with his favourite newspapers. Again and again he turned to the sensible and motherly Cox, who collected the bits that he desired, including everything from toothpaste to field glasses. His ability to acquire what he needed, upon request, and to domesticate his surroundings further differentiated him from many of the enlisted men. He mused over furnishings for his quarters, asking Cox's opinion on how to make his hut more inviting: he was to live in it for seven or eight weeks, and 'one must look nice'. He excused himself these potentially frivolous concerns in military terms as they were there 'To soothe one's nerves after marching'.[31] More grandly, he also requested a car, and asked his mother if he might take over the family automobile, as he thought he could get it registered as government property. With that at his disposal, he argued, he and his fellow officers could more easily travel around the surrounding countryside, and make diversionary trips to London.[32] Camp for Brooke was thus a hybrid civilian and institutionalised experience, combining the social entertainments of the officer class with the marching and training that characterised the daily existence of a soldier.

For Brooke, as for other officers, this concern with material provisions was also a shortcut to leadership, akin to his assuming a lofty and all-knowing tone in letters following the Antwerp expedition as he searched for ways to fulfil his new role as a volunteer soldier after a relatively sheltered life and fledgling literary career. Brooke's concern with providing additional material support and even luxuries for his men illustrates his sincere desire to become a popular and trusted officer, following the expectations set by a still-rigid class system. At this point he was neither the tested 'old soldier' nor a civilian; he lived in a kind of limbo. Meeting daily needs at camp offered Brooke another opportunity to move away from the culture of the latter, to align himself firmly with the military hierarchy, which strictly controlled the roles and relationships of servicemen, and to embed himself in military life. That Brooke remained in England, far from the battlefield where the real tests to leadership, and the opportunity to form and strengthen relationships with the men in his charge still loomed, was for him increasingly frustrating as the months passed. It informed his thinking at the time as he imagined ways to explain the experience – both physical and philosophical – of becoming a soldier.

And yet his civilian identity and existence persisted. He was given various short leaves, and spent a great deal of time visiting, or being visited, or – in the absence of the event – in planning visits. He wrote multiple letters to his mother about securing rooms in the nearby inn, and the logistics of spending tea and dinner with her and his Aunt Fanny.[33] He wrote light-heartedly that perhaps Lascelles Abercrombie could be made assistant clerk to the Admiralty so that he would be included in order to discuss their work on the next issue of the literary journal *New Numbers*.[34] When it was known that Churchill, along with the king, were coming to review the Battalion, Brooke presented the rather formal, morale-boosting exercise as an opportunity to break up the monotony with friends and acquaintances: 'We hope to get Winston down here in the mud'.[35] On this particular occasion he was able to combine socialising with soldiering; Marsh also made it to camp, and they all dined together along with Herbert Asquith, who had come along as well.

*

To counter such semi-civilian diversions, and to offset misgivings about his as yet incomplete shift from martial innocence to experience, Brooke's writing in the first autumn and winter of the war increasingly fixed on paradigm, that of the decadent home front contrasted with the Spartan aestheticism of the self-sacrificing serviceman, adopting a pose of 'critical separation'. Although (as Brooke's experience of camp illustrates) identity was 'braided together', soldiers and civilians in war time saw themselves as clearly delineated, and 'this distinction informed the moral code of austerity and sobriety through which the shirker, the black marketer, and the profiteer became the internal enemy, enjoying the spoils of war while soldiers faced unimaginable hardship'. This sense of a hierarchy of sacrifice became more acute in the later years of the war: Brooke would not live to see the effects of an extended, resource-sapping conflict. But the emergence of the 'two collectives'[36] influenced even his concise experience of the war.

Despite, or perhaps owing to, the fact that he was relatively cossetted in his day-to-day life as a soldier, in his camp letters Brooke introduced an anti-civilian line, critiquing what he viewed as the apathy of the general population and, in particular, the pacifist attitudes of some of his friends. As early as late October, he wrote to Cox that, 'I get more & more sad that England's taking it all so lightly. I'm praying for a raid. No one really knows we're at war'.[37] For Brooke, rumours of the likelihood of an invasion of England served a dual purpose. He hoped – vaguely – that the shock would awaken the population to the realities of war and, more specifically, that this could lead to real, honest-to-goodness 'active service'[38] in defence of the homeland for himself: in other words, movement and direct access to the much-romanticised crucible of battle. Brooke continued his project of constructing personal and collective war identities; he examined the 'good' – or 'straight'[39] – and the bad in himself, continuing through his Antwerp portrayal into camp life and projecting into the future when he hoped to achieve a more heroic version of himself, part of a more heroic version of the English community as a whole.

One particularly lengthy and revealing letter to E. J. Dent illustrates his belief, at least theoretically, of the need to cast aside individual needs and aspirations in support of the general war effort. On 5 November, Brooke responded to an appeal on behalf of a mutual school friend who required financial aid to travel to Los Angeles on account of poor health. He was furious, returning to the plight of refugees to justify his increasingly hard-line stance towards the war and universal sacrifice: 'I feel that if there's a ghost of a chance of Pole doing some good by giving his life, he should try to give it. Also, that if anyone *has* any spare money, that he should be trying to assist with it some of the poor Belgian widows & children. I've seen those widows & children'.[40] Having written to Rosalind Murray of his 'satisfaction' at the prospect of 'avenging the wretched Belgian refugees I saw in the night in Antwerp',[41] he added his voice to the popular, international outrage that met reports of German atrocities in the famous university town of Louvain: 'Cambridge is very fine' for housing refugees.[42] To Dent, he offered an apocryphal story very much in line with the emerging propaganda printed in newspapers in order to illustrate what he felt was an appropriate level of commitment and sacrifice:

> I know a girl who is consumptive. Her doctor said she'd probably die if she didn't spend this winter in a sanatorium. She's doing Belgian refugee organisation & clothing in London: & is going to stay it. One of her three brothers was shot through the head near Ypres a week ago, leading a charge. The other, who has spent a third of the last two or three years in a consumptive sanatorium, is at the front in the Flying Corps: & will stick at it, till a bullet or consumption remove him, – or 'til he returns, whole & hearty, at. There's nothing like disregarding weakness.

He explained his hard-line tone to Dent as resulting from his proximity to those who had experienced war directly, and his belief in the need to build a moral infrastructure around what civilians should be prepared to offer of themselves in war; that is, volunteer to serve in whatever capacity they could, not avoid duty as he felt Dent's friend was attempting to do:

> In the room where I am writing are some twenty men. All but one or two have risked their lives a dozen times in the last month. More than half have gone down in torpedoed ships, & been saved *sans* their best friends. They're waiting for another ship. I feel very small among them.

His perceived personal inadequacies ('I feel very small among them') made him increasingly extreme in his support of the war, and how he conceptualised individual relationships to it. His civilian friends, he felt, ought to feel equally humbled, and further commit themselves, even if they had to rely on their imagination for motivation; 'that, & the sight of Belgium … makes me realise more truly than most people in England do – to judge from the papers – what we're in for, & what great sacrifices – active and passive – everyone must make'.

Brooke's interpretation mirrored broader shifts towards a more hard-line interpretation of patriotism, reflected not only in political debates and shifting allegiances (from the suffragettes' general pause in hostilities with the establishment to the conceptualisation of 'labour' as the material ramifications of the war clarified) but in popular English, and to an extent in British culture also at the time. Brooke positioned himself firmly on the side of honour and sacrifice. Even as his direct experience of war more accurately characterised him as a semi-mobil-ised witness as opposed to an active combatant, it was enough to justify a personalisation of the war and the nation's attitude towards it: 'I couldn't bear it if England does not face or bear what Germany is facing and bearing'. At the close of the letter to Dent he relapsed into a more private, generous, and self-aware tone for a moment, asking that he 'Forgive my tirade', but he still made any financial aid conditional upon Pole's attempting to enlist in one form or another.[43] For Brooke, the war was becoming a polemic battle pitting service against selfish-ness. He had placed himself at his country's disposal, on the side of right, and others must as well.

*

And yet, still Brooke the poet waited, impatiently, to assume the iden-tity of the poet-soldier; criticising civilian attitudes provided a foil to his persistent inactivity. His disillusionment with camp life only increased when promises of deployment to France failed to materialise: upon returning to camp from Antwerp, he wrote excitedly to Gwen Raverat that 'We're going to train for a few months, & then go out to France, starting on the lines of communications: about Christmas time, prob-ably'.[44] This was one of the many rumours in the period leading up to the Royal Naval Divisions eventual embarking to the Dardanelles that ultimately proved a false lead. Another invasion scare prompted a quick farewell to his mother; 'If it's in Kent, we may get to the front, I hope so'.[45] Disappointed that nothing had happened, he again took up his anti-civilian line, describing the situation where, 'Elderly men rushed about pulling down swords from messroom walls and fastened them on with safety pins'.[46] Deployment plans for his platoon remained for much of the time in camp hypothetical up until the point of departure for Gallipoli, and despite his connections at the Admiralty Brooke was as subject to the seemingly inexplicable timetables, calls, and recalls of military life as any other officer or enlisted man. He continued to feel the need to remind those in the civilian world of the importance of what he was doing, and also to remind himself that camp life was worthwhile despite its tedium; they were all working towards a larger test.

Excepting periodic spikes in excitement, mainly inspired by diversions in London, in practice after the initial taste for front-line experience gleaned at Antwerp – altogether 'A queer business'[47] – Brooke was simply bored. He surmised that '"military life", in training, is quite "soft" for officers; not nearly so "hard living" as the larger part of my life has been: an existence endurable by anybody who can endure – say – college life'.[48] Really, he wrote, it was all 'very dull'.[49] By January, Brooke was becoming rather desperate; 'I'm fixed here for God damn how bloody long: waiting till the rest of the Division gets shipshape. Till April I fear. God knows how I shall live through the interval, till we can blessedly get out'.[50]

Brooke's initial horror at the outbreak of war, followed by a sustained period of anxious waiting anticipating the ultimate test of battle and – lurking beneath – the implicit threat of death, are important to understanding the context for his ultimately famous and influential poems, the War Sonnets, which emerged out of this period of waiting. Through these he constructed an aesthetic and moral allegory of volunteerism and military camaraderie, self-consciously separate from, but implicitly informed by, civilian ideals as they emerged and began to calcify in England in the opening autumn and winter of the First World War. Although they can be – and often were – read as unreservedly positive expressions of a mind fully resolved to do his duty, they were as much born of contradictions: of 'the oxymoron of agreeable horror', and of a 'Romanticism … nursed on calamity',[51] as of a pure unadulterated patriotism.

6

The War Sonnets

Our genuine admiration of a great poet is a continuous *under-current* of feeling; it is every where present, but seldom any where as a separate excitement.

Samuel Taylor Coleridge, *Biographia Literaria*,
Part I, Chapter 1

Like many public schoolboys with literary ambitions, Rupert Brooke's poetic mentors shifted over time in response to his passions and tastes. As an adolescent, Brooke preferred the Victorians, particularly Browning. At 18, the list included Rossetti, Swinburne, Dowson, and Wilde. At Cambridge, his interests ran to the Elizabethans, and Geoffrey Keynes, who had been a student at Rugby with Brooke, recalled the fashionable and somewhat affected young poet being given a volume of Baudelaire in 1906.

Keynes, who served in the Royal Army Medical Corps during the war, developing a portable blood transfusion device, later became a great champion of Brooke's. He felt that by the end of Brooke's university years, a combination of awakened political awareness and the

maturation of his emotional life meant that the ephemeral literary influ-
ences faded. From one who 'affected to think Tennyson old-fashioned'
and whose 'enthusiasms were the natural tastes of his age' emerged a
poet of 'genuine feeling', so that in the end his later poems were 'inspired
by his own experiences, though few of his friends knew of the heights
and the depths of the emotional crisis through which he passed'.[1]

This emphasis on authenticity, on reaction and observation free
from affectation or false influence would become a point of praise, as
well as a bone of contention, for many readers of Brooke's poetry – and
in particular the sequence of poems collected as the War Sonnets[2] –
from 1915 onwards. For many readers, these verses, and especially 'The
Soldier', 'The Dead', and 'Peace', in descending order of popularity, rang
with the authenticity of the enthusiastic volunteer demonstrating the
purest patriotism. They represented an update of the work of canonical
poets like Byron, Tennyson, and Kipling, speaking to, and for, a new
generation. Brooke and his poems were an affirmation of the 'English'
values of honour, aestheticised youth and friendship and, ultimately,
self-sacrifice. They were also a product of Brooke's personal experience
of the war, as well as what he perceived to be general 'undercurrent[s]
of feeling', captured and fixed in verse, through which he strove towards
Coleridge's ideal of the 'great poet'.

The timeline that dictated the War Sonnets' creation reveals that,
in truth, Brooke's poems were imaginative exercises anticipating a
direct experience of war. This is not to say that they fail to reflect, or
build upon Brooke's encounters with the war in 1914 and 1915, and
somehow ring hollow as examples of an elusively authentic war experience: 'Fear and mortality were written, tinged with Georgian ardour'
into Brooke's poems, but 'daily degradation was not'.[3] Readers, some of
whom assumed that Brooke had fought for an extended period of time
at Gallipoli, or in France, would posit their own experiences onto the
War Sonnets and the myth of the poet-soldier, but this would happen
later.

*

In the absence of a cathartic experience at Antwerp, and with military life in camp grating on his nerves, what did inform Brooke's particular approach to the War Sonnets in the autumn and early winter of 1914? They avoid – at least overtly – reflection on the confusion and disappointment that coloured his only direct experience of deployment. He was feeling low for much of the winter, depressed at the death of many Cambridge and Rugby friends, and as such felt a personal connection to the growing body of commemorative poetry and literature that emerged out of the ghastly opening months of the war.

Brooke was not explicit, at least in letters, as to the motivations behind the five soon-to-be famous sonnets. He kept rather quiet about them, seemingly mulling over and distilling the complex circumstances of their creation. Before the war, he often discussed his efforts with Marsh, but the relative lack of self-commentary on the poems that would later secure his fame may have been the result of Brooke's consistent attempts throughout the autumn of 1914, carrying on across the winter of 1915, to distance himself in his correspondence from his intellectual, civilian self, and to embody the imagined ideal of a soldier that he hoped to assume, whatever his perceived limitations: 'I feel so damnably incapable. I can't fly or drive a car or ride a horse sufficiently well'.[4]

As his presumed destination, prior to January 2015 when plans for the Dardanelles' action began to firm up, was France, Brooke was embroiled in a cramming course in officer training. Despite his romanticising of soldiering in letters to friends, and his excursions to London, he wanted to be practically prepared: '*Must* have a cloth to tie around action of rifle; *Must* keep ammunition clean … Practise men in cleaning in trench & firing'. Notebooks covering his time in camp are filled not with verse, but tactics: tips on shooting and how to take a trench successfully. He kept folded in his diary a marked copy of 'Hints for instructors on the firing point', a document modelling appropriate officer behaviour: 'It goes without saying that Instructors, besides being well up on all the theory of shooting, should be good shots themselves. A recruit will have little confidence in a man who cannot take up a rifle and prove that it is the man and not the weapon at fault'.[5] Brooke was now actively, not simply figuratively, transitioning from civilian to soldier.

Brooke's attempts to master the basics of warfare were to be expected, but he also recognised that in his role as an officer he was responsible for the lives of others, and that his own heroism was bound up in the test of whether or not he could perform to a standard under fire that minimised loss of life amongst those under his command. While the War Sonnets were criticised by some as intensely self-involved and materialistic in their preoccupation with individual sacrifice,[6] they also represent the glorification of the bonds of friendship,[7] expressing a hope that this would prove the vital ingredient to military success at the critical moment. They act not as a glorification of war, but 'celebrated in exultation the discovery of a moral purpose'.[8]

For Brooke, it was the male group, bonded by friendship and common experiences and responsibilities – the popular ideal of a coming together of individuals, united in their loyalty and fundamental honour, of the military unit as the sum of its collective heroics – that epitomised and affirmed the higher value of war.[9] He based his assumptions about the interactions within military units under fire on ideals as opposed to confirmed experience. With respect to the War Sonnets, this potential limitation compounded their appeal: because Brooke was neither fully civilian nor soldier, they translated well, expounding the common sentiments of a broad readership throughout the war. They explained and elevated generalised emotions that remained comfortably familiar and reassuring, even as the war dragged on and became a test of endurance.

While Brooke may have felt out of his depth at times in many of the particulars of being an officer, glorifying loyalty and national pride both as it related to himself and others through the 'we' of 'Peace' and 'The Dead' – 'we, who have known shame, we have found release there'[10] and 'we have come into our heritage'[11] – was something that he felt qualified to do. His initial attempts to rationalise enlistment, coupled with his stunted experience of combat, influenced by months at camp imagining ways to substantiate the tacit ties of military brotherhood, all contributed to the style and subject of the War Sonnets, which were constructed and revised between November 1914 and January 1915.

*

Having some time in camp to theorise, Brooke integrated the motifs of his general experience of enlistment and self-mobilisation into the positive, yet largely passive images that populate the War Sonnets, which avoid any direct mention of violence or killing. He had occasionally remarked on a desire to shoot Germans in his letters to Jacques Raverat, which overall were more belligerent than others written over the course of the autumn and winter. What mainly concerned him was the desire to defend, or more aggressively 'avenge', Belgium, most specifically the refugees, thereby adopting the popular justification of the British position of moral outrage as a basis for war, aligning this with his own political opinions and limited military experience.

'Belgium' became a kind of generic trope for Brooke as he wrote the War Sonnets, a justification of his wish to fight on the side of 'good'.[12] The acceptance of the ideal of a battle in the name of 'civilisation', sometimes specifically defined – as by Gilbert Murray – as a reaction against German disregard for international law, and of 'humanity', so violently portrayed in the numerous stories, some of which were substantiated by the influential Bryce Report, formed a general background for Brooke's poems. Braiding these discourses together, he also incorporated the idealised vision of the individual's relationship to a liberal and aesthetic 'England' that he had begun to work out in 'An Unusual Young Man'. As a result, the War Sonnets – and in particular 'The Soldier' and 'The Dead' – do fit ideals of what constitutes public poems.[13] However, they are not distillations of specific events: apart from his interest in reports on Antwerp and a more general interest in refugees, from the point of his enlistment in August 1914 until his death in April 1915, Brooke was – at least in the letters that exist

– relatively nonplussed by specific developments that he read of in the newspapers.[14] Instead, his War Sonnets were a general portrayal of the larger themes derived from war experiences.

It is also important to note that the War Sonnets were the products of a career poet confronting the realities of an expensive lifestyle without much family support,[15] someone who hoped eventually to achieve commercial viability through his writings. On 24 October, his publisher Frank Sidgwick alluded to the narrowly patriotic tone of much of the poetry that appeared in the newspapers in the early months of the war. Teasingly, he asked Brooke, 'Does war inspire you? It seems to make worms turn in the vitals of many of our British Singers-on whom be Peace, if Peace will kindly stop their Song'.[16] Brooke's famous poems were not to be 'British' in flavour, or overtly patriotic in the sense that Sidgwick implied and disparaged. They were an attempt to glorify something less temporal or specific, which ultimately proved commercially resonant.

Prior to the war, Brooke had, as practically every other individual who fancied himself artistically inclined, weighed in on, 'What is poetry?', a subset of the overriding question, 'What is the value of art?' He returned to these questions in military camp, and indeed for him, as for many others who voiced their opinions in the numerous articles that appeared from August 1914, hostilities rendered these questions more immediate and pertinent. Brooke agreed that, 'The great poets have always posited some splendid and abiding vision, and that all poetry is, in a sense, the soul's longing for a more lovely life'. However, he went on to question, 'Is poetry the heart of life or a ring on her finger? Is it the delicate whisper among the rare few, or for the sweating many?' Brooke's conclusion was that, with poetry one combined personal and collective experience in the sense that 'everything anyone says about poetry is true. Neither the whole truth, nor the most inspiring and glorious Truth'.[17] While poetry for Brooke represented a fusion of aesthetics and sensibility, it was primarily amorphous: it appealed – and responded – on various levels to poet and reader alike. In the War Sonnets, he wanted poetry to express a complete and transferable ideal.

This was an implicitly savvy but, for Brooke, hardly inauthentic premise upon which to construct a set of war poems. As he worked out his philosophical and practical relationship to the war he simultaneously worked to refine an idealised vision of himself that he fully intended to fulfil, and was based, in part, on his brief but much pondered experiences of the war to date. His verses fell in line with the gentle, personally derived propaganda dominant in British First World War culture throughout the war. They were a distillation of complex ideas into short, easily digestible stanzas that reflected commonly held – and culturally affirming – emotions.

Brooke also demonstrated a cultural awareness that this now world war heightened the debate over art and its value by opening up a field where artists competed as representatives of respective national cultures. Brooke wrote to Dent in November 1914 that '[Charles] Péguy[18], the poet is [sic] killed. Also various other poets. I am envious of our good name!'[19] Conscription, as well as the invasion of French soil and the threat to Paris, particularly in August 1914, where casualties numbered more than 300,000 in less than two weeks,[20] meant that proportionally higher numbers of recognised French poets and artists were being killed in the early stages of the war.[21] For Brooke, the poetry they had produced thus accrued a higher value, just as did the symbolic actions and actual deaths of the writers and artists themselves. 'I want to mix a few sacred and Apollonian English ashes with theirs', Brooke wrote to Drinkwater after he received news of Péguy's death and 'I don't know what others … lest England be shamed'.[22]

Brooke was not alone in recognising the comparative value conferred on writers when they placed themselves in physical danger and especially when they died in service of an ideal. The added moral force of the symbolic act allowed such figures to 'set the favourite pose for the period',[23] but the War Sonnets also allowed Brooke to extend his preoccupation with achieving a fusion between action and thought. Whether or not he did make the ultimate sacrifice, he wanted his experience of the war to mean something beyond the politics, petty bureaucracies, and mundane sacrifices he had witnessed and contrived in over the course of his months of service. The War Sonnets moved beyond these, exploring the larger theme of the individual's relationship to friends – in 'The Dead' offered as consolation for the individual 'wandering comradeless'[24] – to nature and to death: themes that were present in the majority of Brooke's pre-war poetry as well (and, it goes without saying, were central to the European literary romantic heritage). These timely poems offered up these themes in the context of a national – and indeed international – crisis, in response to ideas that were 'in the air'.[25]

Brooke's Sonnets were not simply the products of a visionary inspiration, or unadulterated patriotic fervour, as many obituaries and articles concerned with and contributing to the myth of the poet-soldier would later claim. They were a product of his non-linear personal mobilisation and particular experiences as a soldier. Brooke worked on them as any poet does, trying out combinations and drawing on ideals that struck an appropriate cadence. The poems were completed as Brooke became aware of the Hood Battalion's departure for Turkey, an assignment that he viewed with pleasure and anticipation, and which inspired an outburst of appreciation for what he was now – finally – setting off to defend.

After the long tedious months in camp, he was personally reinvigorated in a way that threw him back to the excitement of the initial days of the war and his enlistment, but with an even greater sense of purpose. A fragment of another unfinished ode to England that Brooke took with him aboard the *Grantully Castle* when he sailed to Gallipoli was found by Marsh on '10 Downing Street' paper, dating from Brooke's brief convalescence there following a bout of flu in January 1915, just as he was completing the famous Sonnets.[26] The fragment centred on a deep pastoral appreciation of England: 'The beds of silver and quiet grow … And the stars wheel and shine, and the woods are fair. / And light upon the snow is there'. This was reminiscent of the tone that Brooke deployed throughout the War Sonnet sequence with a seriousness and fervour that drew not only on the preceding months spent in contemplation of what made the experience of volunteering worthwhile, but from a lifetime of reading and writing romantic poetry. Distilled in the War Sonnets, this became the 'safety with all things undying'[27] promised by aligning personal fates with the nation's moral course, the 'Honour' and 'Nobleness' that 'walks in our ways again'[28] characterising the personal and generational awakening to a collective purpose, and the camaraderie 'And laughter, learnt of friends; and gentleness' born of this newfound identification of the 'body' with 'England', 'A body of England's, breathing English air, / Washed by the rivers, blest by the suns of home'.[29] The poet-soldier imagined an idealised home, just as his later readers pictured 'The Dead' and 'The Soldier' and, in some cases, the ideal of the poet-soldier: each yearned for the other.

With the War Sonnets Brooke also took up the idea – expounded publicly in numerous writings by public intellectuals like Hilaire Belloc, whom Brooke admired – of local patriotism to the national level, presenting 'England' as 'an idea whose reality was rather in the mind than on the map'.[30] Just as Brooke was deeply moved by the plight of the war's refugees, he was also inspired by the 'tragedy' and 'dignity in the people' he had invoked in his description of the war's outbreak on the night of the declaration of war. The 'people' became the soldiers, with himself amongst them; 'all those people fighting for some idea called England – it's some faint shadowing of things you can give that they have in their heart to die for'.[31] Although Brooke's preoccupation with England – as opposed to Britain or the Empire – might have limited his readership, in the end, the vague, bright idea of the nation he expounded in his poetry proved largely transferable to other national contexts.[32]

*

Brooke's War Sonnets were born of an emerging mindset favourable to self-sacrifice, as many obituaries and critical articles would later assert, informed by his particular schooling, and by inherited Romantic ideals of the poet-soldier exemplified by the likes of Sir Philip Sidney and Lord Byron.[33] But Brooke's opinions about the value and appeal of his own death in battle for England were, understandably, mixed. He did not appear drawn to killing, or to being killed: his work does not fit with the 'binary of victim and brute'.[34] He was not religious, and indeed had consistently disdained conventional Christianity. The War Sonnets instead deployed conventional sentiments about idealised youth confronting death, playing to 'an audience bound by a community of values' that considered war to be a heroic activity.[35] The convention of 'To the Death' proved immensely helpful in producing 'instant histories of the war – not of the actual fighting, but of the causes and the issues, in the simplest pro-Allied terms'.[36] Brooke might be sceptical of some forms of popular culture that cheapened or overstated the value of blind patriotism, but he was not immune to it, or to common assumptions of what constituted duty and morality in wartime, particularly when they elevated his and his comrades' activities.

On 13 January 2015, Walter Wilfrid Gibson, fellow contributor to *Georgian Poetry* and now to the forthcoming edition of the literary journal *New Numbers*, acknowledged the tardy receipt of the five sonnets: 'This is fine! It's grand to have your poems at last, and they're well worth waiting for. I've sent them off. Any charge for "holding back" will be deducted from your share'.[37] By 11 February, the poet John Masefield had become aware of the existence of the as yet unpublished poems, but had not seen them. He wrote, 'I hear you've written some sonnets. May we see them, please? We would like to see them as we hear they are very fine indeed. Do send them'.[38]

An additional point should be drawn from Masefield's question. The War Sonnets were not initially published in a form that made them particularly accessible to many readers, and if Masefield in February was unaware of their imminent publication in *New Numbers*, then certainly popular success was not assured. The likelihood of the journal even being published was initially tenuous:[39] ironically, given the success of the War Sonnets it first introduced into the public sphere, it would later become logistically too difficult and expensive to maintain in wartime.

The distance between circulation via a tiny literary publication run by a group of relatively unknown poets and the posthumous success achieved by Brooke's poems relied on a particular set of circumstances, and not least the newspaper obituaries, articles, poems, letters, and advertisements that appeared after his death. The War Sonnets provided a dearth of sombre epigrams: the 'swimmers into cleanness leaping', the 'worst friend and enemy is but death'; 'the rich Dead', 'Honour', 'Nobleness', the 'sweet wine of youth', and 'we have come into our heritage';[40] the 'corner of a foreign field', the 'richer dust', 'a pulse in the eternal mind', the 'laughter, learnt of friends', and 'an English heaven'.[41] These offered, on a platter, an accessible and appealing lexicon to politicians, editors and journalists, writers and readers, because they elide the 'physical realities of war', recasting them through 'a form of romanticised nature worship that moves the warrior out of the context of this particular war'.[42]

The relevance of the language and the ideas found in the War Sonnets, coupled with the manner and moment at which they entered the public domain, would later make all the difference. Championed by connected and anonymous individuals alike, they also tapped directly into a universal vein. A perfect context for success was emerging, and the eventual taking up of the myth of the poet-soldier by the reading public would later raise the War Sonnets above the bulk of patriotic poetry written during the war.

Brooke was never fully convinced of the collective merit of the five poems. While being transported to the Dardanelles in March of 1915 he concluded that 'The Dead' and 'The Soldier' were fine, but the others were 'poor, but not worthless'.[43] This may be an expression of modesty, but read straight it reveals a sharp eye for cultural and commercial appeal: these two poems would be quoted more than any others in the coming years, held up as standards for all would-be poet-soldiers and their audiences.

7

Transport

The machine was working again; it had snatched up their
battalion in its steel claws and dropped them on to its conveyor
belt. Now the belt was moving; whither, they did not know. It
was strange, too, to come into living contact with the machine
for the first time, to see it work.

Alexander Baron, *From the City, From the Plough*
(2010 [1948]), p. 107

Once the Gallipoli invasion was a known fact in the Hood
Battalion in January 1915, Brooke expressed pleasure at the
destination, adopting the trope of crusader in his letters
to friends.[1] Again he was better informed than most soldiers in his
position, as Violet Asquith had leaked that 'Ian Hamilton is going to
command you'. She claimed that this was her father the Prime Minister's idea, and that Lord Kitchener had instead suggested alternatives,
but warned that this was another '*deadly* secret'.[2]

Brooke's one reservation was that he would be far away from
what he considered to be the war's main theatre. Most of his training

in England had been undertaken with French and Belgian trenches in mind. All of his ideological attempts to contextualise his and Britain's participation in the war based themselves not on the Imperial, but on proximate, European concerns, namely on the much-publicised accounts of ethical and cultural outrages in Belgium, the excessive military force against civilians, and sympathy with France as an invaded and occupied nation at the mercy of 'Prussian militarism'. Brooke accepted the common motif of defence of England being defence of 'Civilisation', and subsequently wrote in semi-seriousness to Jacques Raverat that, 'I shouldn't like to get killed in Turkey. I don't mind killing Turks to begin with, but I'd like to puncture a German, before I finish'.[3]

He alleviated these concerns through a series of practical reassurances. In contrast to the bland stasis of camp, it was thrilling finally to be moving somewhere. He tried to prepare by learning a little practical Greek, practising phrases like 'How far ...?', 'sugar', 'cup', 'tea', and statements anticipating discussions of 'After ... the end of the war'.[4] Despite his desire to experience battle, he was not above admitting some (ill-founded, as it turned out) relief at his posting; he wrote comfortingly to Cox, at least 'it's [Gallipoli] not as dangerous as France'.[5] The tone of his letters, particularly those to his primary correspondent at the time, his mother, understandably offered reassurances as to his safety, enjoyment, and sense of well-being as he finally set off.

Brooke returned to the idea of collecting interesting companions for the voyage. Now that he knew more surely of the destination, he took another line, and one that would carry over into his letters aboard the *Grantully Castle* in March. Of Dudley Ward, he wrote, 'I wish he'd enlist. I'd like to enter the Hagia Sophia with him. He would be sensible about God, if we met him'. The 'expedition' now seemed to be taking on the cast of an adventure very much based on civilian ideals of pleasurable travel, a sort of organised cruise infused with a sense of national and moral purpose; the war and its requisite violence provided the backdrop, not the foreground.

Whatever his internal misgivings, the impression he gave of the transport was of a voyage that was neither necessarily sad nor glorious, but highly entertaining. From the time the *Grantully Castle* left England Brooke wrote as one travelling contentedly in the company of friends. Happily, and somewhat cruelly, he wrote to Raverat, who still desperately wanted to enlist despite his ill-health:

> On *Active* Service … with Latin & 6 [volumes of] Greek & Shakespeare … we've been gliding through a sapphire sea, swept by ghosts of Tireseus … Hannibal on the poop, or Hermes. Oh, & we came down by Spain, & say Algiers, & thought of the tribes of dancing girls, & wept for Andalusia. And now we've left Triniacria behind (you would call it Sicily) & soon – after Malta – we'll be among the Cyclades. There I shall recite Sappho and Homer. And the winds of history will follow us all the way, and you will be in Chelsea (pay!) painting gawky picture (ugh!) of green-fleshed northerners (wuff!). Poor devil. I'm a dark-eyed son of the South.[6]

Brooke's manoeuvrings to surround himself with friends made possible the continuance of his sense of exclusive camaraderie. He dined nightly with Dennis Brown, Patrick Shaw-Stewart, and Arthur Asquith, who were also relying on classical Greek references to contextualise their experiences.

One evening, following the departure of the Royal Naval Division after a stopover in Cairo, where on 31 March Brooke had been training his men at firing exercises in the hot sun,[7] there was a fancy-dress ball, from which Brooke had to leave early, as he was feeling ill. This listlessness continued: the somewhat dreamy, surreal, and unfocused quality of Brooke's letters and diaries in this period – when he was not being irreverent about feeling like a war tourist – may also be due in part to the fact that Brooke was mildly feverish throughout the voyage. He had also been inoculated following a visit to the pyramids in Egypt with Asquith, where he was struck with a 'touch of sun',[8] which may have contributed to his fatigue.

*

Brooke used verse as a space for contemplation, even for experimenta-
tion in points of view, and for appreciation of the larger implications
of death in battle. It was the form he took most seriously, and hence
the space in which he was at his most self-aware. This was common
to many of his contemporaries, and would reflect and later be used
to reinforce ideals about the sombre nature of the poet's task and his
right, and indeed duty, to assume a collective voice.

The poetry that Brooke was writing while on his way to Gallipoli
was never published in the newspapers. The most complete, 'Fragment', acts in concert with some of the themes expounded in the War
Sonnets: specifically, appreciation for the physical and psychological
pleasures of friendship. In the poem, fellow officers are viewed through
a window, becoming 'Slight bubbles, fainter than the wave's faint light,
/ That broke to phosphorus out in the night, / Perishing things and
strange ghosts, soon to die / To other ghosts, this one, or that, or I.'[9]
The poem has a particularly detached quality – 'this one, or that, or I'
– with Brooke, the 'I', firmly fixed at the centre, unseen, pitying the fact
that this 'gay machine of splendour 'ld soon be broken, / Thought little
of, dashed, scattered. ...'[10]

Finally, after months of anticipation, Brooke was taking a firm
step away from his former life. Unlike many enlisted men, his vision
of the war – in this unfinished poem and throughout the War Sonnets
– remained self-contained; throughout the transport he enjoyed the
privileges of a middle-class officer, and as such displayed a tendency for
voyeurism that contrasts sharply with the tactile, cramped atmosphere
of troop-ships, let alone that of the trenches.[11] Despite the fact that he
was sailing presumably ever closer to the fate that the War Sonnets had
imagined as a distant reality, everything seemed, to Brooke, blurred,
'faint' and calm as he discovered space for contemplation. Aboard the
ship, what was of greatest importance was the comfort of calm, reflec-
tive friendship with select company (if not close communion with *all*
of the Royal Naval Division). Sailing towards the Aegean, much as

at Grantchester, he experienced the joys of living amongst a curated group of friends, free from the expectations, dramas, and distractions of family and civilian life.

Occasionally in his letters Brooke shifted tone. Even as he wrote, somewhat callously and ironically, to Jacques Raverat, wishing for dangerous duty, he assured his mother that the battalion was unlikely to be placed in any sort of danger. He happily described his time in Malta: 'very like Verona or any Italian town, but rather cleaner and much more Southern. There was a lovely Mediterranean sunset and evening, and the sky and sea were filled with colours'. For the moment, the war was expanding his horizon in just the way he wished. It satisfied the side of him characterised by a certain wanderlust, while allowing him the pleasure of ceding control of his future to the navy, or to a more general, mysterious fate. On this occasion, his travels were less a personal exercise with journalism as the excuse, as in the case of 1913 and 1914, when he travelled through Canada, the United States, and extended his explorations into the South Seas. This was instead a nationally sanctioned quest, a 'Crusade'[12] by a 'Crusader',[13] that turned out to be rather enjoyable, 'one of the best jobs of the war',[14] as well as 'one of the important things of the war'.[15] The two halves of himself had been made into a whole.

He continued working on a poem begun at the Asquiths in the winter prior to his departure, planned as a great ode to 'England'. This in a sense expanded on what were ideas explored in the War Sonnets. He identified England – again not Britain, but instead the gentler, mythical, less politically contested entity – as the 'Mother of men'. The poem, entitled 'I.M. [In Memoriam]', still in manuscript form, explored the interplay between the individual and the eternal motherland as a mirror to what Brooke continued to view as the militant enemy: 'Prussia is a devil' set to destroy the better points of 'Civilisation'.[16] Its concern lay with legitimacy: 'Love is her soil, & the stars her justice' justified the great offering, as did the more sentimental strain of 'The heart and hands and water that we love / And she, for whom we die, she the undying'. 'England' gave purpose to death, anticipated and at moments almost desired. It ended with a reminder that Brooke was looking back, just as he had been in 'The Old Vicarage, Grantchester', now not as a voluntary expatriate, but at the vanguard of the community of defenders; 'Our wandering feet have sought, but never found her / She is built a long way off'.[17]

This partial poem, later published in *Collected Poems* in 1918 with its more personalised appreciation of camaraderie, and the predictable expansion of the ideal of an ageless, benevolent 'England', never amounted to more than a single stanza. Another poem copied in to his diary from the period presents a more graphic, direct example of war poetry. Perhaps this was a nod to the language of the stokers that Brooke commanded in the battalion, men whom he occasionally mentioned in letters to friends in England, and whom he seemed to view with some fear, in a sense trying to avoid novelising them. It demonstrates – 'he left a lump of bleeding jelly' – appreciation of a greater tonal and metaphoric range that may, hypothetically, have come to inform subsequent poems had he lived to experience multiple battles in the presence of men representing a greater cross-section of life-experience:[18]

> 'When Nobby tried', the soldiers say,
> 'To stop a shrapnel with his belly
> He   away
> He left a lump of bleeding jelly.'
> But *he* went out, did Nobby Clark,
> When the illimitable dark
> Out of the field where soldiers stray
> Beyond Parades, beyond Reveille.[19]

This poem did not display the lyric sophistication of the War Sonnets – and in particular 'The Soldier' and 'The Dead' – both natural favourites for readers seeking out a figure capable of distilling ideals of aesthetic, poetic, and patriotic 'England': 'there's some corner of a foreign field / That is for ever England.'[20] But it represented another way to imagine and ultimately describe a soldier's death and his afterlife: 'the field where soldiers stray / Beyond Parades, beyond Reveille'.

*

There was still the impending test, and the possible imminence of death, particularly once the Royal Naval Division departed from Egypt and approached the Dardanelles in April 1915. While in letters home to his mother and to friends Brooke assumed a tone of cheerfulness, his writings from the time also display evidence of what his fellow poet-soldier Edmund Blunden would later identify as 'a depressed forced gaiety then very much the rage'.[21] Brooke had heard rumours that the Hood Battalion would spearhead the attack in Gallipoli, expecting 75 per cent casualties.[22]

Brooke began, tentatively, to engage in the intellectual and practical exercise of preparing himself for death for England. In what would prove a decision with major implications for his posthumous fame, he wrote to the politically and literarily well-connected Marsh off the cost of Greece, appointing him literary executor, noting that 'This is very odd. But I suppose I must imagine my non-existence, & make a few arrangements'. After working out provisions for the division of his manuscripts, he concluded with, 'There's nothing much to say … You've been very good to me. I wish I'd written more. I've been such a failure'. This moment of depressive self-reflection is poignant; again, counter to the image of the confident, even arrogant self-sacrificing poet-soldier, Brooke felt that there were things left undone, that his life was by no means complete.

To other friends Brooke presented additional, if less definitive 'final' testaments. He had no control over the time or place of the massing invasion; he might survive the landing, or he might not. In the end, of course, he did not make it even that far, but in his weeks aboard the *Grantully Castle* he still managed to write multiple 'penultimate' letters. Cox received one penned on 10 March, telling her please to take his papers after his mother had died. He followed up this letter

– which concluded: 'I hope you will be happy, & it's a good thing I die'[23] – with a somewhat less dramatic letter dated 24 March, discussing some lectures on the war given by E. M. Forster that Dennis Brown had received in the post. Perhaps this was a way of dealing with the thought of death, not uncommon to soldiers, for 'the great paradox of death is its certainty coupled with the difficulty of actually imagining it'.[24]

He again emphasised the need for people to witness the war, maintaining that while he was being 'romantic' about battle, he 'can't tell most of the romantic things, at present. My own lot have seen no fighting yet, & very likely won't for months'. But he was tense with anticipation and a quiet terror: 'The only thing that seems certain is that one doesn't know from day to day what's to happen'. Cut off from well-connected friends, he was as unsure as his comrades as to when they would actually join the attack. He described having prepared for the landing with a few thousand other men after eating a large breakfast, an activity that he admitted did not agree with his stomach. Then, following several hours of silence while patrolling along the shore, which 'looked to be crammed with Fate', they were told that the attack was postponed. One stoker quipped, 'when's the next battle?' Brooke described being gripped with a feeling of having failed a test of responsibility as an officer, 'I was seized with an agony of remorse that I hadn't taught my platoon a thousand things more energetically & competently'.[25]

Letters like these, written to friends and family, served both an emotional and a practical purpose. They sorted out Brooke's affairs at home, and established him as ready for whatever test or sacrifice was to come. Brooke often cast himself as someone removed from the war, as, for the most part, he was. As a citizen and as a poet he was interested in its effects – poetic, aesthetic, and cultural – but he was never, in the end, despite all of his efforts at home to portray himself as a soldier first, fully engaged with, or exposed to its horrors. To Raverat on 18 March, again anticipating the long-awaited invasion and his imagined, impending death in battle: 'There are only two decent reasons for being sorry for dying, and one against. – I want to destroy some evils, & to cherish some good. Do it for me'.[26] Brooke's personal conception of the soldier was ultimately benign and, although, of course, not predicted, in his own death he fulfilled this ideal. As he had written from camp on 21 December: 'I've a restful feeling that all's going well, and I'm not harming anyone, and probably even doing good'.[27] He never found himself amongst the killing and the dying, or undertook the killing himself.

Brooke's writings offer evidence of an individual using poetic ideals to elevate what is expected of the soldier in war, and of his society in sacrificing him, supposedly for higher ideals. Although he never could be entirely aware of the appeal of his particular story, of the figure he cut and of the poems and writings he produced, he did write, teasingly, to Violet Asquith, describing a meeting with General Hamilton just prior to his death on 23 April as 'our greatest poet-soldier and our greatest soldier-poet'.[28] In the end he seems to have counted himself the former: still the 'poet-soldier', emphasising his literary identity first despite his months in uniform. However, he did not explicitly specify a preference. His letters and poems of the war hint at a desire to become more the man of action, 'soldier' first and 'poet' second. Like the instinct that led him to identify 'The Soldier' and 'The Dead' as his most appealing War Sonnets,[29] the sum of his writings recognised and commemorated the voluntary death of the soldier. This would prove fertile ground – and provided a fair amount of material – of use to those who worked to popularise Brooke's poetry and person after his death. The myth that emerged appealed to a variety of audiences, some with vested interests – be they private or public – who used it to define ideals of national honour and sacrifice, and for the individual and collective management of grief.

II

Afterlife

8

Patriotic Poetry

Throughout the First World War, official and unofficial propagandists alike stressed the idea of cultural superiority as justification of war in defence of 'Civilisation'. In 1916, official German propagandists released a poster offering portraits of great artists alongside comparative illustrations of social welfare as a refutation of Allied charges of 'barbarism' in conquered territories.[1] In London, the 'most effective series of recruitment posters' quoted lines of William Shakespeare on war as a reflection of the tradition of poetry, language, and resolve.[2] Spearheading British propaganda efforts in the early years of the war, Charles Masterman, at Lloyd George's behest, enlisted the services of various writers and poets for Wellington House, and saw that their endorsement of the war was published not just in England but on the front page of the *New York Times*.[3] The American poet-soldier Alan Seeger, who joined the French Foreign Legion at the outbreak of the war, from 1915 until his death in 1916 published excerpts from his diary as well as occasional editorials urging American intervention.[4] Writing from the trenches at Aisne, he presented his case on the grounds of the cultural and moral superiority of the Allied cause, invoking the universal duty to march 'forth with haste'.[5] *The Times* sent Robert Bridges to report on factory conditions:[6] his piece was consciously poetic, as was Rudyard Kipling's 'The Battle of Jutland', when describing the plight of British ships under attack.[7] It can even be argued that the persistent appeal of Brooke's War Sonnets to wartime readers was at least in part down to their echoing the rhetoric of war correspondents, who saw it as their duty to explain the war in aesthetic – as well as political and logistical – terms to the readership.[8]

From its start, writers and public figures defined, recast, expanded, and narrowed the war's philosophical terrain. Journalists and editors responded to war news by fitting their copy to the accepted ideals of justification, which fell under the consensus principle established in August 1914: the actions of the Triple Alliance nations, and in particular German aggression, meant that the Allies held the moral imperative. Through the various media available, they strove to provide and promote examples of cultural superiority. Rupert Brooke's life and afterlife provided useful material: fitting the popular sentiment, and pliable in terms of application.

The official British propaganda organisations, including the Press Bureau, Wellington House, and the Parliamentary Recruitment Committee recognised the importance of employing poets in some capacity to support a liberally patriotic interpretation of the war. John Masefield, Thomas Hardy, and Kipling were all established men of letters in 1914, and their endorsement of the war was presented to the public as an organic, independent reaction based on sensitive, balanced consideration of the cultural and moral values of the competing belligerents. Government officials – first Masterman and later Lord Beaverbrook – acted behind the scenes, providing some financial and logistical support. Masterman's influence was more benign than his replacement's; in 1917, the government began to pay closer attention to how it might overtly and covertly influence public opinion. But, for the first two years of the war, lack of an organised governmental structure monitoring and contributing to the national discourse on patriotism meant that the media – and specifically newspapers – were highly influential in setting the tone for patriotic expression.[9]

With respect to managing the formal relationship between the government and the press, for F. E. Smith, former editor of the *Westminster Gazette* (and the man who commissioned Brooke's 'Letters from America' in 1913), the aim was to maintain a sense of goodwill and inter-party cooperation in order to present a unified front supporting the war. He wrote to Lloyd George in September 1914, 'Winston tells me you thought the constitution of our [Press] Bureau unduly Tory ... In fact *all our rows without exception* have been with Tory papers ... You know me too well to suppose I want party capital out of the damned office'.[10] As much as possible he wanted the Press Bureau to behave in a manner that raised patriotic rhetoric above political infighting. While individual acts of censorship resulted in complaints, generally speaking, the Press Bureau and Wellington House managed to avoid appearing as uncritical mouthpieces of the government, whereas, for instance, in the United States, George Creel's conception of the Committee for Public Information as a 'plain publicity proposition'[11] would get it wrong.[12]

Furthermore, as opposed to viewing the press as hostile, many political leaders fully endorsed the notion of close cooperation. In March 1915, Ivor Nicholson instructed Lloyd George of his opinion that 'There is a need of a frequent and stimulating contact between the people and their rulers, in order that the tendency to slackness of interest in the War may be counter-acted'.[13] Cooperation between the government, the Press Bureau, newspapers and various commercial publishers produced a broad consensus about the fundamental ideals of the war that held firm, for the most part, throughout the war.[14] The line between news as information and news as propaganda – even news as entertainment – was necessarily blurred. The majority of those directly in control of the close, cross-referring official and supposedly critical estates of state saw no problem in collaboration. They naturally turned to whatever was at hand, and specifically to the heritage of Edwardian 'imaginative literature' to understand pressing political and social problems.[15]

The Press Bureau also encouraged greater collaboration between newspapers, particularly at the early stages of the war when they were dependent on the same government and military sources for news of the fighting. In the resulting semi-vacuum, editors looked to one another for stories. The press, in particular *The Times,* with its highbrow reputation for serious political and cultural discourse, from 1914 succeeded in reaching an even wider audience by acting in close cooperation with mass-market dailies such as the *Daily Mail* and the *Daily News. The Times,* with its middle- and upper-class readership particularly keen to be updated on political developments in wartime,[16] could introduce a story, and allow its fellow papers to continue and expand and reprint elements of it, producing relatively uniform writings of similar focus and tone.

The Times was not the only paper to report on the total nature of the war abroad and at home – about major battles, German atrocities in Belgium, debates at Westminster, or the death of a poet-soldier – only to see them reappear, in part and in full, in local, national, and international media outfits. The establishment consensus on how to approach the war, and the level of contact between Fleet Street editors – enshrined in practices like the *Nation* lunches – ensured a consistency of subject; each was aware of one another's stories, even up to anticipation of the day of printing. Institutions like the Press Bureau and the office of the Censor structurally conflated the community's already concentrated networks.

After his death, Brooke, 'an English hero',[17] would emerge as a particularly useful figure for newspaper editors, convinced of the need to promote the British cause in as many ways as possible. He could be presented as apolitical: the poet-soldier who also inadvertently provided his own epitaphs in the form of the concise, reprintable War Sonnets. He appealed to editors keen to inspire readers enthusiastically to support the war, and concerned that the general public might not fully understand the gravity of the task the nation had embarked on. This preoccupation persisted, and provides an insight into what many newspaper editors and their subordinates saw as their primary function in wartime.

By example, Geoffrey Dawson,[18] the editor of *The Times* who would play a central role in drafting the newspaper's influential obituary of

Brooke, explained what he saw as most important to convey consistently through the daily leaders: namely the need for the nation to take the war as seriously as he felt were he and members of the government. Despairing, in June 1915, he wrote that he had 'doubts whether the Nation realises the war'.[19] He was moved by, and continued to urge his journalists to try to balance accounts of, the heroism and pathos of the war. Eventually, although he appreciated the spirit of the volunteers, he – and *The Times* – came to support conscription on the basis of its great organising potential, and its ability to 'put a stop to an immense amount of ill feeling between classes and individuals'.[20]

In July 1915, writing about the Dardanelles campaign, he offered the following instruction:

> I should take the same line we have always taken about the light-heartedness, the want of coordination, and the general muddle in which the Expedition was begun … I do not think you can place heroism too high. To me it is perfectly amazing that so many of these people – only partly trained and quite unused to battle – should have done so splendidly.[21]

Dawson did not want to obscure the grave situations the war introduced; he wanted to manage them. Sometimes this translated to too much control and advice, encapsulated in a complaint from one of his writers: 'I think that at present you are trying to do too much. The net result of the present method is that you are in effect providing all the leading ideas to which the paper gives publicity'. *The Times* was in danger of becoming a single-voice political platform for its editor: 'Without in the least lessening your control, I think you should encourage, more than you do, the propounding of ideas. I don't mean little ideas, but the broader lines of policy'.[22]

The 'propounding of ideas' required a broader brush. Sidney, Shakespeare, Milton, Byron, and, it would emerge, Brooke, exerted a hold over people's imaginations, especially in wartime. Even such subjects as a walk outside could be turned into an opportunity to remind readers of the sacrifices of the soldiers, and the cultural heritage they died for: 'these things have a beauty through their sacrifice which they have not had before'.[23] The shock of high casualties could be softened, and death in war – at least as a theoretical proposition – made more appealing when placed in this continuum.

*

The 'larger ideals' informing the case for total commitment to the war, so clear to editors and journalists, could thus be conveyed to the readership in a manner appealing to their particular tastes. Poetry and poets, past and present, provided a useful alternative register counteracting more visceral patriotic expressions. The precedent of 'public poetry' written with the aim of distilling and expressing a national sentiment was well-established. Both Kipling and Hardy had contributed poems upon the occasion of Edward VII's death that sublimated personal politics for a general presentation of national grief and sadness.[24] Examples of poetry exalting death in battle were numerous, with poems such as Tennyson's 'Charge of the Light Brigade' and Sir Henry Newbolt's 'Vitaï Lampada' influencing the public's imaginative expectations of later conflicts.[25] Contemporary examples included Hardy's 'Men Who March Away', included in his *Satires of Circumstance* at the last moment in August 1914. The volume was set for printing, but the poet did not feel that the overall tone was appropriate given the changing political context, and hence included the single patriotic verse to acknowledge the historical moment.[26] Not only the subject matter, but the specific language deployed by the popular press overlapped with poetic spheres. Rudyard Kipling's poem 'For All We Have and Are' included the lines, 'The Hun is at the Gate', a phrase that initially turned up in the *Daily Mail* as part of its coverage of the sacking of Louvain.[27]

Early in the war, *The Times* published a brief article under the title, 'War Poetry',[28] outlining a lecture given by Sir Herbert Warren, the Professor of Poetry at Oxford, who spoke at the Sheldonian Theatre (the Examination Schools, the usual venue for public lectures of this kind, had been turned into a hospital). The correspondent, echoing Warren on Tennyson, was impressed by the relevance of the poet's 'patriotic songs' from the preceding century: 'How strangely much of it again seemed to fit the present moment! The great scene had been re-enacted in the streets of London and in St. Paul's'.

Warren began his lecture by praising a 'fine article' in *The Times* on 'French War Poetry', which had asserted that the English had no tradition of war poetry. Warren argued that while this may have been true in the sense that England had been without 'its agonies on her own soil', poets, in this case Tennyson, who had grown up during the Napoleonic wars, had contributed to the nation's substantial book of 'war songs', primarily with the verses that 'made him, more than any one had ever been before, the Laureate of the nation'. These were 'The Charge of the Light Brigade' and its epilogue, 'The Charge of the Heavy Brigade', which gave 'most precisely and concisely his view of war and of the soldier's duty'. The article concluded with the lines: 'Man needs must combat might with might / Or might would rule alone', and:

> Who loves war for war's own sake
> Is fool or crazed or worse.
> But let the patriot soldier take
> His mead of fame and verse.

The lecture – and subsequent article – stressed the value of patriotic verse to the soldier and to the nation, and the relevance and rightness of the poet's valuation of war as a necessary evil.[29]

The patriotic discourses that Brooke's semi-private mobilisation, his death, his public image, and the War Sonnets were shaped by and would later contribute to, were constantly reiterated and reworked throughout the war: in the daily political leaders and opinion pieces, in obituaries, literary reviews, religious articles, and even advertisements. The *Times Literary Supplement* provided a literary compliment to the news reported in *The Times*. Prior to the war, in February 1914, Dawson had discussed with Lord Northcliffe the idea of greater interaction between the two; 'He tells me that you want to introduce the ordinary *Times* measure into the *Literary Supplement* next week, from which I infer that you would like reviews of books to begin to appear in the paper'.[30]

An article published on 3 September 1914 illustrates the tone adopted by the *Times Literary Supplement*, which shifted only occasionally over the course of the war. 'Patriotic Poetry: Articles in the Literary Supplement' was published in the wake of the retreat from Mons; at such a moment, it seemed appropriate to discuss the 'varied ways in which singers of our country have expressed the love which England inspires in her children'.[31] Like the report on Warren's lecture, 'Patriotic Poetry' presented a reasoned case for the war, using Tennyson (again), Kipling, Wordsworth, and Scott to reassure readers about the nature of the current conflict:

> Two noble nations of a noble tradition may be at war, and each be moved by truest patriotism, if each is striving not only to prove itself but to win a little nearer to that ideal self which is the hope and justification of life on earth. It is the one condition, the one problem, the one aspiration of life – to be the best one is; and that can only be attained at the expense of one's own and of other men's worse. English patriotic poetry reflects all this – from the grave, far-sighted stability of a Wordsworth to the antique chivalry of Scott.

The article does not explicitly damn Germany; given reporting on Belgian atrocities, the reader is left to make up their own mind about whether or not, in the enemy's case, the 'noble tradition' is being adhered to. It acknowledges the particular drama of this new war, and the shifting alliances to secure the future of 'Civilisation':

> Is not our once sweet enemy France now our armed and bosom friend? Is it possible that Englishmen will ever forget the instant courage of Belgium, of a little people that without

a moment's pause faced extinction rather than submit to the mercy of the aggressor?

By coming to the aid of these new allies, and by throwing the collective and formidable cultural weight of its literary heritage behind the struggle, the 'truest patriotism' can be achieved.

There was a commercial element to all of this earnest discourse about the role of newspapers and poets in times of war. Warren's lecture coincided with the publishing of a volume entitled *Tennyson's Patriotic Poems*, released a few days prior by Tennyson's son and 'published for a penny'.[32] Such articles were timed to coincide with, and reflect on, particular opportunities and events as they arose.

*

Articles like these, published daily throughout the war, legitimised poetry as a politically and aesthetically valid form for interpreting the war and defining the experience of death and mourning. The extent to which recognised literary figures held sway over and were afforded space in popular discourse can be explained by the longstanding 'political failure' of English intellectuals who, generally speaking, did not engage in critical public debate about major cultural issues (Gilbert Murray being a notable exception). This concentrated power in the hands of individual authors,[33] thereby creating a situation where a relatively minor poet like Brooke could secure establishment recognition, popularity, celebrity, and critical literary success.

Brooke's initial injection into the wider public culture of the war as an emerging patriotic poet, on a much larger scale than with respect to the *New Numbers* release in the winter, was orchestrated in part by the *Times Literary Supplement*, which reviewed the War Sonnets and – crucially – reprinted 'The Soldier' on 11 March 1915. This is probably how the Dean of St Paul's Cathedral, William Ralph Inge, was alerted to the existence of the sonnet. While the favourable review raised Brooke's literary profile beyond – albeit influential – King's College,

Poetry Bookshop, and *Georgian Poetry* circles, the Dean helped to put in motion the process of moral promotion and sanctification of the poet-soldier when he read the poem in the Easter sermon at St Paul's entitled 'Why the dead shall rise'. His role as head of a national institution reaching a significant religious public[34] helped to establish Brooke as a potentially notable public figure at a timely moment: in advance of the death of the poet-soldier and the Gallipoli landings. Marsh made sure that the news about the sermon and the article was sent, by telegraph, through Admiralty channels, and Brooke's friend and fellow officer, the musician Denis Brown, alerted Brooke to his London success;[35] Brooke was listless, fatally ill, his response muted as he contemplated what he expected would – finally – be his first full experience of battle.

Marking the first Easter of the war, Inge's sermon attempted to explain, mourn, and memorialise the nation's war dead, taking inspiration from the 'sons and daughters who have died in exile' in the desert from a passage in Isaiah 26:9; 'The Soldier' was deployed as a modern-day foil in order to draw a moral parable. Inge praised the poem, written by 'A young soldier', as an example of 'pure and elevated patriotism, free from hate, bitterness, and fear', but also warned that Christian patriots must go further in their faith. The expectation of commemoration, and 'The Soldier's preoccupation with the physical body', raised too many conditionals; 'The spirit of heroism and self-sacrifice knows no restriction of this kind'.[36] Inge's careful, considered reading served to emphasise above all else the universal opportunity the war provided for men and women to achieve a spiritual selflessness, solemnly disposing of any expectations of individual recognition or material reward. 'The Soldier' could then be accepted as detailing a pure martyrdom, a modern update on the lives of the saints, with each death adding a layer to the communal story, attesting to the power of faith and loyalty.

This presentation of 'The Soldier' also leant itself to mass communication, providing a moral touchstone for readers within and beyond formal religious contexts.[37] Religion played a conventional role in

Brooke's actual death – the Chaplain read the burial service of the Church of England at Brooke's funeral on Scyros – and exerted an even lesser philosophical influence on his life. However, popular religious rhetoric fed the chorus of praise for the poet-soldier, with the formal and informal ecclesiastical infrastructures providing a conduit between the British front and home front. Faith played a key role in shaping linguistic and visual iconography of the war. Its influence was both institutional and personal: the Y.M.C.A. organised material and spiritual support for soldiers; Isaac Rosenberg wrote letters and poems home from France on paper provided by the association. Soldiers carried pocket Bibles with them in the trenches, and quoted from them in their letters home. Military chaplains provided continuity between military and civilian life, transferring and adapting the home parish and religious community to serve the provisional needs of the front: they conducted services and internments in battle zones, and provided absolution, becoming closely associated with death and burial. Playing on the authority of religious figures and institutions, and their presence both at home and in military sectors, politicians invoked religious language to justify specific policy initiatives: appeals to limit alcohol consumption and increase productivity amongst soldiers and workers were endorsed by religious leaders, who urged citizens to rise to the war by foregoing drinking in the name of self-sacrifice.[38]

After learning of Brooke's death, in May 1915, Inge sent the manuscript copy of his sermon to Mary Brooke. He urged her not be offended by his criticism of 'your boy's beautiful sonnet' from which he had attempted to express a 'large hope for immortality of the personal life'. He went on to note, 'I shall always feel a special pride in this last addition to the role of honour of my college' (the Dean had been at King's College, Cambridge as well).[39] By this point Brooke's death and 'The Soldier' had become public entities; his letter recognised and attempted in some small way to ease the private grief. Inge's sermon deplored the cult of the individual, but his reticence and careful, intellectual assessment of the poem was largely obfuscated by Brooke's popular reputation as it evolved after his death. When the *Christian*

World Pulpit reported on a sermon delivered at the Lyndhurst Road Congregational Church in Hampstead, it did so under the headline 'Rupert Brooke and the Rest of Them'.[40]

The Times reprinted the Dean's sermon on 5 April. Wishing to make a broader point about faith and sacrifice, Inge had not mentioned Brooke directly by name, but in an early act of cross-promotion and syndication, *The Times* editors included a footnote alerting the public to the fact that 'The sonnet quoted by the Dean is by Mr. Rupert Brooke and was printed in a review in the *Times Literary Supplement* of March 11'.[41] Guided by Dawson (who would play a key role in shaping Brooke's public image through the obituary), the recognised function of *The Times* was to serve as the nation's and Empire's political recorder and arbiter, especially at this moment of unprecedented rupture and violence. It also played a central role in establishing and shaping cultural discourses; 'The Soldier' and its author's potential symbolic value brought together political, religious, literary, and commercial spheres, all part of the newspaper's – and the broader press and literary establishment's – existential brief during the war. Poets and poetry fulfilled a cultural need for gentle propaganda, and many over the course of the war would choose to channel and express their patriotism by contributing to the Brooke myth.

9

Public Death

Geneneral Sir Ian Hamilton's dramatic comment, that after Brooke's death 'The rest is silence',[1] proved incorrect, as the memorialising commenced immediately: it quickly took on a significant symbolic value. Reviews of the War Sonnets, and the incorporation of 'The Soldier' into the Easter sermon at St Paul's were one thing, but the death of the poet-soldier in April 1915 would come to represent something beyond individual tragedy. The genre that first raised Brooke and his poems in the public consciousness was the obituary.

The obituary was already a prominent, recognised literary genre in 1915. In outlining major life achievements, it also reaffirmed consensus social values. It developed out of the tradition of private death notices designed to announce the commencement of mourning. Numbers rose substantially in parallel with expanded literacy rates and the rise of newspapers.[2] In wartime Britain, social historians have pointed out that the encounter with the death of large numbers of young men was at odds with progress in mortality rates made in the late Victorian and Georgian periods.[3] Death – from injury, accident, and illness – once a private and fairly regular element of family life, was again, shockingly, claiming large numbers of young men and women. The genre both informed and depended on a larger cultural shift relating to death as a social experience, as rituals surrounding the death of royalty and politicians evolved from private affairs to public pageants. Death was (for lack of a better word) *accessible* to all, and communal participation, either organised or spontaneous, substantiated awareness of the national community.[4] The obituary functioned not necessarily in order to emphasise ideals important to the deceased or to his or her family, but instead to present a valuation of the individual's cultural contribution. This was particularly important during wartime, and was in great demand given the sudden preponderance of death.

This meant that from 1914 to 1918 the war forced the government and the public to develop ways of coping with death in practical and symbolic ways. Charles Masterman later observed that while at Wellington House he had 'only been able to write occasional articles … for the most part obituaries for friends'.[5] As for writing obituaries specifically for poets, Wilfrid Meynell wrote to Masterman asking him if he had been the author of a 'Leading Note' on Francis Thompson at the time of his death.[6] The practice of writing obituaries to commemorate public as well as private citizens continued in wartime with a national purpose more patriotically attuned than during the prior years of peace.

Communal, as opposed to private, mourning rituals also provided a pretext for an increasingly organised, state-managed and owned process, and made it easier to talk about death in war as an abstract cultural ideal. In Britain this process was not only confined to the post-war years with their preoccupation with memorial building; it was a continuous project that began as soon as the first casualty lists were published, born of a need to signal that not only individuals but, in solidarity, all of British society was in mourning, even if actual sacrifice could never be shared or equal.[7] The ideals around death in service of the nation conveyed by obituaries and memorial practices, be they spontaneous or official, centred on common themes: even street shrines of East End immigrant communities largely adhered to a 'conformist' message.[8] Obituaries written to mark Brooke's death reflected this expectation.

*

In January 1915, Brooke had himself been asked by *The Times* to write an obituary for the poet James Elroy Flecker under the headline, 'A Loss to English Poetry'. His piece followed the conventional form, noting first the cause and place of death, his father's name and profession (women being almost entirely absent from public obituaries), his university associations and professional work. Brooke then went on to detail Flecker's tastes, highlighting his love of 'Greece and the East' in addition to England, attesting that 'He sought beauty everywhere, but preferred, for most of his life, to find her decoratively clad'. As to personality, Brooke stressed Flecker's 'conversation', which was 'variegated, amusing, and enriched with booty from the by-ways of knowledge'. Finally, the most important aspect of Flecker's life was the 'strength and clearness' he had attained in his 'craft'. This was directly tied to his 'character', which was very clearly reflected in his writings'. Brooke's literary epitaph – the quality of the writing being tied to the esteem afforded the dead – for his friend and fellow 'Georgian' poet, was that 'By his death there passes away a poet whose accomplished work was equalled by few of his coevals; his promise by still fewer'.[9] Both in its form and its preoccupations this obituary anticipated many similar pieces that would be written about Brooke who also, with this piece, participated directly in the culture of remembrance that continued along inherited lines, and would necessarily expand in the coming years to encompass the ever-growing numbers of war dead.

Obituaries were not just important for families and friends of the diseased. They were a way of fixing the reputation of a person in death, and as such were particularly significant for other members of the literary establishment and the avant-garde who also engaged in this particular commemorative practice. T. S. Eliot[10] and Ezra Pound both utilised the form to promote their particular views on the evolution of the literary canon, and to fine-tune emerging 'high Modernist' ideologies.[11] In Eliot's review/obituary of Alan Seeger, one can see this attempt to order and assess the poetry and the man (the two were in the same class at Harvard) while signalling points of professional divergence or criticism: 'The work is well done, and so much out of date as to be almost a positive quality … Alan Seeger, as one who knew him can attest, lived his life on this plane, with impeccable poetic dignity; everything about him was in keeping'.[12] This could be a tricky exercise, balancing genuine admiration and warmth for the individual while avoiding loading uncritical praise onto work that was not necessarily to taste. In this way for writers like Brooke and Eliot, and for those who elected to write about the dead, the obituary functioned as a vehicle of public self-definition and critical expression. In the case of major figures like Eliot, these literary memorials, while associated with particular historical moments, live on as testaments of evolving literary philosophies.

During the war obituaries like these transcended their more traditional role as mere notices of death. Both Brooke's and Eliot's obituaries were literary reviews as much as they were standard obituaries, offering meditations on death in war and on literary legacies. This merging of forms would become important for coverage of Brooke as, in his afterlife, he achieved his apotheosis as 'England's Poet-Soldier'; neither the tragic and honourable fact of his death nor any assessment of his work could be separated from the other. Expectations about what could and should be included in any assessment of the honourable dead informed the subsequent writing of editors, journalists, poets, writers, and, in turn, readers confronted with expressing personal and national loss. The obituary, while more ephemeral than other versions of literary epitaphs, in Brooke's case was repeated and reworked in various forms until it became its own kind of shrine.

*

The Times had a longstanding tradition of publishing obituaries of national and international interest. Many years later, reflecting on the public value of the form in an article for *The American Scholar*, Sir William Haley, editor of *The Times* from 1952 to 1966, wrote,

'Obituaries in *The Times* and in the world's other serious newspapers are a better measure of merit than any official citations or honours lists, which in England are largely controlled by politicians who cannot resist playing to the gallery on occasions. The great newspapers of the world have no such temptations.'[13]

This was either a rather earnest or a decidedly tongue-in-cheek assessment of the role of newspapers. While, collectively, editors and journalists might endeavour to avoid signalling overt support of any cause or person as Haley asserts, newspapers traditionally do collect – and reflect – political opinions. Particularly in wartime, even seemingly benign and generic writings take on a political cast. When Brooke wrote of Flecker that he 'loved England ... always with more passion than affection,'[14] he may or may not have been intending this as a comment on Flecker's (or even Brooke's) patriotism. However, in January 1915, a statement such as this in an obituary carried more political and sentimental weight than in peacetime. Topics perceived to be 'above' politics were, in themselves, presented as emblems of national character and cultural superiority.

Brooke's *Times* obituary serves as a case study of estates coming together to promote a common cause, and engage in an act of public mourning. A politician, a senior officer of the press, a civil servant (and influential cultural patron), and a journalist united to create a memorial in words that commemorated not only Brooke, but attempted to answer questions as to what was important to protect and defend in English 'Civilisation' at a moment when military failures and the high casualties associated with modern, attritional warfare demanded a public redefinition of acceptable sacrifice.

The full-length obituary appeared in *The Times* on 26 April 1915, one day after the commencement of the much-publicised invasion of Gallipoli. They also printed a brief death notice on the 25th. Interestingly, *The Times* was not alone in covering the death of the 27-year-old sub-lieutenant. Just how the *Globe* and *Pall Mall Gazette* obtained information about Brooke's death on the evening of his demise is unclear. News may have leaked from the Admiralty either via Churchill or

Marsh or someone else in the office; as previously discussed, the world of elite Westminster politics and press was a small one in 1915. The *Globe* entitled its 24 April article, 'Whom the Gods Loved', praising the War Sonnets, promoting the 'sentiments and ideals of the clean young Englishman fighting for a just cause', assuring readers that 'Rupert Brooke died as he would have wished, in the service of his country, and in the prime of his young manhood'.[15] The *Pall Mall Gazette*'s obituary, also published on the 24th, reported 'a real loss to the future of English literature', and, echoing the *Globe*'s take on the symbolism of the romance of death in Greece, drew the comforting conclusion that, 'One who gave his career to his country will sleep well on an Aegean isle'.[16] Both of these obituaries advanced themes that would become central pillars of the myth of the poet-soldier: the pristine, 'clean' Englishman, the 'just cause',[17] and death as quiet, painless 'sleep'.[18]

The Times obituary contained two sections: first, the standard paragraphs relating the facts and dates of Brooke's life, and second, a three-paragraph tribute signed with the initials 'W.S.C.' – Winston S. Churchill, First Lord of the Admiralty, who, as previously mentioned, had met Brooke on a number of occasions. Marsh, as Churchill's Private Secretary and Brooke's close friend, probably contributed most of the detail relating specifically to Brooke, and may have drafted significant portions of the expositional section,[19] but Churchill's 'house style' is evident in its language and emphasis. (In the obituary itself Churchill makes no mention of personal connections having influenced his decision to focus on this particular dead soldier.) Geoffrey Dawson, editor of *The Times*, approved the Churchill contribution in full, signing-off on the text in the marked copy. He also personally drafted the majority of the standard obituary. Leader-writer Arthur Clutton-Brock,[20] a Rugby alumnus who also wrote a pamphlet on behalf of the Propaganda Bureau at Wellington House in 1915,[21] added the final half of the third paragraph of this section; Dawson's and Clutton-Brock's contributions were not acknowledged in the press copy of the obituary. From the outset, Brooke's posthumous identity was in the hands of gifted, influential, and shrewd definers of patriotism as they went about

The Times from 26 April 1915, including Rupert Brooke's obituary.

creating their epitaph to Brooke and, more broadly, to all of the young men who must be sacrificed in defence of the nation.

*

Churchill's motives for contributing the obituary are worth pausing over. He had been held personally responsible for the debacle that was Brooke's first and only experience of direct action: the failed defence of Antwerp in October 1914, a heavily publicised defeat that resulted in public criticism of the First Lord's decision to deploy the Hood Battalion. Privately, Prime Minister Asquith expressed concern, not least due to the presence at the retreat of his son Arthur, whom he cited alongside 'Rupert Brooke (the poet) & one Denis Browne (a pianist) who had respectfully served 1 week, 3 days, & 1 day'. Their deployment at Antwerp was, Asquith judged, 'like sending sheep to the shambles'.[22] Reservations like these, particularly coming from the Prime Minister, necessarily shifted as the full scale of the war dawned on those charged with winning it, the politically charged conscription debates failed to secure a resolution in favour of mandatory enlistment, and the principle of volunteerism was maintained.[23] The obituary helped to promote the idea that even poets made, and would be expected to make, fine soldiers.

Churchill's acquaintance with Brooke alongside the First Lord's personal knowledge of the emerging situation in the Dardanelles in April 1915 provided sufficient cause for him to monitor closely Brooke's illness and, upon being the first to receive word by telegram of his death, to involve himself in the rites both in London and on the island of Scyros. Churchill sent word to Major John Churchill at 11:50 p.m. on the 23rd to attend the funeral as his personal representative.[24] The Major received the telegram too late, as the burial took place that evening, but he sent a full description to Churchill.[25] Marsh was kept informed of the situation by no less a figure than General Hamilton, who related that he had recently offered Brooke a position on his staff, but that Brooke had turned him down in favour of remaining with his men until after the operation.[26] It is not going too far to say that Churchill was both genuinely interested in Brooke's welfare, and simultaneously recognised his potential symbolic and political value, once news of his death was confirmed. The idealisation of voluntary sacrifice, of devotion to one's men and to the common good, provided the central theme of *The Times* obituary. Brief and coherent, it stands as an impressive piece of improvised propaganda through its derivation, from the death of one, of a resonant idealisation of collective identity in wartime.

The obituary began with traditional notice: 'We regret to record the death, on April 23, at Lemnos, from the effects of sunstroke, of Rupert Brooke, the poet, a sub-lieutenant in the Royal Naval Division.' Right from the outset, *The Times* obituary displayed certain slight alterations to the factual record: Brooke died on a hospital ship, not at Lemnos, and was buried at Scyros. Furthermore, he died not of sunstroke, but of septicaemia – a blood infection – originating from a mosquito bite received in Egypt. With respect to the details, Major Churchill had written to the First Lord to describe the 'most romantic burial' on 'Scyros Island' on 24 April, the day after the cable exchanges between Churchill and Major Churchill, and Hamilton and Marsh; however, specific place names were left out of the cables, and the letters describing exact locations would not have arrived in England in time to inform the obituary. Both the *Globe* and the *Pall Mall Gazette* had written about 'sunstroke' and 'burial at Lemnos' on 24 April; it is possible that Churchill, Dawson, and Clutton-Brock simply repeated these details, under pressure of time, for the sake of convenience. Brooke had also written to his mother on 5 April that he and his friend Patrick Shaw-Stewart had had 'a slight touch of sunstroke a few days ago,'[27] and then wrote to Marsh about 'a touch of sun, in Egypt',[28] so this could account for the initial discrepancy. It is also possible that from a military point of view Churchill may have obscured the exact location of part of the fleet on the eve of the Gallipoli landings. The second paragraph of the secondary section of the obituary corrected the mistake, citing 'death from blood poisoning', but reaffirmed the death at Lemnos. 'Sunstroke', with its classical and romantic connotations, and with Brooke becoming an Icarus-like figure, sounded good, and many obituaries would follow the lead of *The Times* in reprinting the idealised trope.

Dawson took a moment to remind readers of earlier coverage of Brooke in *The Times*, referring to 'the one [poem, 'The Soldier'] which the Dean of St. Paul's quoted in his sermon on Easter Day'.[29] He went on to assert how Brooke had 'found in his readiness to do his duty for his country a high religious joy'. Churchill's section of the obituary was highly charged, filled with popular cultural references and generalised romantic language: this was an obituary as well as an epitaph for the mobilised youth of England, brought to the forefront by the death of Brooke, representative of many. Brooke's life 'has closed at the moment when it seemed to have reached its springtime'. Despite the tragedy of death at such a 'moment', Churchill contended that Brooke as a poet became transcendent in life and in death through his ability to 'do justice to the nobility of our youth in arms', by expressing their 'thoughts of self-surrender'.

These lines from Dawson and Churchill also allude to a fundamental paradox of the war. While it was on the one hand significant and reassuring that the established generation of 'self-acclaimed moral authorities'[30] in the person of editors and politicians endorsed the 'self-surrender'[31] of young men like Brooke, this also spoke to a potential, as yet only implicit rift between generations and the sexes.[32] It was very well for men past the age of service (and, for that matter, for women) publicly and vociferously to voice their support for the war. But in testifying as an informed volunteer no voice was more valuable than that of a young man in uniform. Brooke, who, Churchill wrote, 'expected to die … was willing to die for the dear England whose beauty and majesty he knew',[33] represented just such a witness. Despite his promise and youth, he had advanced 'towards the brink in perfect serenity, with absolute conviction of the rightness of his cause'. Brooke became the embodiment of the rational, 'highly instructed', 'youth of England'. He epitomised the ideal of volunteerism, even as the nation bedded in for a long and costly war: 'in days when no sacrifice but the most precious is acceptable, and the most precious is that which is freely proffered'.

Notably absent from Churchill's section of the obituary was praise of any specific military ethos, writing that as Brooke took up his 'country's cause' he did so with a 'heart devoid of hate for fellow-man'. The poet-soldier's involvement in the Antwerp campaign and membership of the Hood Battalion were included as factual background; as a result, he joined the ranks as one of 'England's noblest sons'. Churchill instead stressed Brooke's literary and civilian virtues, only tacitly linked to the war by the circumstances of death. His central achievement was not military glory in battle, but the willingness to offer up his mind and body, becoming not only a soldier but a 'poet-soldier' in 'this, the hardest, the cruellest, and the least rewarding of all wars that men have fought'. He was an example of the best thoughts and actions of all of the volunteers, and through his war poetry he had succeeded in aesthetically condensing the noble ideals of his generation: from the War Sonnets the obituary featured sections of 'The Dead', with its 'laughter', and 'white / Unbroken glory',[34] stressing the painless, clean nature of Brooke's death. This, of course, was very much in contrast to the violent nature of many deaths in the field throughout the war, which the authors of the obituary and later contributors to the serene myth of the poet-soldier as the inviolate 'body of England's'[35] no doubt recognised.

The two sections of the obituary carefully reinforced further ideas about what made Brooke worthy of singling out as well as being representative of the youth of England. Dawson also turned literary critic in his section of the obituary when discussing the War Sonnets, judging that they expressed a pure 'joy without the misgivings and emotional insecurity of his earlier verse'. The lyrical beauty of the poetry reflected and reinforced the purity of the individual and of the national cause. Both Churchill and Dawson asserted Brooke's appreciation for bucolic England, playing on a common cultural and poetic trope made all the more relevant by a mechanised war.[36] Dawson wrote of Brooke's love of the Cambridgeshire countryside, and Churchill spoke of the 'dear England whose beauty and majesty he knew'. Both lingered on his physical beauty: Churchill's praising of his 'classic symmetry of mind and body' echoed Dawson's assertion that 'few men have been so interestingly and lastingly attractive'. Clutton-Brock reiterated almost verbatim the sentiments of Churchill's final paragraph: the 'freely proffered' sacrifice willingly laid down in the 'joyous' service of the nation, with the final lines of the obituary also stressing the continuous honour in sanctified death in battle; 'if any seeming waste is not waste, there is none in a life full of promise and joyfully laid down'.

Overall, the obituary stressed what its authors felt was important to recognise and praise in Brooke, as well as what he represented as an archetype of his generation. In so doing, they began to establish Brooke, or more specifically the ideal of the poet-soldier, as a *lieux de mémoire* of the war.[37] He was 'typically' English – intelligent, well-educated, with good looks and excellent connections – and he had chosen to offer up his pleasant life and promising career in defence of the nation and its ideals. The obituary consciously ignored the complex temporal realities of the war: Gallipoli, after the initial success of the costly landings, settled into a long, grinding, and equally costly stalemate, resulting in complete withdrawal from the peninsula in January 1916. Yet Brooke's positive image – representative of 'the thousands'[38] – would remain useful in countering both specific and general losses on the battlefield.

*

The Times obituary was powerful not only because of what it contained, but because of who wrote it, and who published it. Both the *Pall Mall Gazette* and the *Globe* in a sense 'scooped' *The Times* by introducing tropes that would long remain associated with the death of the poet-soldier, but *The Times* played a central role in legitimising and confirming Brooke as a national symbol. The *Globe* acknowledged the influence of *The Times* obituary in a follow-up article of 27 April, which began with a quote from 'The Soldier' and went on to confirm that 'He was the most promising of the young Cambridge poets, says *The Times*'. The article reiterated Churchill's positing of Brooke as a model figure, 'part of the youth of the world'.[39]

Brooke's was, of course, not the only obituary to appear in *The Times* during the war in the coming weeks and months. The Royal Naval Division, with its bevy of well-connected officers, enjoyed a prime place in coverage of the Gallipoli campaign. But the poet-soldier was never far away. Brooke's name was included in the 'Roll of Honour' alongside others killed in the initial stages of the landing and the subsequent occupation of the peninsula on 6 May. *The Times* published 'Biographical Notices' of Lieutenant-Commander G. H. Pownall, R.N. and (drawing further attention to the obituary) 'Sub-Lieutenant Rupert Brooke, R.N.V.R.' on 3 May and 26 April respectively. William Denis Browne, friend to Brooke and Marsh, received individual attention in '*The Times* List of Casualties' for the Dardanelles of 17 June. His family, school record, and contributions to the *New Statesman* and *The Times* were mentioned, as well as his musical talent. Also included was the point that he 'joined the R[oyal] N[aval] Division last September with his friend Rupert Brooke, and took part in the Antwerp expedition'.[40] An article entitled 'Heroism at Gallipoli' updated readers on the Division's exploits, and then invoked 'Rupert Brooke' as the balladeer of their valour.[41] The 'Losses in the Ranks' with '174 Men Dead and Wounded'[42] were recorded, although, of course, not in full; only later in the war and post-war period would the nation engage in a systematic, collective memorialisation of the fallen, ultimately resulting in the anonymous dead achieving a near cult-like – if homogeneous – status.[43]

The Times Brooke obituary illustrates how a group of influential persons turned the individual loss of one soldier into a metaphor for collective loss, and in turn presented the poet-soldier as a repository of virtue and 'self-surrender'.[44] Various publications – locally, nationally, and internationally – would amplify Churchill's, Dawson's, Clutton-Brock's and Marsh's initial effort. They did so through consistency of language, theme, and argument, and in a fair volume: Mary Brooke kept an album, beginning in April 1915, that contained 147 obituaries and similar tributes, the majority concentrated between 26 April and the end of May 1915.[45] In the end, Brooke's life was reduced to the following, edited by Marsh, and inscribed in *1914 and Other Poems* and in the public consciousness thereafter:

> Rupert Brooke, born 3rd August 1887.
> Fellow of King's, 1913.
> Sub-Lieutenant, R.N.V.R., September 1914.
> Antwerp Expedition, October 1914.
> Sailed with British Mediterranean
> Expeditionary Force, 28 February 1915.
> Died in the Aegean, 23 April 1915.[46]

On these bones, broader ideals about what it meant to be 'England's Poet-Soldier' were hung.

10

Syndication

In the middle of May 1915, the *Sketch* published an article demonstrating to what extent, in the weeks and months following his death, awareness of Rupert Brooke – or more specifically the idea of Rupert Brooke that emerged out of the obituaries – and his War Sonnets proliferated. The article details a conversation (real or imagined) between two men in the heart of London on Regent Street, at what might be considered the intersection of its commercial and political districts, one already familiar with Brooke, the other not:

> I was walking up Regent Street with a friend. Suddenly he said
> – apropos of nothing that I can remember: 'Do you know the
> poems of Rupert Brooke?'
> 'I don't think so,' I replied.
> 'Then you should be ashamed of yourself'.
> 'I am. Tell me about him. Who is he?'
> 'He's dead. He went out to the Dardanelles on active service,
> and died there of sunstroke'.
> 'Was he a real poet?'
> 'In my opinion, one of the very few real poets we have ever
> had'.

'Then he should have been looked after. A real poet is a precious thing. Why was he allowed to go at all?'

'He would do. He was twenty-seven, and, as far as I know, unmarried. And he was an athlete. I suppose the call was irresistible'.

'Perhaps it was destiny'.

'He seems to have thought that himself. One of the finest things he ever wrote was a poem in which he seemed to expect death'.

'What a pity'

'Yes, a thundering pity ... Hullo! There's my 'bus!'

And so he rolled away, and the world of London rolled by, and the soul of the poet hovered over the England he so passionately adored.[1]

The exchange neatly catalogues the themes asserted repeatedly in numerous obituaries, including *The Times*, the *Pall Mall Gazette* and the *Globe*, to name but three. Calling attention to the fact that Brooke was 'twenty seven', 'unmarried', 'an athlete', and perhaps seeking adventure introduces a new facet, and paints a more practical approach to enlistment than the fervid articles asserting 'readiness to do his duty for his country' being evidence of 'a high religious joy'.[2] The two men fix on the point that he was a 'real poet ... one of the few poets we have ever had' (note the collective 'we' of the reading nation) – as all 'intelligent' citizens must acknowledge, who 'seemed to expect death' and in the end fulfilled his 'destiny'. By the end of the exchange, the man only just introduced to Brooke offers this judgement: 'By dying a hero's death – one might say, without exaggeration, a martyr's death – he had achieved fame, for what that is worth, and maybe immortality'.[3]

The conversation also indicates the speed with which Brooke's place in popular culture was secured: in less than a month he was well on his way to assuming the title, introduced by the *Morning Post* on 27 April, of 'England's Soldier Poet', or 'England's Poet-Soldier', as claimed by the *Westminster Gazette* on 1 May 1915. During the First World War, citizens of Britain searched for ways to 'turn the sublime and abstract emotions of grief, pride, and hope into tangible symbols'.[4] Given the heady combination of worthy sacrifice, literary promise, and general appeal condensed in Brooke's story, in the *Sketch*'s rendering the narrator ought not only to be aware of an up-and-coming poet; he 'ought to be ashamed' that he is not. In the end, there is no escaping Brooke's legend: the piece concludes with the acknowledgement that, 'Of course, as always happens, directly I had heard of Rupert Brooke. I came across his name everywhere'.[5]

*

Brooke's visibility, as well as his literary reputation, were aided by the timely publication of articles affirming his place in the national consciousness alongside his poetry and prose. Not just national but international communications systems had been modernised in the years leading up to the war, and were in the spring of 1915 well-placed to syndicate material for consumption by an increasingly literate public.[6] The accessibility and the transferability of the myth of the poet-soldier benefited from this, as newspapers, publishers, and readers exchanged ideas more quickly and in a greater number of formats than would have been possible during previous conflicts.

Even as the sobering casualties undermined the excitement of the opening months of the conflict, the 'pleasure culture of war'[7] persisted hand-in-hand with a curiosity bordering on voyeurism: public demand for linguistic and visual orientation in a time of great upheaval posited greater control in the hands of commercial vendors.[8] In publishing, communication advances taking place in modernising cities in the period leading up to the war meant that 'unprecedented circulation ... connected words and images as never before as general readers could for the first time read words and then directly encounter a referenced image'. In the past, the 'society of spectators'[9] might only comprise condensed urban populations; in 1915, regional and local press networks passed on news considered to be of national signifi-cance to a disparate readership.[10]

These networks relied on the close interaction between public and private sectors. With respect to literature, throughout the war publishers displayed 'a commitment not only to commerce – to profit – but also to country and their own consciences'.[11] The resulting dialogue between governments and publishers (utilising design, image, and language to market their products) and the consuming public contributed to the success of the popular myth of Rupert Brooke as the national poet-soldier, an emblem of collective sacrifice. In the autumn of 1915, *Book Monthly* published an article entitled 'Soldier Authors: The Writing-Man turned Fighting Man in Armageddon', claiming that it was 'high time that a Literary Roll of Honour be inscribed'. This should be created at the nomination of the public, compiled and circulated by the periodical. And, it claimed, there was no doubt that 'In such a list of heroes there is one entirely worthy of standing first … and that is the late Rupert Brooke'.[12]

*

The syndication of language and ideas reached its peak in the spring of 1915. In the articles that appeared, made up of a mix of obituaries and literary reflections assessing his published works, Brooke's life, death, and poetry provided a template for describing collective loss. Newspapers across the country printed *The Times* 26 April Brooke obituary, in part or verbatim. The *Westminster Gazette* published its poetic obituary along the lines articulated by Churchill and colleagues: 'The unuttered beauty of their hearts who went / Like him, from joy, aware and not afraid / To meet the obscure event'.[13] Direct quotes from the obituary itself were often unreferenced, as in the case of the aptly named *Echo*.[14] Proximity to – and personal knowledge of – the poet was important: the *Daily News* obituary, also citing *The Times*, ran under the headline 'By One Who Knew Him', and the *Northampton Mercury* prefaced their reprint of Churchill's piece with 'One who knew him well writes in *The Times*'.[15]

Obituaries stressed the loss to the nation's literary culture: 'The war is exacting its toll of genius'.[16] H. W. Nevinson, who had known Brooke personally and also covered the Gallipoli landings, wrote an obituary for the *Nation* that also focused on his poetic potential: 'His grip on the larger issues of the world might have been like Byron's'. He went on to state that in his rumpled bohemianism, 'No one could less resemble the canonical British idea of a poet, and yet in reality he was a poet of the type particularly English, both in his modesty and in his love of action'.[17] In his leader for the *Daily News*, Cecil Roberts was even more explicit in drawing a direct line between Brooke's deserved popularity in death and the effects of the obituary on his literary reputation: 'Dying at an age when his fame was scarcely extended beyond a circle of intimates, who, perhaps marvelled more at his personal beauty than his exquisite verse, it is well that public attention should be called to the work of a young poet whose performance gave promise of a great future'.[18]

In his obituary Nevinson also testified to Brooke's physical attractiveness: 'Evidently he did not want to be conspicuous, but the whole effect was almost ludicrously beautiful'.[19] Other publications carried this forward, balancing semi-sexualised language with respectful assertions of purity:[20] 'Youth' – 'beauty' – 'His beautiful golden head and his athlete's body'[21] came together to form the picture of the 'clean young Englishman'.[22]

Drawing on Churchill's observation about Brooke's 'classic symmetry of mind and body'[23] as the *Globe*'s line that the poet had died 'in the prime of his young manhood, as those whom the gods love',[24] the *Daily News* injected their obituary with a dose of popular Hellenophilia, explaining Brooke's 'view' of death as expressed in 'The Soldier' as revealing how the war 'put an end to his splendid boyhood and gave him a man's vision and a man's utterance', which made appropriate his death 'among the isles of Greece', home to 'many English poets who have died in their time of promise … who have died soldiers of liberty'.[25]

'Grantchester' warranted repeated mention. Under the title 'Where Rupert Brooke Wrote His Poems', the *Daily Sketch* painted a charming picture of Brooke's pastoral intellectual life: the poet, a 'Cambridge Man' had 'lived for many terms at the Orchard, in Grantchester, where in the summer time the happy boating parties pull in and land for tea under the apple trees. It was there that he wrote most of the lovely and delicate poems that are his legacy to the University'. To the university, the poetry: 'To England he left his youth'. Transporting the reader even further back into an imagined pre-war idyll, the *Daily Sketch* even implied (incorrectly) that Brooke had written the War Sonnets at Grantchester or Cambridge.[26]

Most of the obituaries offered a brief assessment of Brooke's War Sonnets as testimony to a willingness to die in battle, concluding that they – and 'The Soldier' in particular – were written 'In his own epitaph'.[27] He was portrayed as 'a gallant and joyous type of poet-soldier',[28] who, 'Like Shelley ... had a premonition of his death, and his epitaph is to be found in his own verses'.[29] Drawing on older and more established figures in an attempt to situate the young poet-soldier in the English literary canon, one obituarist asserted:

> I think that Rupert Brooke in his essence was nearer to the Elizabethans than to the Victorians. There was in his genius a touch of Sir Philip Sidney and Sir Walter Raleigh and of Shakespeare himself. He had a strain of their noble sweetness and serene chivalry and knightly tenderness.[30]

Brooke's death, potentially portrayed as arbitrary and irrational, was thus placed in the literary continuum; after all, 'Perhaps it was his destiny'.[31]

*

Obituaries implicitly mixed commemoration with commerce. The *Sunderland Echo* noted with satisfaction the timing of the initial – albeit limited – appearance of *New Numbers*: 'so full of Fate's exquisite ironies, has nothing more poignantly ironic, and nothing at the same time more beautifully appropriate, than the publication of Rupert Brooke's noble sonnet-sequence, "1914", a few swift weeks before the death they had imagined, and had already made lovely.[32] The *Pall Mall Gazette* anticipated a more accessible publication shortly, predicting a short popular anonymity for the poet: 'If he had as yet no name in the publisher's sense, those who watch and sing of promise in prose and verse were keenly alive to the freshness and charm of his talent'.[33]

If in any market timing is everything, in May 1915, Brooke's increasingly common tag as the nation's poet-soldier, as well as the public's general receptiveness to the sentimental, increasingly standardised,[34] even journalistic language[35] of the War Sonnets, assured the popularity of the poems. As it became more difficult to maintain that the actual experience of the war was any sort of physical or aesthetic pleasure, the demand for a type of language that could elevate the individual and the nation at war to a higher plane increased, as did the need for reassurance as to the certainty of British ascendance, moral and military. Brooke's publishers Sidgwick & Jackson moved quickly to take advantage of the moment so that, in the words of the essayist and poet Arthur C. Benson, 'the survivors of a shipwreck'[36] could quickly get their hands on the poems written by the beautiful young martyr-poet whose 'name' they now came across 'everywhere'.[37]

The ideal moment almost passed them by. *New Numbers* had only ever enjoyed a very limited circulation, with sales set via subscriptions in advance. Future issues had been suspended by agreement of the contributors in December 1914 owing to the rising cost of paper and production as a consequence of the war.[38] Even as public awareness of Brooke grew following the review of the War Sonnets in the *Times Literary Supplement* in March 2015, and the subsequent coverage of Dean Inge's Easter sermon, there were no immediate plans to reprint the poems in another format or volume: Brooke was on his way to the Dardanelles, and Edward Marsh was busy at the Admiralty. Frank Sidgwick, who had considered *Poetry* (1911) to be compelling if rather slight, was unlikely to be motivated to respond to the appearance of a mere five new sonnets. No one was pressing, there was no great urgency, and it was assumed that Brooke had many more verses – war poems or not – left to write.

As the preceding chapters illustrate, Brooke's death, and coverage of it, changed all of this. The myriad obituaries provided the public with a taster, linking the publishing of the poems to the national ideal of 'freely proffered' sacrifice.[39] Brooke's verses were thus plucked out of the 'abundant poetry produced by the war'. They now had a distinct public value: 'few lines have given stronger comfort to those whom the war had bereaved than these'.[40] Brooke's loss was not only a private personal tragedy: his poems – forming part of the common cultural heritage of the war as it unfolded – and increasingly his story, now belonged to the nation. 'Rupert Brooke's Promise',[41] coupled with the 'Spirit of the Martyr-Poet',[42] gave the act of purchasing the volume of Brooke's poetry an added solemnity. Potential consumers would not only be buying a volume of poetry, but recognising – and in a sense endorsing – the image and self-sacrifice of the poet-solider. As such the purchaser was also making tactile those 'abstract emotions of grief, pride and hope'[43] felt by and for all of the war dead within the bounds set by the prevailing cultural authorities. Brooke's *1914 and Other Poems* duly appeared in May 1915, and thus entered the popular culture poised to take advantage of this demand. In promoting the poems, newspaper and periodical headlines alike capitalised on the idea of a final poetic utterance: 'Rupert Brooke's Last Poems';[44] 'An English Soldier-Poet';[45] 'Rupert Brooke's Last';[46] the direct testimony of 'A Young Poet's View of the War'.[47]

One major unexpected benefit to Brooke's publishers was that the War Sonnets' initial debut in *New Numbers* allowed for a propitiously loose interpretation of copyright. The poems were printed over and over in the weeks following Brooke's death, as well as in reviews of each subsequent edition, offering lines from, and in a few cases printing in full 'The Soldier', and occasionally also portions of 'The Dead'.[48] After his death, Brooke's estate and the rights to his writing had passed to Marsh and Sidgwick & Jackson.[49] Neither was motivated to be too strict about what was printed when so many were writing reverently about Brooke, whom they each admired in different ways. Their potential risk in allowing relatively unfettered reproduction paid off, as newspapers offered free promotion, first for *1914 and Other Poems* and subsequently for *Letters from America* and *John Webster* (1916), and the *Collected Poems* with Marsh's 'Memoir' (1918), all published by Sidgwick & Jackson during the war.[50]

*

There was a blanket, all-consuming element to the coverage of Brooke's death and the syndication of his image; he cast a long shadow. Alfred Brooke was a new volunteer to the British Army in 1915. When his older brother died he was serving in France with the Post Office Rifles. After learning of his brother's death, Alfred wrote to his mother: 'I quite agree that it is as well that Rupert died before reaching the Dardanelles. That landing must have been terrible and frightening, though at the moment necessary, is not an experience to be desired'. Informing this opinion was Alfred's own, more-extensive exposure to the trenches. For him, war was 'terrible and frightening'.[51] A quiet death was preferable.

When Alfred was killed in France on 14 June 1915, the *Daily Sketch* published an article lamenting 'how many ex-presidents the Cambridge Union Society is going to lose in this war. The latest is poor Rupert Brooke's younger brother'.[52] This was published under the headline, 'Rupert Brooke's Brother', the more recognisable name deployed to draw the reader in to its account of yet another valiant if, by implication, less notable volunteer. In the *Rugby Observer* Alfred's obituary ran under a similar notice: 'Late Mr. Rupert Brooke's Brother Killed'. The obituary went on to restate the poet-soldier's many achievements, and to report that Alfred 'had not the brilliant literary attainments of his brother, but a distinguished career in politics had been predicted'. Alfred exhibited potential, whereas Rupert, despite the predicted unwritten masterpieces of the future, had through the War Sonnets fulfilled his. To close the obituary, the writer again compared the two, emphasising the common cause of service and sacrifice: 'like so many British officers, he [Alfred] laid down his life for his country nobly in doing his duty. As with his brother Rupert, war was abhorrent to him, but this did not deter him from at once offering his services to his country'.[53] Even in the official account of the Post Office Rifles, Alfred's service and bravery mentioned his famous sibling: he was noted as 'the brother, and fit to be the brother, of Rupert Brooke, the poet'.[54]

The intense period of mourning and commercialisation following Brooke's death meant that, commencing in April and May 1915, 'England's Poet-Soldier' became a logical and, indeed, almost unavoidable point of reference through which to channel patriotic literary expression. In the years to come established patrons and readers would come together to further his reputation as the nation's 'Chief Poet'.[55] The intensity and immediacy of the public's endorsement of the myth secured this title and ensured the success, particularly of *1914 and Other Poems*, as well as anything that appeared ascribed to – or in association with – the nation's poet-soldier.

11

Image

The visual assault of the war took place not only at the front. In a much less threatening but by no means obscure manner the war occupied every newspaper, from articles to obituaries and, finally, in a shortened, simplified form, in the advertisements banking the texts. Newspaper layouts presented large amounts of information in fine type; headlines offset important ideas, and drew the reader's attention to a featured topic. The image of the soldier became associated with the commerce of war, and was used to advertise everything from cigarettes to field glasses to footwear: Craven 'A', a mixture of 'soothing, comforting' tobacco, employed the image of Field Marshal Sir John French smoking a pipe, creating a narrative context for purchase:

> Somewhere in France at the back of the fighting line – sometimes in it – guiding the Empire's might to overthrow the bully of Europe is the man on whom all our hopes are centred … But, midst the turmoil of war comes a time when the tired brain demands rest and solace – and what could be more refreshing and comforting than a quiet half hour with a good briar and a tin of Craven 'A'?[1]

Repeating the word 'comforting' reminded the public of what they could do for the men on the line: provide a taste of the solace of home by purchasing pipe tobacco, either to send to the soldiers on active service, or for investment and consumption by patriotic civilians. Equally, by association, one could be like the Field Marshal by smoking what he smoked. This form of endorsement worked to promote the interests of the Carreras tobacco company, but it also furthered the notion of a fully participatory war, just as Brooke's image and poetry 'endorsed', through association and self-epitaph, the values of volunteerism and sacrifice.

Newspapers also set themselves up as the public's direct link to the front. Most newspaper advertisements in *The Bookman*'s Christmas issue of 1917 trumpeted their coverage of the war. For the *Saturday Westminster*, the notice went: 'POLITICS. THE WAR. LITERATURE. ART. THE DRAMA. All have their space in the SATURDAY WEST-MINSTER. The Weekly Magazine-Review for the Man Who Thinks'. The *Daily Chronicle*'s began with the question, 'What is happening at the Front?', followed by a list of its various war correspondents and their locations on the Western, Italian, Russian fronts, as well as Frank Dilnot whose 'Dispatches tell what America is doing'. The *Times Literary Supplement*, presenting itself as 'The leading critical literary journal', also noted it would make a wonderful 'WAR-TIME PRESENT'.[2] All of these publications counted the entertainment and 'pleasure culture'[3] aspect of war as their special preserve.

War culture was made up of a variety of registers, all available to the public as required, whether solemn or silly. With respect to news-papers, layouts could be eclectic. On 26 April 1915, Brooke's obituary in *The Times* competed with descriptions and illustrations of 'Distinc-tive Headwear' for ladies, 'Vive La France! Why not Claret?', 'Viyella: Shirts and Pyjamas', J. W. Benson's 'Luminous "Active Service" Watch', Vittel 'The Famous French Medicinal Mineral', and Luntin Mixture Tobacco. This was not the exception but rather the rule when it came to articles about Brooke that ran in more popular publications. In other instances, Brooke was visually singled out for attention, as when in May 1915 *The Times* ran with the following the headline:

CAMBRIDGE IN MAY TERM

HEAVY WAR LOSSES

RUPERT BROOKE[4]

Here, Brooke's name itself was representative, visually as well as conceptually, for collective loss at the university, with the different type-scales signalling his relative importance.

Notices of Brooke's work also drew the eye to the margins of newspapers, supplementing the longer articles by reminding the reader of the accessibility of Brooke's poetry. As his name and legend became public property, advertisements alerted the reader to the fact that they could now possess the much-discussed War Sonnets, in full. *Punch* pushed this idea in its review of *1914 and Other Poems*, asserting that 'of this little volume, which contains the last things written by RUPERT BROOKE, it can be said that no one who cares for the heritage of our literature should omit to read or possess it.'[5] On 9 August 1915, Sidgwick & Jackson's advertisement for 'RUPERT BROOKE'S *1914 and Other Poems*' included, as evidence of its runaway success, a listing of each of the impressions to date, as well as a notice that a photogravure portrait of the poet was included in the volume.[6]

The advertisement also listed, in order of descending popularity, '*Poems* by RUPERT BROOKE' and *Poems of To-Day*, described as, 'An Anthology of Contemporary Poetry for Schools Selected by The English Association'. The 47 authors selected appear only by surname, with one exception: 'Meredith, Stevenson, Kipling, Davidson, Gosse, Bridges, Thompson, Yeats, Newbolt, Masefield, Belloc, Chesterton, Flecker, and Rupert Brooke, &c., &c ...'[7] Brooke's poetry – and image – were increasingly co-opted and anthologised, a well- established educational practice that allowed literature and ideals about a common cultural heritage and national identity to reach audiences not only across England and the British isles, but the Empire.[8] As *Land and Water* noted in 1915, acknowledging the reach of *Poems of To-Day*, 'we have anthologies of "Poems of To-Day" read and re-read by all the boys and girls in every sort of school in the kingdom'.[9]

By 1917, the efforts of Marsh, Sidgwick and numerous identified and anonymous editors, critics, and journalists had made Brooke into one of the most commercially successful and culturally recognisable figures of the war, his fame expressed through a variety of media. In 1917, John Ireland set 'The Soldier' to music, composing an original score for the verses sung by a solo male voice accompanied by the piano.[10] In 1918, *Musical Opinion* published an article that included a poem in memory of Brooke and 'many others besides … who have carried out the doctrine to the full'. In somewhat less formal prose, its author observed that 'It is a self-stultification to imagine that the artist or poet is a separate species. Man he is, and man he must be first', otherwise his work becomes 'namby-pamby', and lacking in any relevance.[11] In its various permutations, Brooke's poetry and image had maintained their popular appeal.

*

For its 1917 Christmas edition, *The Bookman* put together a special issue for its advertisers and readers. Within were pages of advertisements for books, including a number of cover photographs. Many were aimed at children; most concerning themselves in some way with the war. The central image of the issue was a photograph of 'England's Poet-Soldier' – a full-page headshot of Brooke in shirt-sleeves, jacketless but wearing a tie, gazing intensely away from the camera in semi-profile.[12] This issue of the magazine conspicuously brought together the worlds of poetry and commerce, presenting the poet-soldier as full-on celebrity.

The photographs published in newspapers and various periodicals and magazines during the war played a key role in establishing the idealised myth of the poet-soldier more generally, and in securing – and sustaining – Brooke's specific popular reputation. The images can be broken down into two categories: those concerned with Brooke's grave in a transposable pastoral landscape, and photographs of the poet-soldier himself taken in April 1913. In contrast to many poet-soldiers who published works during the war that included, as their frontispiece, the standard studio shot in uniform,[13] no such image of Brooke was ever included in any of his volumes.[14] These attractive civilian images amplified the range of his popular appeal to those desiring an alternative to the nation as modern military state, and to death as fierce, graphic, and terrifying. They undermined the war's 'particularly symbolic transgression' and culturally destructive capabilities, helping to make the '"self-mutilation" of humanity'[15] opaque and palatable.

As much as the obituaries and articles about 'England's Poet-Soldier' contained discussions of voluntary sacrifice and of a classical and romantic aesthetic heritage fulfilled in his person and verse, many admirers also concerned themselves with qualities specific to Brooke: namely his physical attractiveness. The poet-soldier's noted attention to the male body – his 'own epitaph'[16] – in the War Sonnets provided a respectable context for readers to ponder not only whether or not he had been 'one of the handsomest men in the University',[17] but 'one of the handsomest Englishmen of his time'.[18] The picture of the cleanliness of the swimming youths reinforced notions of communal purity even as the 'red / Sweet wine of youth' transformed bloody death into a metaphor for pleasure made noble through the 'Holiness' and 'Honour' of death for England. Scanning the images offered in these verses, one could fully believe the assertion that 'his last poems show that he looked forward to the idea of death for his country bravely and even joyfully'.[19] The poems were evidence of the 'sentiments and ideals of the clean young Englishman fighting for a just cause',[20] the ultimate physical manifestation of the modern poet as 'man of action'.[21] Thus Brooke was presented – and, it was agreed, presented himself – as a pristine example of perfect youth in death: the 'clean young Englishman' unblemished, obfuscating the broken bodies that returned from the front to live amongst his readers during the war. The 'allure of a clean death was pervasive.

The vision of death during war – painful, humiliating, ugly – intensi-fied the urge for its immaculate counterpart'.[22] The poems and the images fixed youth – and in this case a very handsome example of youth – forever: Brooke became, at a time when this idea was partic-ularly poignant, a boy who never grew up.

*

The decision to publish photographs of Brooke from the American photographer Sherill Schell's 1913 series vastly increased the public's access to his person, and created an image directly in accord with these idealised characterisations. The images also increased the appeal of volumes of his poetry as objects to be possessed, for now everyone could own and study not only the most famous English poems of the war, but a photograph of the nation's handsome poet-soldier.[23] Brooke, who never directly participated in the marketing or distribution of the photographs in his war volumes, had not particularly liked the shots later used for *Letters from America*, *Selected Poems*, and *Collected Poems*. Although he thought them more typical than what became the most iconic image, included as the frontispiece to *1914 and Other Poems*, he claimed that they made him 'look like an amateur popular preacher'.[24]

Both the *1914* image and 'Number VI', from *Letters*, were sold separately from the volume in April and May 1915. Once they were available to the public alongside the poems, demand for copies of the latter fell.[25] This did not signal a lessening in demand for Brooke's image, but instead was a response to its availability in other formats, even as it confirms the general preference for the *1914* image. In 1919, Emery Walker wrote to Marsh, informing him that:

> We have scarcely left off printing the portrait for the first volume of 'Rupert Brooke', which we call 'No. I', since we started four … years ago – never for more than a day or two. Orders have come in one on top of the other.[26]

Specialist magazines and periodicals took an interest in the *1914* image, praising its 'form' and composition, as in *Amateur Photographed and Photographic News*'s article on the 'Photograms of the Year' from May 1915, which also reprinted 'No. I'. The photograph was also shown by Schell in an exhibition at the London Salon of Photography; it reached a visual as well as a literary audience.[27]

For this most widely circulated image, Brooke was shot in profile, from the neck up. No clothing distracted the viewer. As with the other portraits in the series, Brooke had not been wholly convinced of its worth, or appropriateness. He described it to Cathleen Nesbitt as 'very shadowy and ethereal and poetic, of me in profile, and naked-shouldered. Eddie says it's very good. I think it's rather silly'.[28] Unsurprisingly, despite the repeated emphasis of obituaries and articles on 'purity',[29] its sensual qualities were obvious. Brooke's Cambridge friends thought it more akin to kind of prim, middle-brow pornography: the poet-soldier as 'Your favourite actress'.[30]

Selected Poems, brought out first in the United States and then in England in 1917, also included a photograph. It showed Brooke jacket-less, close up, and in half-profile, presenting a semi-casual image of the poet-soldier as handsome intellectual. Reviews of *John Webster and the Elizabethan Drama* that included the photo in its 1916 edition noted the pictured author's 'very subtle intelligence' and 'perfect ear and eye', evidence of the still-vital appeal of his work and the myth; 'It is posthumous and it is young'.[31]

The photograph included as the frontispiece to *Letters from America* (1916) was the most formal photograph of Brooke from the Schell series. In this instance, he was not to be made, at least overtly, into a figure of silly romance or, worse, an object of what was viewed by many as explicitly sexual, a manifestation of 'khaki fever'. This was the worrying (for some, throughout the war) phenomenon wherein youths of both sexes 'were drawn to the men, many hardly older than themselves, who were often full of bravado about what they hoped would be a short and glorious campaign'.[32] While most agreed that this trend dissipated slightly in accordance with war-weariness, sexual and gender management continued throughout the period, and indeed beyond.[33]

Previous chapters have discussed how, even as obituarists and critics consistently asserted that Brooke was exceptionally honourable and gifted, they also promoted the idea that he was exceptionally attractive. They did so in a way that avoided any appearance of impropriety, or fetishising. It was more acceptable for the public to order up images of the half-naked poet-soldier or the intense close-up of the young man in his shirtsleeves, and to linger on Brooke's 'beautiful golden head and his athlete's body'[34] because established figures such as Henry James[35] and H. W. Nevinson at the *Nation* did so as well, with the latter remembering how Brooke's entry into the offices of the *Nation* in 1913 produced an 'effect' that was 'almost ludicrously beautiful'.[36] The very proper and staid *Country Life* would go on to reproduce the *John Webster* image when they printed a long article on Brooke's old school, Rugby, in April 1916. Brooke was identified as a notable alumnus, a representative of the 'spirit of the twentieth century, a graciousness, a tolerance, a human sympathy', one of those who 'have fought the good fight and finished their course, almost before the echo of their schoolboy feet has died in Quad and Cloister'.[37]

Brooke's celebrity – and the photographs of him that contributed to it – emphasised both his physical appeal and his poetic sensibilities. They appealed to the public irrespective of age or gender. While Brooke's own homosexual experiences remained a private matter during and long after the war,[38] there was nothing stopping men and women from identifying the poet-soldier as a sexual object or fantasy. This was troubling to a society that was, at least publicly, aggressively condemning of homosexuality. It was easier to direct the reader of an obituary or article to react in a particular way to the poet-solider than it was to control reactions to photographs of him. Brooke had been presented as a symbol of the explicitly male military domain, but the images accompanying the published poems simultaneously made available the image of the attractive semi-bohemian poet, now draped in – and made doubly attractive by – his patriotic sensibilities.

RCB/Ph/188. Sherril Schell, Portrait of Rupert Brook in profile, with bare
shoulders, taken in London in April 1913.

Reactions to the images could not be entirely fixed. His physical appeal, like his poetry, benefited from its adaptability to whoever was utilising or consuming it.

*

In part owing to the wide dissemination and resulting popularity of the *1914* photograph, Brooke's face became archetypal. The photograph was deemed recognisable and sufficiently solemn to be reprinted on a souvenir for the Royal Naval Division. The four-page pamphlet included the shot of Brooke, collaged with a masted ship, a copy of Brooke's War Sonnet 'The Dead', a bugle score including the lines, 'Don't let us forget the Mates who have Fallen', and the quote, 'If blood be the price of the Admiralty, Lord God, we ha' bought it fair'. Profits from the souvenir went to the Division's Prisoners of War, many of whom were captured during the Antwerp retreat.[39]

The *1914* photograph was also the inspiration for memorials unveiled during the war. Brooke's mother Mary commissioned a bust based on the image that she intended to be placed in Rugby Chapel; the event was to be marked by a ceremony with various speakers, including Marsh, Ian Hamilton, and Walter de la Mare. Initially intended for unveiling in 1917, Mary Brooke postponed the memorial 'In view of the appeal by the Government to abandon all avoidable occasions of travelling ... till after the war'.[40] The photograph later formed the basis for another, less personal memorial to the dead. In included a figure not overtly identifiable as Brooke but inspired by the poet-soldier, in Aldeburgh, Suffolk, by Gilbert Bayes. Incorporating lines from 'The Dead', the sculptor used Brooke's profile for the model of a dead youth, uniform fashionably dishevelled, rocks pillowing the body, with the sea in the distance. The critic Charles Marriot praised the sculptor's restraint as contextually appropriate; 'There is a moral discipline as well as aesthetic guidance in the limitation of the stuff', as the marble medium 'saves its face ... giving all the necessary relief to the design'. Fittingly, the artist created an abstracted version of Brooke, with the poet-soldier becoming the 'illustration to the verse ... leaving the moral to that, rather than an attempt at symbolism by the sculpture'.[41] The furthering of a message of physical and moral purity embodied in a single mythical figure continued, this time captured in stone.

Brooke's failure to sit for the standard war portrait was, in the end, a blessing in disguise. Despite the fact that part of Brooke's fame rested on the success in particular of 'The Soldier' at a time when the English public was especially enthralled and even fixated on the man in uniform as national defender, the opportunity to imagine the poet-soldier in uniform – or not – proved popular. It further allowed Brooke to be associated with something transcending the war, and to assert the English ideal of the 'part-time soldiers' with an identity 'rooted in civilian life'[42] that countered the image of an enemy obsessed with militarism. Nevinson, in his review of *1914 and Other Poems* for the *Nation* specifically recognised this as central to understanding Brooke, who died 'for England's life against the ideal of efficient officialism', thus offering readers the example of a 'legacy of protest'.[43] The Schell images, published alongside the poems with their abstracted portrayals of war, allowed for an attractive flexibility: in death Brooke could move from peace to war and back again, taking on various forms, appealing to those who desired nostalgia for a world that seemed to be fast slipping away, as well as to those who appreciated aesthetic and in some cases sexualised depictions of the male form. The photographs fixed – and preserved – the perfect body of the poet-soldier, in death as in life.

*

Images of Grantchester and of Brooke's evolving gravesite at Scyros also provided a foreground and background in which to project the poet-soldier. As with all such images, the poetry added multiple layers of meaning. They drew on a long tradition of the 'cultural politics of countryside imagery'.[44] In this case, English ideals colonised a foreign landscape, providing a backdrop to the death of an English hero.

One recurrent theme of the War Sonnets, already touched on in previous chapters and often brought to the forefront in obituaries and articles about Brooke, was the poet's relationship to death and, to an extent, burial. In 'Peace' death becomes the 'worst friend and enemy' that ends the 'agony'[45] of the body; in 'The Dead' it is traded for 'that unhoped serene, / That men call age' and for 'immortality'.[46] The most quoted lines – 'there's some corner of a foreign field' – throughout the war whenever Brooke was discussed came from the 'The Soldier', with its melding of the body of the soldier with England.[47] The image of 'rich earth a richer dust concealed' invoked the familiar 'dust to dust' of Christian burial and to the interment of the dead soldier, a scene set in an imagined pastoral: 'hearts at peace, under an English heaven'.[48] As the war forced more and more people, and English society more generally, to confront death on a mass scale, the idealised image of 'Rupert Brooke's Resting Place in Aegean Sea'[49] became an increasingly important element of the myth of the poet-soldier, 'One who gave his career to his country will sleep well on an Aegean isle'.[50] The idea that wherever a soldier fell and was buried became England and, it followed, 'home' resonated with many.

Photographs of Brooke's grave at Scyros during the war were not as accessible or in demand as the Schell photographs of the living poet, included in the published volumes of poetry and prose. Throughout the war, Mary Brooke managed the grave, which evolved from a simple white cross to a more substantial marble tomb. Only later, in the late 1920s, did pilgrimages to the site begin to receive coverage in the press and these articles more often than not included snapshots of the grave and its surrounds.[51] However, 'buried at Lemnos' or 'buried at Scyros' was a constant refrain of the obituaries, articles, and reviews. Having obtained an American edition of *Selected Poems* in 1916, the *Sphere* reported approvingly that the volume's introduction concluded with the lines:

> There is a grave in Scyros, amid the white and pinkish marble
> of the isle, the wild thyme and the poppies, near the green and

blue waters. There Rupert Brooke was buried. Thither have gone the thoughts of his countrymen, and the hearts of the young especially. It will be long so. For a new star shines in the English heaven …[52]

Unofficial pilgrimages were already taking place. One reader and soldier, Captain Fred Pepys Cockerell, took it upon himself to write directly to Brooke's publishers, including photographs that he and friends had taken in 1917 during a brief leave from service. He described the scene as he found it; 'Although it differs from those Cambridgeshire lands which he loved, this place which is forever England is meet enough for him. At his head is a wild olive, the reward, for the soldier, of the winner of the race; and five paces away a bay-tree for the poet'. He hoped the publishers would pass on to Brooke's grieving mother 'These little photographs … taken at a hazard, rather with the idea of giving those for whom he cared a general impression of the surroundings among which he lies'.[53]

Imagined versions of the site proved so appealing that they even inspired a long article in the *Mercure de France* entitled 'Le Premier Mort des Dardanelles',[54] which was then translated and included in a small book reprinted in limited number in Britain and the United States as *Rupert Brooke's Death and Burial*.[55] Purported to be 'Based on the Log of the French Hospital Ship *Duguay-Trouin*', this offered a highly sentimental account of the burial procession, and contained as its frontispiece a photograph of Brooke's grave with a simple white cross, described as an appropriate setting for 'the first Englishman fallen by the roadside', a 'deserted place' where 'the sun will shift the strip of shade cast by the small olive trees'. Over this tragic, but appropriately romantic, scene, 'The Muse watches, and the obscure colloquy in which she is absorbed alter her immemorial presence little by little'.[56]

The musings show the extent to which imagined landscapes – particularly in times of conflict and cultural upheaval – 'can be self-consciously designed to express the virtues of a particular political or social community'.[57] Together with the photographs of Brooke, the burial site, compared and occasionally coupled with an imagined 'Grantchester', provided a comfortingly familiar space for the poet-soldier to exist in the minds of readers. They actively countered more disturbing thoughts about death in modern war. Instead, 'England's Poet-Soldier' lived on in a perennial pastoral twilight, a comforting image that was aesthetic, peaceful, and patriotic.

*

In a time of war, even commercial success sometimes required a temporary sacrifice of profits. As the price of paper increased, meeting the public demand for the Schell photographs of Brooke – as for his poetry and prose – placed pressure on the publishers and the engravers.[58] In September 1916, Sidgwick wrote to Marsh, wishing to renegotiate the terms of the royalties, which despite Brooke's posthumous success had not been altered after the original 1911 *Poems* agreement. Sidgwick hoped to increase profits from the sales, which could in turn be reinvested to keep up the printing stocks.[59] The photographs were especially problematic. Even after the war Sidgwick complained that, in particular, dealing with photogravures meant that the production timetable increased to the point wherein they could not keep up with clamour for the volumes.[60] Walker, the original engraver, remembered that he had worked as quickly as possible under 'difficult conditions' during the war; only later could they recover to the pre-war schedule as well as the 'old quality of printing'.[61] Despite these challenges, no one appears to have suggested omitting the photographs from the volumes altogether as a practical remedy to the situation.

And no wonder. Brooke's popularity showed no sign of abating; each reinforced the other, as the press, literary patrons, fellow poet-soldiers, and readers maintained a ready audience for the poetry and images. Practically speaking, keeping multiple editions with various photographs and prices on offer meant greater circulation, as did allowing reproductions of 'The Soldier' and 'The Dead' in as many newspapers as possible. Advertisements continued to illustrate the exemplary sales figures to the public, listing the dates of each impression of *1914 and Other Poems*, which already totalled seven by August 1915,[62] reaching fourteen by October 1916[63] (it was produced in runs of 5,000 per printing). By 1920, this volume would sell 105,155 in Great Britain alone.[64] It remained Brooke's best seller throughout the war, followed by *Poems* (1911), which, combined with modest pre-war sales, reached an impressive 59,346 copies sold by 1920. *Collected Poems*, with Marsh's *Memoir* from 1918, ran third, followed by *Selected Poems*, which was published in Britain in 1917 after a similar American edition performed well in 1916.

Table 1 Rupert Brooke, sales, Great Britain, to 1920

Volume	Sales
Poems (1911)	59,346
1914 and Other Poems	105,155
Letters from America	5,982
John Webster and the Elizabethan Drama	1,886
Selected Poems	17, 545
Collected Poems	20,407

Source: RCB Xf/11, Mary Brooke, Sales Figures to 31 December 1920.

All in all, it was Brooke's poetry that sold best, in various forms, throughout the war. The journalistic *Letters from America*, with Henry James's appreciative preface, and the more academic *John Webster and the Elizabethan Drama* displayed different facets of his literary talents. During the war the reception that all of his prose and verse volumes received contributed to Brooke's success, but he was first and foremost the nation's poet-soldier, an icon that achieved a visual ubiquity and cultural currency that worked hand-in-hand to establish and sustain his literary celebrity.

12

Patrons

The influence of the war as an everyday reality – social, political, commercial, and material – pervaded as the imagined and hoped-for victory failed to materialise. For Brooke's publishers, as his popularity soared in the months after his death, it became clear that their early investment in the young poet would be recouped. In a note to Marsh from September 1915 reporting on the £176. 19s. 3d. made from the publication of *1914 and Other Poems* between May and June 1915, Frank Sidgwick predicted that, 'The next cheque will be even larger'. He followed this up with the wry comment, 'I trust the beneficiaries will not be taxed on war-profits'.[1] This was a fair assessment of what Brooke's profits were.

Table 2 Rupert Brooke, royalties, Great Britain, 1915–18

Period	Royalties	2016 Value
January–June 1915	£667.0s.0d.	£213,700
July–December 1915	£3,566.2s.4d.	£1,143,000
January–June 1916	£3,206.9s.8d.	£945,400
July–December 1916	£3,944.7s.8d.	£1,163,000
January–June 1917	£1,940.6s.8d.	£503,300
July–December 1917	£2,800.6s.0d.	£726,300
January–June 1918	£1,392.8s.4d.	£274,700
July–December 1918	£3,648.1s.2d.	£719,700

Source: RCB Xg/9, Lascalles Abercrombie and Fuller & Son, Ltd., Figures for Tax Purposes, Abercrombie to Marsh, 29 November 1920.

Brooke had many patrons, in life and in death. He also, through circumstance, posthumously became one. Through his generosity, his fellow *New Numbers* poets shared in the proceeds that accrued from the War Sonnets.[2] Lascelles Abercrombie, one of these beneficiaries, noted the strange circumstances of his inheritance: 'I received from you yesterday a fortune, embodied in a form which somehow gives the sense of self-sacrificing patriotism in addition to that of immense wealth.'[3] Half-yearly royalty payments throughout the war period remained consistent, with the periods between July and December recording higher figures than months from January to June (Table 2):[4] however much omnipresent patriotism motivated Brooke's would-be fans, in publishing then, as now, sales increased parallel to the traditional Christmas rush.

Abercrombie, as well as John Drinkwater, Wilfrid Wilson Gibson, and Walter de la Mare, who had all been friendly with Brooke and had shared his ambitions of making a living by writing, published numerous poems and articles testifying to Brooke's substantial talent and general significance in the months after his death.[5] De la Mare was also chosen by Marsh as the representative to attend the ceremony posthumously awarding the Yale University Henry Howland Memorial Prize to Brooke in June 1916.[6] Some of the poets' writing was more substantial; for a time they became something akin to Brooke scholars or fellows (although they continued with their own work as well). Drinkwater completed a long piece bringing together material from his laudatory obituaries and articles entitled 'Rupert Brooke: An Essay', in 1916.[7] He wrote of the 'rare perfections that attain greatness by their very symmetry and fortune'.[8] In a similar vein, de la Mare delivered a long lecture at Rugby in March 1919, later published by Sidgwick & Jackson as *Rupert Brooke and the Intellectual Imagination*. For the four surviving *New Numbers* poets, the supplement to their income provided a degree of freedom for which they could feel nothing but gratitude. As Wilfred Gibson wrote to Marsh in April 1917, 'It really is wonderful'.[9] The poets demonstrated their genuine appreciation by helping to shape the posthumous reputation of their young patron, attesting to his literary merit and praising his pure and patriotic sacrifice.

*

Patronage – both as benign support and as an expression of unequal power relations – took on a variety of forms during the war, and played a key role in the formation and dissemination of the Brooke myth: it could be collective or personal. Much has been written about divisions between 'historical generations'[10] and the guilt many in the older generation felt about unequal sacrifices. As Coulson Kernahan recorded in the preface to his *Experiences of a Recruiting Officer*: 'I admit that the unheroic and humiliating task of persuading younger men to a duty and to dangers, which one's own more advanced age prevented one from sharing, was not, and is not, congenial'.[11] In June 1915, Marsh wrote to Denis Browne, who was killed shortly after, that 'it's really almost unbearable to be a gentleman of England at home at ease and in safety when the real gentlemen of England are doing the exact opposite'.[12] These sentiments led many on the home front to seek out 'the duty which lay nearest, and in which I could at least be of some small personal service',[13] and to throw themselves behind the war effort, feeling that this was the best way to support the soldiers.

The dynamic played out in the army and navy as well. Officers acted as temporary patrons for the soldiers in their charge, as Brooke demonstrated in camp in 1914, trying to secure as many comforts for them as he could,[14] or might become involved in commissions, as when Churchill helped to get Brooke assigned to the Royal Naval Division. Patronage extended across the political, civil service, and military spheres as well. In October 1914, Charles Masterman at Wellington House received a plea from Herbert Asquith, forwarded to him by Lord Durham, who wanted to do something on the soldiers' behalf: 'I receive letters nearly every day from Durham recruits asking me to help about bounties and wives' allowances and their own pay which are in arrears. They don't understand red tape'.

He suggested that Asquith and Masterman in his role as semi-official propagandists might 'Use me as a stalking horse if you like'.[15] Churchill also got involved in issues like these, which mixed policy with the righting of individual wrongs expressed through personal appeals. In September 1914, he wrote to Lloyd George in response to an article in the *Nation*: 'The 5/- pension is a scandal. No soldiers should be dependent on charity. Your large outlook should be turned on this'.[16] Thomas Marlow, editor of the *Daily Mail*, complained to George about a speech made by a Captain De Knoop reported in the *Manchester Guardian*, wherein references to lack of shells were omitted by the censor: 'At the front they read of fellows going to strike for another halfpenny an hour or because they were asked to do a bit of extra work and the men in the trenches looked on those at home as stark staring mad'.[17] Such intercessions were born of a desire to do one's utmost on behalf of the fighting men, even as they served particular political agendas.

For men of this older, established generation, commitment to the soldiers and to the war became self-justifying. In October 2016, Gilbert Murray wrote in *The Times* of the need to maintain not only material support, but to shore up the ideological framework justifying so much death:

> You ask me to go on facing death, or facing my children's deaths; you ask me collectively to endure more and more, to give more and more of all that is dear to us; and we are ready to both endure and to give. Of course we will go on. We have no faintest temptation anywhere to refuse the last sacrifice that is needed for victory. Only, for heaven's sake, in mercy to the dying and respect for the dead, do not lower or forget the cause for which we are giving it![18]

In the end the absolute commitment to the war proved difficult to let go, even as the dead piled up and some began to question: what is this all about, and is it really worth it?

*

Many established critics and would-be literary patrons responding to 'the radiant, perfectly posed story of Rupert Brooke',[19] worked to secure his literary reputation during the war. They admired the sacrifice of the man at least as much as his poetry, recognising all the while the role of the latter in defining the war's philosophical terrain, in commemorating the war dead, and in making it all more endurable. In so doing, these writers – even those who remained hostile to what they considered to be the vulgarity and sensationalism of the emerging modern media as it responded to the war – contributed to Brooke's popular reputation as it developed outside of more closed and regulated intellectual circles. For 'lovers of literature', his death was an 'affecting national interest', and hence 'appreciations' of Brooke were 'most welcome' in the pages of newspapers as were more cerebral literary assessments.[20]

Murray, whose writing on the war Brooke had so admired, added his voice to the chorus recognising the young poet's achievements. He had continued his role as a public academic and moral arbiter. In November 1915, he was one of the signatories of 'A Duty of the Hour', a public letter published in *The Times* calling for 'sacrifice' of a 'self-denying economy' that promoted abstention from drink.[21] In October 1916, he wrote again to the newspaper about the need to keep the ideals that he had identified as justifying British entry into the war at the forefront, thus countering 'the gradual forgetting of the cause in the mere struggle'.[22] In 1918, *The Times* covered his Creighton lecture at the London School of Economics, which proposed a parable for the current 'great war' in the all-consuming Peloponnesian Wars.[23]

In assessing Brooke, Murray quickly pinpointed his appeal. In a May 1915 article for *Cambridge Magazine*, he predicted that: 'I cannot help thinking that Rupert Brooke will probably live in fame as an almost mythical figure'.[24] A week later, *Public Opinion* used Murray's quote to frame their article on Brooke, 'An Almost Mythical Figure'.[25] Murray's published writings on Brooke included both personal and professional insights. He was 'entirely unaffected, so simple and friendly and

modest' that 'Neither his genius, nor his good looks, nor his numerous
adorers seemed to spoil him'. He was simultaneously rarefied and
'prosperous, much beloved', a 'delightful companion', someone with a
'great gift' for 'friendship'.[26] Evidence of this could also be found in his
poems: Murray argued, against the actual timeline of their construction, that having had the 'experience of facing death in Belgium and
the Dardanelles', Brooke transformed it into a 'deeper music', drawing
on his 'deeper experience of the imagination' as well as an 'intensity of
perception',[27] an attribute especially developed in the poet-soldier. His
War Sonnets owed their power to the 'sensitive' and 'honest' personality of their author. The final poems were his inspired testimony, 'for
the most part he [Brooke] never wrote unless he had something quite
definite to say'. In conclusion, Murray asserted that, 'Among all who
have been poets and died young, it is hard to think of one who, both in
life and death, has so typified the ideal radiance of youth and poetry'.

Other critics went on to endorse and expand on these themes,
proposing Brooke as a testament to the continuities of culture and a
rich, ever-renewing literary heritage. With a nod to popular classicism,
the writer and lawyer E. S. P. Haynes wrote that 'English poets, with a
few exceptions, like Sir Philip Sidney, have rarely fought and died for
their country, whereas it was all in the day's work for the Greek poets'.
Brooke the poet-soldier was both 'ancient' in his response to war as a
'compelling duty', and an embodiment of the Greek ideal renewed by
the self-sacrifice of Englishmen of his generation. He was 'Greek in his
appearance',[28] and, as such, in the popular shorthand version of such
articles, a 'hero' and a 'martyr' as well as an immortal poet.[29] Writers
also linked Brooke to an idealised Elizabethan past: 'Until April 23rd
in this year, when this greatly loved boy died at the Dardanelles, Philip
Sidney had not found his fellow'.[30] For the poet, essayist, and academic
Arthur Benson, Brooke was the epitome of the 'high-minded and gifted
young man' carrying with him the 'continuance of a noble poetic tradition', and a poet-soldier carrying forth the 'meteor flag of England'.[31]
Sir Henry Newbolt, the influential poet who spent part of his war
as Controller of Telecommunications at the Foreign Office and was

knighted in 1915 for his services to literature and the government, in a lecture on 'Georgian Poetry' given at the Royal Society of Literature in January 1916, went on to compare Brooke to Donne, concluding that 'the right poetry for any age was not the poetry of the future, but the poetry of the past and, above all, of the present'. Brooke's sort of poetry, however much it anticipated some 'treasure of greater beauty', was a product of the present conflict, and, as such, 'the right poetry' to instruct and inspire readers and writers.[32] For the poet, critic, and author Edmund Gosse, he was a 'genius … sustaining the majesty of English, as long as English exists'.[33]

Brooke's was not the only loss noted by the literary London establishment, but when writing about any other representative of the war dead, he was often brought in to the discussion. The journalist and poet Cecil Roberts wrote an article about the loss of Brooke, 'the lover and singer of Greece' and James Elroy Flecker, who 'is closely followed by his younger friend'.[34] Murray also brought the two together in his *Cambridge Magazine* article for May 1915, positing that Brooke and 'James Elroy Flecker, extraordinarily different people, seem to me to have been quite the best of their own remarkable generation' and, tragically, 'they are both gone in one year'.[35]

Edward Thomas, the poet and critic who briefly also became a poet-soldier, wrote a careful, considered review of Brooke's 'promise', fulfilled through his poetry and by his actions as a soldier. When reviewing *1914 and Other Poems* in 1915 Thomas noted the tendency of many to describe the War Sonnets as 'very personal' expressions. In his view, the 'impersonality is more striking'.[36] Having known Brooke, he agreed that the loftiness and brilliance of the poems 'reminds everybody who knew of Rupert Brooke' of his personality. He was consistent on this point in his article for the *English Review*: 'No one that knew him could easily separate him from his poetry; not that they were the same, but that the two inextricably mingled and helped one another'.[37] With regard specifically to 'The Soldier', it was 'those things that he puts by' without complaint, the result being that he 'ceases to be metaphysician or aesthete, to become something above either, above a union of the two'. Although he did not particularly appreciate Brooke's portrayal of self-sacrifice in the poems, Thomas understood and approved of how he 'embraced England and eternity', uniting the '"kindred points of heaven and home", and shows them to be one'.[38] This resonated with Thomas. As he had written earlier in 1915:

> I believe that England means ... that all ideas of England are developed, spun out, from such a centre into something large or infinite, solid or airy, according to each man's nature and capacity; that England is a system of vast circumferences circling round the minute neighbouring points of home.[39]

Thomas portrayed Brooke's 'sacrifice ... for the idea of self-sacrifice' as legitimised by an England where one could remain free from overt coercion and make up one's own mind to serve, as Brooke had. In the end, his daring to be 'an Apollo not afraid of the worst of his life' assured that 'His reputation is safe: it was never greater than now, when he stands out clearly against that immense, dark background'.[40]

These established writers and critics fully believed that they owed it to posterity and, more immediately, to the war dead (and specifically to England's emerging poet-soldier) to recognise their self-sacrifice: they could not allow 'for the death of a singer ... to pass unnoticed'.[41] They wrote 'from life, from the heart, and, also, for strategic value'.[42] They used their public influence to direct readers – 'the people' – who 'will also desire from time to time to discover some eternal symbol of the nobility that is in them also, patiently keeping the balance of the world'.[43]

*

The Belgian poet Emile Verhaeren offers another example of an established poet who advanced Brooke's reputation, within and beyond English literary circles. Verhaeren translated Brooke's poems into French, and his volume of poetry *Les Ailes rouges de la guerre*, published in 1916 in Paris, included a lengthy tribute poem to Brooke. Claiming to be 'D'après une lettre d'un de ses amis et compagnons d'armes qui l'enterra à Scyros', the poem 'Rupert Brooke: Poète et Soldat' conflated the distance between the reader and Brooke, offering a romanticised imagining of the penultimate moment of sacrifice: the 'dénier souffle' of the poet.

Verhaeren's poem echoed many of the themes present in English obituaries and articles about Brooke. He exemplified 'les hautes idées' of his generation made manifest in action as 'Etant poète, il se promit d'être soldat'.[44] Although he had only briefly joined the fight in defence of Belgium, more broadly speaking he had joined the struggle against the prime enemy and perpetrator of the war: for Verhaeren, 'la pesant et féroce Allemagne',[45] the terrorisers of innocent Belgian citizens and the sackers of Liège. The gentle Englishman, 'En uniforme roux coupé en son milieu / D'un seul rang de boutons aux fleurons militaires', presented a civilised counter to the aggressive German soldier.[46] Happily, Brooke had not suffered violations of the body: instead his memory conjured images of the 'blanc marbres' of 'Sa tombe, au cœur d l'île', a commonly sanctified place where 'nous irons rechercher sous le thym et la mousse'.[47]

Verhaeren's death in 1916 was, like his young subject's, recorded in *The Times*. The obituary argued that he had provided his own 'graphic summary of his spiritual life', translating 'all that he loved and suffered into his poems of proud but frank intensity'. The obituary also alerted its readers to the presence of the Brooke poem in *Les Ailes*. This 'graceful tribute'[48] to the nation's poet-soldier and 'nos bras sanglants' of 'La France et l'Angleterre'[49] provided 'a fine apostrophe to the grandeur of England, at last abandoning her splendid isolation and leading the brotherhood of nations'.[50]

*

Henry James's 'Preface' to Brooke's *Letters from America* appeared in 1916. It also drew on the general themes of the obituaries and articles published in the months following Brooke's death, elaborating on them in James's particular circling style. In so doing he further endorsed the ideal of the poet-soldier for readers in Great Britain, the United States, and beyond. The *Glasgow News* alerted its reader to the fact that 'Some unpublished prose will be included and a long tribute to the author has been written by Mr. Henry James. This tribute, in view of the serious illness of its writer, will be read with great interest'.[51] James was dying when he wrote the piece, and this heightened its value, offering an 'inspired account' of Brooke's life. Both the *Daily Chronicle* and the *Liverpool Courier* publicised this fact in their headlines: 'The Prose of a Poet. And Henry James' Last Writing'[52] and 'Mr. Henry James, O.M., Posthumous Tribute to Rupert Brooke'.[53] In amongst the hagiographies, in a rare moment of levity, the *Sunday Chronicle* took a moment to draw attention to the contrasting styles of the two authors:

> If we were not still so poignantly conscious of the loss of both of them, we might be tempted to a merry jest at the idea of the late Henry James getting out to explain the late Rupert Brooke. The situation is unparalleled for unconscious humour in the history of letters. Rupert Brooke was many charming things; but above all he was the most brilliantly explicit of our twentieth-century writers.[54]

Still, it concluded solemnly, the 'intention of Henry James was most laudable'.[55]

'The Preface' maintained the message of fatalism so prevalent in many obituaries and articles about Brooke. James matched this with a recognition of the poet-soldier's particular nationalist appeal to readers. When he learned of Brooke's death he wrote to Marsh, with all the fervour of a convert to the mystique of his adopted homeland, explaining that 'he penetrates me most when he is most hauntingly (or hauntedly) English – he draws such a real magic from his conscious reference to it'. Although he confided in Marsh that he found the War Sonnets to be rather less 'natural', or natural in a different way to his other works,[56] he argues that they presented 'a meaning still deeper seated than their noble beauty, an authority, of the purest, attended with which his name inscribes itself in its own character on the great English scroll'.[57] 'How', James asked, 'could he have shown more the young English poetic possibility and faculty in which we were to seek the freshest reflection of the intelligence and the soul of the new generation?'[58] His life and death 'makes a monument of his high rest there at the heart of all that was once noblest in history'.[59]

The *Liverpool Post*'s reviewer was somewhat unconvinced of James's earned familiarity in speaking of 'Rupert' as a 'proprietary right'.[60] In an interview with the *Daily Mail*, James's secretary Violet Hunt attested to James's 'emotional' closeness to the young poet-soldier: 'I remember his passionate cherishing of young Rupert Brooke ... He could not even speak of Rupert Brooke after he died'.[61] One English newspaper concluded that 'The Preface' was 'not a panegyric: it is a jubilee'.[62] The *Sunday Times and Sunday Special* happily concurred: 'For Henry James he [Brooke] represents the fine flower of our culture, of the English tradition and school system'.[63] The *Dundee Advertiser* argued that:

> For a hundred years poets sang of that [English] aspect, but never once did they see it in all the grandeur of sacrifice as we see it now. Henry James, a great American, who adopted Britain as his country, has written to this book an introduction which is an inspiration to all who read.[64]

It articulated the literary (and, it was hoped by many in 1916, the political and material) 'sympathy'[65] between the two nations represented by their respective poets and authors. Again playing up the idea of 'a mourner now himself amongst the mourned',[66] reviewers praised the 'great master of human elaboration and civilised beauty who has just left us',[67] with the *Manchester Guardian* characterising the 'beautiful piece of writing' as 'very friendly, noble, and illuminating'.[68]

Letters from America subsequently appeared in the United States in January 1916, published by Charles Scribner's Sons. In many

American newspapers, the virtue of the volume, and its most explicit selling point, played on the idea of continuity between literary generations and peoples. Like their British counterparts, many advertised Brooke's work in the same line as 'With a Preface by Henry James', reinforcing the argument that Brooke's death became notorious as the parable of the 'Fine Young Genius Lost to England'.[69] This 'Genius' was not the judgement solely of the majority of prominent British critics, but was supported by none other than 'a great man of letters, at the eminence of fame and experience'; hence the value of the 'Preface' as James's personal testimony. Brooke as a figurehead represented 'youth on the threshold' of the 'fame and experience'[70] already secured by James. 'With friendly, affectionate manner', James

> ranges round about his subject, going off into excursions of comparison and speculation, putting here and there a touch of observation or of fact, and presently there emerges from under his hand the bright and gallant figure of a youth, pressing onward eagerly into life, loving the world, beloved by all about him.[71]

This particularly glowing review characterised the piece as 'the most perfect of its kind in the history of literature',[72] solemnising the relationship between generations; the old, established figures paid tribute to the young who have unnaturally died before their time in a noble cause.

James's main value as a literary patron was in offering any substantive testimonial in favour of Brooke's exceptional achievement. The *Westminster Gazette* promoted this idea in its review of the 'Preface', noting approvingly that 'Henry James returns again and again to the one thought, under ever-varying aspects, of how perfectly Rupert Brooke responded to all that could have been asked of a young poet of this, his own time and generation'.[73] In pressing this view in conjunction with assurances about a common literary sensibility and – to an extent – a common political cause, in *Letters from America* James presented Brooke as evidence of 'general [English] community of feeling',[74] and fulfilled Marsh's 1915 prediction of his value as a cultural ambassador.[75]

*

If Henry James was arguably Brooke's most vaunted international literary champion, Edward Marsh was his most hard-working and devoted patron throughout and after the war. Quietly, behind the scenes, drawing on his extensive literary and political networks and as Executor of Brooke's literary estate, he had a hand in much of what was published about his friend from 1915 to 1918. But he was not omnipotent and as the ideal of the poet-soldier slipped from his hands and into the public domain he also felt the need to record his opinion of what made Brooke so special and important.

Initially, his tribute was envisioned as collaborative effort, fully sanctioned by Mary Brooke, who perhaps more fully than Marsh felt that she had lost her son to a voracious, if largely adoring, public. But the relationship eventually soured, with Mary increasingly critical of Marsh's management of the estate[76] and of the planned 'Memoir'. In May 1916, Marsh – who still had his full-time job as a civil servant alongside commitments to projects like *Georgian Poetry* to balance with work on the piece – wrote to Mary to explain his approach: '"Literary merit", in the humble sense in which I am using the words, is not a scholar's fetish, or a mere inessential ornament; it is the quality which makes the difference between a book that will do, and a book that won't'.[77]

She was unimpressed, and dug in: 'You couldn't bear me taking my stand as his mother'.[78] Exasperated, Marsh later wrote to Frank Sidgwick, who was very much on his side in the feud, wondering (rather cruelly) 'How Rupert could be produced by a woman without sense of humour or beauty, and narrow to that degree, I shall never understand'.[79] The *Collected Poems of Rupert Brooke* with Marsh's 'Memoir' eventually appeared in July 1918. Mary Brooke offered a short introductory note, attributing the delay – and the fact that the volume was not all that she hoped it would be – to the 'desire to gain the collaboration of some of his contemporaries at Cambridge' that had been made impossible by the death of so many of them. She offered a fig leaf to Marsh: 'I cannot speak strongly enough of the ability and loving care that Mr. Marsh has brought to the work'.[80]

The *Memoir* boosted sales of the *Collected* edition in 1918; it was also printed separately as a stand-alone volume. Marsh's extended obituary featured his own writing with Brooke's alongside letters and anecdotes supplied by a variety of friends and acquaintances, and further affirmed many of the general themes established over the course of nearly three years of praise and reflection on the poet-soldier. It spoke of Brooke's development as a poet, of his love of Grantchester, and of his careful volunteerism, 'seeking out the best way to serve as a soldier'.[81] Marsh alluded to Brooke's sadness at the death of friends who went before him, conveying the general tragedy of the early war period. Addressing Brooke's death, Marsh chose to include Denis Brown's final letter to him, written two days before his own death on 2 June:

> Coming from Alexandria yesterday we passed Rupert's island at sunset. The sea and sky in the east were grey and misty; but it stood out in the West, black and immense, with a crimson glowing halo round it. Every colour had come into the sea and sky to do him honour; and it seemed that the island must ever be shining with his glory that we buried there.[82]

It was as though Marsh could, still, not bear to speak directly of the loss of his friend.

Responses to the *Memoir* were broadly positive. Many noted Marsh's 'rare self-effacement', noting that the author 'has withheld his name even from the title-page, and allows his hero throughout, as far as may be, to be revealed in his own letters or through the words of his friends'.[83] However, some of the people close to Brooke who hoped that it would offer a more definitive account of their friend to counter the distilled version that now dominated public discourses were disappointed. An article in the *Cambridge Review* argued that the 'Memoir' existed only so that 'the legend of Rupert Brooke' could be 'magnificently endorsed'.[84] The *Oxford Magazine* observed, 'Such an atmosphere of eulogy and thanksgiving renders the task of those who are anxious to form a sound judgement as to the man himself, and the intrinsic value of what he has left behind him, more than ordinarily difficult'.[85] Virginia Woolf concurred in her review for the *Times Literary Supplement*, characterising the piece as another form of entombment.[86]

Marsh was hurt by these responses. He saw his role as existing 'for R.'s credit', to 'safeguard' his public image. This was something that he viewed as his 'sacred trust'.[87] One public exchange illustrates how sensitive he could be when executing his perceived duty. In August 1918, a rare critical review in *Town Topics* drew on a letter written by Brooke and published in the *Memoir* to attack the 'egotism' of the War Sonnets. Brooke had compared himself to Keats, and the writer took exception.[88] After requesting the exact passage,[89] Marsh replied, arguing that the original Keats' quote had been taken entirely out of context. He went on to question the reviewer's 'critical accuracy' in failing to recognise that only one of the poems was 'even nominally about himself [Brooke]'.[90]

Marsh was by this point understandably testy, worn down by years of a punishing schedule, balancing official work with literary and artistic patronage, and, like many others left behind to defend the home front, mourning the unrelenting loss of friends to the war they worked so hard to service. His friend and biographer Christopher Hassall offers an account of Marsh in April 1918, after receiving word of the death of another friend and poet-soldier, Isaac Rosenberg. Marsh ran into an old acquaintance in the street who praised his abilities as an editor by exclaiming, 'Well, Eddie, your Georgians certainly know how to write!', and Marsh, normally genial, replied, 'And how to die', and walked away.[91] The sacrificed generation and, for Marsh, in particular, Brooke, existed above the fray. It was up to him – and the various other literary patrons who bore Brooke on 'nos épaules fraternelles'[92] – to ensure that he remained there.

13

Readers

We are accustomed to thinking of early twentieth-century publishing and other media providing a one-way means of exchange between established writers and critics and their audiences. In this model, readers consume what they receive, which in turn shapes their mental and linguistic landscapes: 'the knowledge, the beliefs, the understanding, the opinions, the sense of identity, the loyalties, the moral values, the sensibility, the memories, the dreams, and therefore, ultimately, the actions of men, women, and children.'[1] With respect to coverage of Brooke, much of what appeared in national newspapers and periodicals was provided by established writers and critics, but in some instances reactions to their work went beyond a passive absorption. Amongst different reading 'constituencies',[2] consideration and discussion initially took place privately, and sometimes remained there, implicitly influencing future poetic responses as witnesses to the development of the ideal of the poet-soldier as it emerged reflected on its power and relevance to their experiences of the war. In other instances, responses became public, reaching new constituencies as the reading nation found ways to interact with and contribute to the Brooke myth.

Such responses from the public also show the extent to which the War Sonnets, and in particular 'The Soldier', had become bona

fide wartime 'hits'. They were so recognisable, so replete with culturally consistent, accessible themes and images that they created what
has been identified by economists as a 'multiplier effect'. The poems,
and in more abstract ways the ideals associated with the myth of the
poet-soldier, inspired – to use a more modern phrase – their own
spin-offs.[3]

*

During the war patriotism was no longer necessarily equated with
a rough, aggressive, overtly masculine ideal of violence and killing.
Instead, the civilian soldier, whose most definite act was volunteering,
became an increasingly sanctified trope as the war turned attritional,
testing mental, physical, and material endurance. Both soldiers and
civilians, including men and women of all ages, came to view their
contributions to the war as forms of 'military service' even as they also
came to view themselves – to different degrees – as 'victims' of the
conflict.[4]

Tribute poems were a particularly accessible way for members of
the public to express their appreciation for Brooke as the poet-soldier,
and for men-in-arms more generally. The *Westminster Gazette* first
included an anonymous poem with its May 1915 obituary, published
under the headline 'Mr. Rupert Brooke: The Poet and Sub-Lieutenant
Killed by Sunstroke'.[5] This opened the door for inspired members of
the public to submit their verse tributes, which provided a means not
only to endorse, but to shape the public discourse as it formed around
and in response to Brooke's death and poetry. These expressions also
offered a culturally sanctioned outlet for private anxiety and grief in
wartime.

Unlike much of what was published about Brooke in the months
and years after his death, many of the authors of this particular verse
genre were women. Their contributions to the war effort were often
of a more mundane, private nature than those of men who went off
to fight. Although the formal political campaign of the suffragettes

was tacitly suspended for the duration, women still searched for ways to signal their support and commitment to the higher ideals that the poet-soldier invoked. The widow and mother of the war dead became a recognised, semi-sanctified figure, but in terms of the hierarchies of sacrifice, the soldiers held sway.

Another (like Brooke) middle-class writer of poetry and prose, Vera Brittain, catalogued how the initial excitement and pageantry of August 1914 gave way to sustained, oppressive anxiety and fear: 'So I wonder where we shall be – what we shall be – if we all still shall be – this time next year'.[6] Ultimately, her personal loss was substantial: first her fiancé, Roland Leighton, after whose death she wrote, 'All has been given to me, and all taken away again – all in one year'. Her brother Edward was also killed, as were a number of close friends.[7] These losses were spaced throughout the war, meaning that grief was constantly reasserting itself.

While Brittain was by no means representative of all British women – her particular personality, tastes, and education made her more likely to respond to the particulars of the poet-soldier's story and the War Sonnets, and to leave a record of self-reflection on them – her experience of loss in the war was not unique, and as a result the pressure to manage and define the resultant grief was constant. Writing poetry, and writing about poetry, for Brittain and others, provided a means of channelling emotions that aided in the process of ordering independent experiences. Feeling 'sorrowful and heavy-laden' at Oxford while Leighton was away at the front, Brittain noted that, 'the thoughts of Roland & Rupert Brooke's sonnets mingled in my mind'.[8] In moments she conflated the two young men: 'Somehow I think Rupert Brooke must have been rather like Roland', linked through their common commitment to an honourable cause, a love of language and literature, and loyalty to friends.[9] Her experiences with Leighton, even when he was at the front, were direct, with channels of communication maintained through the regular exchange of letters and poetry; her impressions of Brooke were derived, but she found Brooke useful in mediating between the initially imagined horrors of combat,[10] and a more proximate anxiety and grief. For Brittain, as for many British men and women, Brooke reconciled opposing realities: peace and war, liberalism and militarism, exultation and weariness, pride and despair.

*

Brooke became a point of reference for Brittain, inspiring both poetry and a renewed passion for the national cause, particularly as it pertained to caring for the soldiers. For other women, expressing their appreciation for Brooke as the handsome young poet of England provided an outlet through which to participate in the war itself, if only 'on the fringes of the male domain'.[11] For some, momentarily at least, Brooke became the representative son, husband, or lover. Reading and writing about him offered a way to narrow the divide between the sexes that carried over from the tumultuous Edwardian period; when war broke out 'men and women seemed more thoroughly alienated from each other than ever'.[12]

Tribute poems arrived from a variety of sources, with many once again reinterpreting and expanding on the themes outlined in the obituaries and articles. In December 1915, the *Millgate Monthly* reported on the publication of a volume prepared by publishers Erskine Macdonald entitled *A Crown of Amaranth*, 'a collection of noble poems to the memory of the brave and gallant gentlemen who have given their lives for Great Britain'. The first poem in the book, setting up the collection, was entitled 'To the Memory of Rupert Brooke', and was contributed by S. Gertrude Ford. Ford's poem echoed obituaries and articles about the poet-soldier, drawing inspiration from 'The Soldier' and in particular the lines of the first stanza invoking the 'richer dust' of the body 'whom England bore, shaped, made aware, / Gave, once, her flowers of love'.[13] This poem paints its own fanciful portrait of the gravesite: 'young flowers and fair, / Not hoary yews, may wreathe the statue's plinth!' represents the perfect dead body, marked by clean marble. Around this 'the mourning Muses strew / Amaranth'. These Muses play an active role in maintaining the burial site of the 'Chief

Poet'[14] as they instruct the winds to 'Waft' this 'scent of English earth' over what Brooke famously identified as 'that rich earth a richer dust concealed'.[15] The poem is virtually buried under references to flowers: 'stricken Hyacinth', 'rue / And rosemary and rose', 'wood's whisper' and 'wood-flower's breath',[16] countering any whiff of death and decay.

While Ford's relatively exultant poem was directed to the 'Mothers of men',[17] as the final stanza states, as much as it was towards the poet-soldier's memory, Brooke's poetry could also inspire a quiet feminist protest against the war, and the nature of the sacrifices required of women. *T.P.'s Weekly* published May Herschel-Clarke's 'The Mother' under the inscription: 'Written after reading Rupert Brooke's sonnet'. The poem opens with, as epigraph, the much-quoted first three lines of 'The Soldier': 'If I should die, think only this of me: / That there's some corner of a foreign field / That is for ever England'. It sets up a dialogue with the lost 'lad'. Reversing the trope of the reader who looks with pride at the men in uniform, the dead youth now regards 'The Mother': 'She lives as though for ever in your sight' (note the mirroring of 'for ever') and hopes, 'If you should die, think only this of me':

> That in some place a mystic mile away
> One whom you loved has drained the bitter cup
> Till there is nought to drink; has faced the day
> Once more, and now, has raised the standard up.[18]

Herschel-Clarke's 'tribute' to Brooke, while by no means a direct attack on the poet-soldier, is a meditation on loss, on absence, and on broken hearts that mingled pride and grief: 'For country, honour, truth, traditions high, / – Proud that you paid their price'.

Seeking ways to engage in the war, the language and images repeatedly utilised in association with the Brooke cult provided an example of how women could frame their sacrifices, while still recognising those made by men, utilising conventional language and tropes, such as those offered by and in association with 'England's Poet-Soldier'. Highlighting the efforts of fellow nurses, Brittain entitled one of her poems

'The Sisters' Graves at Lemnos', dated 1916.[19] The choice of 'Lemnos' was not arbitrary or purely biographical; it was initially the reputed site where the nation's premier poet-soldier was buried, and proximate to Scyros, the location of one of England's most famous, imagined war graves. Reflecting the moral and aesthetic tropes reprinted in articles and obituaries about Brooke, she drew on the myth for her own memorialising, working within a common dialogue of canonisation of the war's heroes and heroines.

*

Both male and female poetic responses fetishised the ideal of the poet-soldier even as they adopted and adapted the inherited, respectable discourses solemnised by public figures and established writers. The burial site continued to serve as a focal point for many tribute poems to Brooke. In yet another variation on a theme, it becomes the chief 'possession' of the poet whose death 'Hallowed his bit of English earth'. This line is inflected with the language of conquest, born of a long history of Imperial wars and occupations, also bought at the price of far-off graves. For another poet, comfort was secured through the image of the 'cool moon-way of the waves at night' now softening 'the flowered earth of Lemnos isle'.[20] Another wrote of the 'Dreaming' youth hearing 'the great winds blow unceasing, / And over him, about him, and around him / The music and thunder of the sea'.[21] These readers and writers appropriated the War Sonnets' language and metaphors – of 'Slumber and waking', of hearts 'Washed marvellously with sorrow',[22] and of 'A body of England's … / Washed by the rivers, and blest by the suns of home'[23] – for their own expressions of aesthetic patriotism and commemoration.

Many found inspiration in Anglophone idealisations and appropriations of classical Greece. For a First World War audience familiar with metaphors and parables, Brooke was cast as 'England's living Helicon', whose 'loveliness is light unto the dead'.[24] Along with the importance of fate, death amongst 'ships on Hellespont' linked the poet back to 'the harp of Homer' and the 'knightlier' spirit of Hector:[25] Brooke encompassed both: Homer the poet and Hector the soldier. In another poem, Brooke became the son of 'Lord Apollo', born for poetry and war, whose death 'near windy Troy', when coupled with death for the British cause meant that 'we cannot wonder at your joy'.[26] The tendency to idealise the moment of sacrifice owed its popularity as much to pre-war newspapers and novels stressing the value of bravery in death for the national cause as it did to a sentimental reduction of the values of *The Iliad*.[27] Both happily elevated both the nation and the poet at war to the realm of the timeless.

While many of the poems stressed the idea that the loss of the poet was irreparable, none claimed that it was unjustifiable. The cause for which he had died was the most important factor in secular or religious redemption, as his was a 'sacred courage', sacred 'For the cause of divine liberty'.[28] Brooke died, as others killed in service of their nation had, in a sanctified cause:

> Honour unmeasured, Love complete
> Have All, in army or in fleet,
> Who, be their doom to die or live,
> Give England all they have to give;[29]

This poem, published in May 1915, ended by singling out Brooke's talent and the place of the War Sonnets in the national canon: life for 'England's Poet-Soldier' – the 'youngest voice in English song'[30] – was thus 'complete … for this special Grace you had, / Allowed us to be glad'.[31] Another, appearing in 1918, returned to the same idea:

> Thereby thy song, thy art,
> Shall take a strength,
> A power, at length,
> Shall catch a thrill, a glow,
> Naught else can give.[32]

Brooke was a singular figure, and a worthy one for such tributes, these newspaper poets argued. Ultimately, it was the poet's insight, talent, beauty, and gallant contribution to the nation that allowed the 'fates' to lift him 'out of the fight', singling him out, 'not willing that the boy should lie among the nameless dead'.[33] Like many established writers who took up his cause, these less-established, often anonymous poets and writers saw Brooke's popularity not only as resulting from material factors of timing, the work of patrons, and cultural and commercial accessibility: it was the poet-soldier's destiny to comfort and inspire his compatriots in a time of war.

*

One figure for whom Brooke's loss was by no means an abstraction was his mother, Mary. In the early summer of 1915, she was the sole remaining survivor of Brooke's immediate family, left thoroughly alone to grieve: a sympathetic national figure, both a widow and a bereaved mother. On 18 June, the *Rugby Observer* acknowledged this in an obituary for Alfred Brooke: 'By his [Alfred's] death, Mrs. Brooke has lost her only surviving son. Two of her sons have died in service of their country ... The heartfelt sympathy, not of Rugby only but of the whole country, will go out to her in her terrible bereavement'.[34] Many were deeply moved by her loss. Lawrence Binyon, the poet of 'For the Fallen', sent her an unsigned tribute poem to Brooke in 1917, asking her to 'forgive my liberty', but 'Your son is a radiant memory to me'. It included the comforting lines, similar to others printed in the popular press, 'There was wrong / Done, and the world shamed. Honour blew the call /And youth's high answer was as natural / And quiet as the needle's to the pole'.[35] By way of Brooke's very public death, Mary Brooke's private grief became a matter of wider concern.

The conflation of very real, private loss with the emerging myth of the nation's poet-soldier did not sit comfortably with her. This was partly because, apart from acting as the requisite chief mourner, she played only a limited role in how the myth around her son developed.

She was understandably interested in what was said. Initially, she and Marsh worked closely to monitor responses, employing a cutting agency to collect related obituaries and articles, some of which were arranged in albums as early as May 1915. Later, as the years passed and Marsh was primarily identified as the official keeper of the Brooke flame, their relationship deteriorated, and she was left in her small house in Rugby, 'brooding over' accounts of her son's death with 'morbid intensity'.[36]

Mary Brooke turned to the idea of a public memorial; something that she could exert some control over. In February 1916, a committee was formed, responsible for commissioning a plaque to be placed in Rugby Chapel, bearing a carving replicating Schell's photograph and frontispiece for *1914 and Other Poems*. The memorial was paid for by public subscription. Officially she maintained a dignified distance, but behind the scenes she asserted her opinion about its design and aesthetics through Robert Whitelaw, a close friend and headmaster at Rugby, who served on the committee and, at her behest, provided the plaque's inscription:

> Dear to the Graces we knew thee, thy life long, dear to the Muses:
> Ah but – while valuing these, valuing Liberty more,
> Gladly thy choice thou madest, to fight for her.
>   Now, we salute thee:
> Lovely wert thou, and thy songs lovely – and lovely thy death.[37]

In this way Mary Brooke had a role in commissioning at least one tribute poem to her son. Marsh, who also served on the Rugby committee, may not have totally approved of the inscription, with its rather precious, old-fashioned language, but probably felt that in this particular matter deference to his friend's mother was advisable.

Like many readers, she pondered her son's actual, far-off grave. As with other matters regarding Brooke's estate, when it came to considering replacing the makeshift marker to the Scyros grave with a more

permanent memorial, Mary Brooke initially allowed Marsh to corre-
spond with the British legation, and subsequently the eventual British
Ambassador in Athens, on her behalf. Sir Francis Elliot took a personal
interest in the project, writing to March in June 1915: 'I have been much
struck by the specimens of Rupert Brooke's poetry which have been
published in the papers since his death, and feel deeply that his loss is
greatly to be deplored'.[38] Mary Brooke later reasserted herself, insisting
that Whitelaw's 'R.B.' stanza from the Rugby plaque be translated into
(ancient, not modern) Greek. She also chose the type of marble and
the shape of the tomb.[39] The result was a simple white block, completed
in June 1917.[40] When it came time to ship the marble tomb, she paid
for an agent to accompany it, and make sure all went according to plan.
From Piraeus to Scyros the tomb went by way of a British warship.[41]
Ambassador Elliot again interceded, helping to find banks capable of
dealing with the foreign transactions required in Greece.[42]

Mary Brooke was able – unlike many mothers and families grieving
the deaths of soldiers abroad – to exert an influence over Brooke's
gravesite at Scyros. The memorial acknowledged its mythic location
and context, as well as her son's 'choice', inspired by the 'Muses' to
give his life in the fight for 'Liberty'.[43] Unlike with respect to his public
reputation, through this venture she exerted direct control, realising
her private ideal of what a public monument to her son should be.
Despite her wariness of Marsh's influence, and of the semi-regulated
nature of public demand for – and consumption of – Brooke's legacy,
the ideals, symbols, and language she returned to in Rugby as in Scyros
reaffirmed much of what had already been consensually fixed as the
chief virtues of the nation's poet-soldier. Just as members of the public
had attempted to do with their tribute poems, she established a physical link between the plaque in Rugby and the tomb in Scyros, further
ensuring that both memorials reflected the popular myth, rendering
the literary and physical shrines as 'English' as possible.

*

Brooke's well-placed collection of influential friends and acquaintances undoubtedly helped to place him front and centre in the public's gaze, but their influence does not entirely account for his popularity. Tribute poems were written in active recognition of ideas as much as of Brooke himself. Most readers were in no way acquainted with the dead man, yet they recognised the power of his story and embraced the sentiments of the War Sonnets, both of which resonated with the reading nation. Some even went so far as to accept the poet-soldier as a proxy for other soldiers, meaning that the ideal played at least a small part in the management of private grief. These writers and readers also helped to ensure that the Brooke myth was continually recast and reinserted into the public domain, even without the continued, invested effort of friends, publishers, writers, politicians, and newspaper editors.

14

Poet-Soldiers

S oldiers – and within this group would-be poet-soldiers – formed another of the reading 'constituencies',[1] and one keenly invested in the developing Brooke myth. The more extreme, jingoistic expressions of wartime patriotism were not always welcomed by soldiers on active duty, as 'celebration and civilian commemoration unwittingly highlighted and to some extent deepened the divide between soldiers and non-combatants'.[2] During the war few viewed Brooke's War Sonnets and the responses his death inspired in the press as falling into this category. Soldiers and civilians alike accepted and in some cases adopted the language expressed by 'England's Poet-Soldier' and reiterated by his many established and emerging champions, which worked to elevate the sacrifices of the war dead above the day-to-day degradations of a dirty, extended campaign: 'There's none of these so lonely and poor of old, / But, dying, has made us rarer gifts than gold'.[3] The Brooke myth mediated between soldiers and civilians – and poet-soldiers and their potential readerships – locating ideals common to all: 'There was never a moment of the war … when, to the majority of Englishman, including those in the trenches, his rhetoric did not seem the most appropriate way of speaking and writing about the ideals of war'.[4]

In the spring and early summer of 1915 many poet-soldiers expressed their sorrow at Brooke's loss directly to Edward Marsh, friend and patron to many of the emerging generation of artists and writers. Many had admired Brooke's poetry before the war, and continued to admire it after his death, seeing the War Sonnets as part of a whole body of work. The acceptance of Brooke as a fellow chronicler of the war experience working within an inherited poetic mode of expression persisted throughout the war period.[5]

Many aspired to it. Robert Graves was one of these, writing to Marsh from France in May 1915 to say that he was 'truly grieved ... generally for all of us who know what poetry is'. He concluded consolingly, aware also of Marsh's personal loss as a friend, that 'we can only be happy that he died cheerfully and in such a good cause'.[6] In a later letter he described to Marsh a dream in which he meets Brooke at the front and discusses poetry.[7] Graves was quite capable of differentiating between the sorrow over the death of a fellow poet and serviceman and the quality of their work. He wrote to Siegfried Sassoon in April 1917 that 'I'm sorry about [Francis] Ledwidge's death, but he wasn't a very good poet'.[8] Brooke, in contrast, particularly with '"Heaven", "The Great Lover", "The Soldier", and all the rest'[9] was an individual to aspire to, like Charles Sorley (one of Brooke's more outspoken critics),[10] whose poetry Graves also viewed as exemplary. He felt that Brooke had been like an 'older brother' to aspiring poet-soldiers: 'I feel in reading him that his is exactly the language I am floundering to catch – musical restrained, refined, yet not crabbed or conventionally antique, reading almost like ordinary speech'.[11] Isaac Rosenberg also wrote appreciatively to Marsh of Brooke's pre-war poem 'Clouds', which he read in *Georgian Poetry* in 1916 and considered 'magnificent' in its gentle metaphoric evocation of the dead.[12]

*

Brooke's poems were taken as the 'personal'[13] evidence of one volunteer by many readers in uniform. These were the poems of a soldier who had never been and never would be exposed to extensive and unremitting warfare. They were not the poems of the Western Front, even if they became associated with that generalised national experience.[14] Brooke's limited exposure to war was by no means grounds for dismissal of either his poetry or image by many readers in uniform. As one anonymous soldier wrote of 'The Soldier':

> those fourteen bars of melody somehow manage to cage, more completely than ever before, one of the dimmest and deepest, one of the most active but most elusive of all the many mixed motives, beliefs, longings, ideals, which make those of us who have flung aside everything in order to fight still glad and gratified that we took the course that we did.[15]

The poems could encompass a variety of opinions and experiences. The Brooke myth provided everyone with the opportunity to discuss and refine definitions of honour and virtue in an aesthetic context.

In the weeks and months after his death, and even after the introduction of conscription in 1916, Brooke's lexicon of volunteerism proved particularly attractive. It testified to an idealism that had not worn out its welcome with many soldier, or poet-soldiers. As Edward Thomas put it, in England it was still possible to make up one's own mind despite the reputed virulence of public sentiment in favour of service: 'It is, perhaps, curious also that I never was in company where any man or woman said that somebody else ought to enlist. When they have expressed an opinion, soldiers and civilians have said that they cannot understand anyone pointing out his duty to one another'.[16] Wilfred Owen, for one, writing in the summer of 1915, also felt the war similarly as a deep emotional experience born of personal choice, something demanding greater commitment than simply donning a uniform: full, mental enlistment of the kind Brooke had also undergone was required. 'It *doesn't* matter 'for my purpose' that the Dardanelles are closed; but it matters to my sentiment that Belgium is; now I don't imagine that the German War will be affected by my joining in, but I know my own future Peace will be'.[17] Owen, like Brooke, framed the war as a personal moral test, relaying a series of theoretical motivations paraphrased in 'The Soldier': beauty, resolution, brotherhood, and belonging.

Thomas's interpretation of voluntary patriotism unsurprisingly took on a pastoral cast: 'If England lies like a vast calm around you, and you a minor, you may find faults without end. If England seems threatened, you feel that in losing her you would lose yourself; she becomes plainly and decidedly "this dear realm of England"'.[18] As Thomas concluded after having read an article on patriotic poetry in *The Times*, 'There may be pleasanter places; but there is no *word* like "home"'.[19]

These poet-soldiers found in Brooke's poetry and philosophical approach to the war much to admire. His poetry, like much of what was produced and read during the war, mapped out the fraternal bonds of military units, even as it based these on models of close, civilian friendship. This spoke to the war's enabling of greater 'emotional interaction between men in which the individual identifies himself as an integral part of an all-male group', resulting in a 'romantic masculinity'.[20] The soldier as written by the poet-soldier was filled with, in Owen's formulation, the 'urgency of concern'[21] for his comrades. Siegfried Sassoon, who of this eventually canonical group of writers came closest to denouncing the war in any public way, became a different sort of 'political poet'[22] from Brooke as a result of his statement of 1917, but he remained intensely loyal to his fellow soldiers. Despite the potential for press coverage of this act of resistance and disgust, much feared by Graves and Marsh at the time, during the war Sassoon did not achieve – at least in a popular or commercial sense – the public influence of the posthumous Brooke, testifying from and for the dead about the serenity of self-sacrifice and the 'clear eye, and sharpened power'[23] of the all-male military units that so entranced many would be poet-soldiers.[24]

*

Glorification of Brooke in the press, presented as the 'Chief'[25] poet-soldier to die in the war, also helped to create a market for the poems of his fellow men in arms: of this they were aware, and grateful. Writing aesthetically about the war was a commercial activity for many young poets attempting to publish their verses and to establish literary reputations that would carry them in good stead after the war ended, should they be lucky enough to survive to see it. Graves wrote often to Marsh and Sassoon about the sales of his volume of *Over the Brazier* (the volume was dedicated to his regiment, which 'I have learned to worship').[26] When in 1918 Sassoon criticised the tone of much of Graves' published poems as being too romantic and saleable, Graves retorted by writing that, 'I can't afford to stop in these precarious days, and anyhow my "antique silk and flower brocade" continues to please the seventeen year old girls, and other romantics for whom they are intended; and why not?'[27] Sassoon, Graves implied – better off than many others – should not be so critical of commercial success. Sassoon later and rather wryly observed that generally speaking being a poet-soldier had its economic advantages.[28] Rosenberg wrote to Marsh from France in 1917, conscious of the need for a responsive audience, which could lift an amateur poet out of obscurity: 'I'll soon begin to think myself a poet if my things get admired so'.[29] Having read an article on Brooke in which his name was mentioned, the American poet and soldier Alan Seeger wrote in his diary that it, 'gave me rather more pain than pleasure for it rubbed in the matter which most rankles in my heart, that I never could get my book of poems published before the war'.[30]

Seeger's first volume of poetry would appear after his death in France in July 1916. Brooke's death and the myth it created helped to carve out an audience that extended across the Atlantic, as many more letters, diaries, and poems of the soldier could now find publishers.[31] The *Bookman*'s Christmas edition of 1917 alerted its readers to a collective genre, one begun by Brooke and carried out by 'subsequent' contributors to the national poetic 'Roll of Honour', including Julian Grenfell, who died just a few weeks after Brooke in May 1915; the Irish

poet Thomas Kettle, who was killed in September 1916; and Edward
Thomas, who died in April 1917, to name but three. A. St John Adcock
contributed the accompanying article 'For Remembrance: Soldier-
Poets Who Have Fallen in this War'.[32] Commercial success and public
recognition went hand-in-hand with patriotic death and sacrifice.

*

The writings of British servicemen in the First World War display
evidence of attempts to carve out a place within the collective national
narrative. When the war ended, no soldier wanted to return home
and find himself in a completely foreign culture unrelated to the one
that he remembered from his pre-war years. Published volumes and
newspapers alike provided a consistent, practical, and mobile bridge to
civilian life, with popularity at the front determined by the interrelated
factors of demand and access; newspapers and publishers responding
to soldiers' appetites for reading material secured and maintained a
steady and rapt audience.[33]

The prevalence of the Brooke myth in the press meant that he was
not only recognisable at the front, but that his poetry and the manner in
which it and his death were discussed served as a potential model. The
anonymous diary of a French interpreter serving with the Post Office
Rifles in June 1915 recorded the death and grave of 'Lieutenant [Alfred]
Brooke, brother of the poet'.[34] Even this soldier, away from the English
home front, was familiar enough with Rupert Brooke to include him
in his personal memoir. Explicitly through the simple and consistent
repetition of his name, and implicitly by writing in a similar tone and
style when defining patriotism, a common language emerged, useful
for discussing the popular topics of personal and cultural motivation,
honour, and death, all values associated with 'England's Poet-Soldier'.
This language interwove itself with letters, trench newspapers and
journals at the front, providing a way for men to make sense of 'the inco-
herence of war' comprised of their own fractured experiences. Model
personal narratives created 'a kind of collective memory',[35] even as the

war unfolded around them. Brooke's poetry, and the manner in which it was presented in a variety of media, aided in personal and national self-definition by helping to create a conventional mode for discussing one's own ideals and experiences, and the sacrifice of fellow soldiers.

The appeal of Brooke and the War Sonnets to this particular audience was increased by the impressive amount of mail reaching soldiers, particularly on the Western Front, facilitating the sharing of newspapers, books, and ideas about the war. Letters, diaries, and memoirs from the period describe the trading of literature between soldiers who were often bored, homesick, and hungry for reading material.[36] Graves wrote to Sassoon in France in May 1916: 'By this post I am ordering Rupert's two books for you'.[37] Graves received his copy of *Letters from America* from Marsh while at the front.[38] Rosenberg, despite, as a private, being stuck in France without leave from 1916, managed two letters to Marsh in 1918 discussing the newest edition of *Georgian Poetry* and inquiring as to the publication date of the long-awaited Brooke 'Memoir'.[39]

In Flanders, Roland Leighton became aware of Brooke's War Sonnets, and wrote to his fiancée Vera Brittain that 'I am very fond of the sonnets ... There is a grave a few yards away from where I am sitting – a private of the Somerset Light Infantry killed in December: which makes the two poems on "The Dead" more real than ever'.[40] Reading the poems, particularly in the presence of one's fellow comrades, in billets near the front line, helped to order and contextualise death, and to remind him of the overriding ideals informing his efforts. Leighton received his copy of *1914 and Other Poems* from Brittain in August 1915, and carried on their discussion of the verses from the trenches. Brittain had anticipated that he would 'love them all, as I do; not the War Sonnets only, though they are perhaps the most beautiful'.[41] Leighton wrote back from France, thanking Brittain for the gift: 'I have just read it straight through. It makes me feel as if I want to sit down and write things myself instead of doing what I have to do here'.

Leighton had not so much changed his mind about the capacity of war to result in noble actions, for 'Sometimes by dint of an opportunity a single man may rise from the sordidness to a dead of beauty: but that is all'. His concern was for the myopia imposed by the daily grind of life at the front, with all of its necessary 'soul-less nonentities', which generally obscured a higher purpose. Brooke's abstractions provided a model of these thoughts, and Leighton welcomed the way that the volume 'stirs old forgotten things',[42] recalling for him the principles underlying his own voluntary enlistment. The exchange of the volume also afforded an opportunity to explain his aesthetic and emotional reactions to the war to his fiancée, maintaining a common topic through which to explore diverging personal experiences of the war.

Further afield another older soldier, General H. G. Chauvel, received a copy of *1914 and Other Poems* in July 1917 after his wife called them to his attention. The couple had lived for a time in Grantchester, and she thought the connection close enough to interest her husband at his command post in Southern Palestine. He wrote on 21 July that he would be happy to read them,[43] and reported on 9 September that he did not think much of the War Sonnets.[44] He did, however, like 'the one about the old Vicarage', that is, the one most associated with home. For this higher-ranking officer, of Australian birth, 'Grantchester' in Brooke's pastoral vision offered a link to something familiar, of the memory of time spent with his family in Cambridgeshire. As with Leighton and Brittain, the poetry formed a thematic and emotional bridge between himself and an ideal of home.

*

Conversations about Brooke's literary merit could and often did revolve around published volumes. However, newspaper printings of the poems, and the various ways in which the idea of the nation's poet-soldier was passed on, increased their availability to readers abroad. Domestic newspapers were sent abroad for distribution to the troops, where reading material appears always to have been welcome. If one chose to, as, for example, did Graves– and this was often logistically easier for officers – it was quite possible to maintain contact with the literary and political scene in London. His letters make numerous references to articles in the daily press. When he wrote to Marsh on 22 May 1915 from France in response to a letter from Marsh about the death of Brooke, there was not too much of a delay to their conversation. In February 1916, he wrote again to Marsh: 'Did you notice in *The Times* about three weeks ago a poem by Siegfried Sassoon about the woeful crimson of War etc.?'[45]

Keeping right up with the political events in London, another soldier, Andrew Stewart, who was in 1914 acting as a stretcher bearer for the British Army in France, observed the evolving criticism of Lord Northcliffe and the *Daily Mail*'s calling for greater shell production in the autumn of 1914.[46] Following a particularly bloody period of the war, the *Fifth Glo'ster Gazette* turned to a recently published poem from *Punch* to express the heroic fate of fellow soldiers:

> Be their name
> Sacred among us! Wouldst thou seek to frame
> Their fitting epitaph? Then let it be
> Simple, as that which marked Thermopylae,
> 'Tell it in England, thou that passest by,
> Here faithful to their charge, her soldiers lie'.[47]

The easy exchange of words and broader political and cultural commentary allowed for dissemination of the ideals associated with Brooke as the nation's premier poet-soldier to the men and women serving on the various fronts, thus bridging the distance that separated them from civilian life.

*

The different registers in which soldiers expressed their reactions to the brutal conflict filtered into trench journals as well as letters, diaries, poetry, and later memoirs. Some, as their later publications would show, did in parts become alienated from the patriotic discourses that prevailed during the war years.[48] By 1917, Sassoon, for example, was increasingly negative about the war in his poetry and letters, not understanding how Graves could maintain the role of 'sound militarist in action however much a pacifist in thought'.[49] Graves wrote in some exasperation in response to Sassoon's criticism from Liverpool in August 1918: 'you might let me be sentimental where sentiment is true: good God, *didn't* they sing, those chaps, anyhow? Like hell they did … and in tune'. While it was not possible in the final year of the war to locate the capacity for 'such prehistoric happiness as Rupert had',[50] in Graves' estimation Sassoon's more graphic examples of death at the front were anti-war 'propaganda' because they did not allow for the possibility of any experience of war but a negative one, whereas others attempted to convey both the courage and levity of the soldiers under very difficult circumstances.[51]

In practice it was difficult for anyone to maintain a consistent tone, even for Sassoon, who also wavered after his anti-war statement of June 1917 criticising the 'callous complacence with which the majority of those at home regard the continuance of the agonies which they do not share, and which they do not have sufficient imagination to realise'.[52] He emphasised the 'majority', not 'all' of those at home: even in his extreme frustration and despair Sassoon recognised and respected the widespread suffering of the many victims of the war. Although not renouncing his critique of some citizens' – particularly politicians' – behaviour during the war, Sassoon returned to his preferred subset of the national community, the soldiers, described in the poem 'Night on the Convoy': the 'inarticulate patience of the men … joins the mystery of his own lonely but thrilling tragedy'.[53] As Brooke had done in 1914 and 1915, Sassoon, like most soldiers who wrote about their experiences, did so in part to try to make sense of their varied reactions to the war through poetry, his chosen genre, as fellow soldiers did in various other media.

Trench journals mimicked the national newspapers in form, with editorials, coverage of Parliamentary affairs, letters to the editor, cartoons, and advertisements, allowing soldiers to extend a civilian institution to the surreal world of the front, and exert editorial control over the content. Unlike the national press, the journals were non-commercial entities, with prices designed not to accrue profit but to keep the paper in print.[54] Their editors fashioned the trench journals after – not in competition with – newspapers from home: they often copied and reprinted articles and poems from the national and international press. They never attempted to replace the established publications, but instead to act as supplements to them as, for example, a local or school newspaper would to a small body of readers with, it was assumed, much in common with one another.

The passing of interesting news, jokes, and satirical essays appeared side by side with commemorations. Especially after a large loss of life in a given unit, editors and poets deployed a common language of commemoration. To mark the leaving of the Ypres Salient by the Sherwood Foresters, one contributor wrote: 'Always, when the strain of the Salient may have left us, the memory of those crosses will remain, and those true hearts who sleep there may rest assured that we, who worked with them, fought with them and hoped with them, will exact the price'.

Printed on the same page was a notice that 'The Editor would be obliged if a few of the poets would break into prose as a paper cannot live by "poems" alone'.[55] Trench journals drew attention to the achievements of their battalion's and division's soldiers, and their own 'house' poet-soldiers, for example including Gilbert Frankau for the *Wipers Times*. When Lieutenant F. W. Harvey published his book of poetry *A Gloucester Lad* in 1916, his regiment's journal, the *Fifth Glo'ster Gazette*, noted the publication, reprinting the *Morning Post*'s review of the book as revealing a 'brilliant aptitude for the vocation of arms. He is also a poet of power and subtle distinction ... [the volume] will give him a high place in the Sidneian company of soldier-poets'. Both the *Fifth Glo'ster Gazette* and the *Morning Post* printed Harvey's inscription to the volume: 'To all comrades of mine who lie dead in foreign fields for love of England, or who live to prosecute the war for another England', reinforcing the rhetoric shared between newspapers, trench journals, and another, unnamed, but well-established poet-soldier.

Poetry was, for many soldiers, the chosen medium for presenting and discussing the war as an existential reality. It was also a link to beyond the immediate experience of the various fronts, where one did not often 'see' poetry.[56] Writing from the trenches in France in 1917, Rosenberg confided that though 'often a troublesome consolation', given the difficulties of constructing verse under battlefield conditions, 'poetry is a great one to me'.[57] Another editorial spoke of their readership's 'constant appeals for poetry'.[58] These demands were met by publishers and private citizens on the home front as well as by fellow soldiers, providing a lifeline through which a common language for describing death and loss – such as that associated with the Brooke myth – was developed and maintained.

In January 1918, the journal of the *British Prisoners of War* published the poem by 'E.H.B.' entitled 'Epitaph – On a Comrade', including the lines:

> Past yon green field, neath whispering trees,
> Which nodding, seem to guard your perfect rest,
> Sleep on, though battlefields and troubled seas
> Divide you from all you loved the best.[59]

Another example, by 'R.F.C.', published in the *Gasper: The Unofficial Organ of the BEF*, memorialised a famous soldier in 'Kitchener of Khartoum', turning his sacrifice into a call for perseverance: 'Farewell, the task is ours, and ours the part / to wield the weapon that thy courage wrought, / To stick the blow thy patient toil prepared'.[60] A poem for the 7th Canadian Infantry Battalion advanced the ideals of Imperial unity and self-sacrifice:

> When Britain calls her sons come forth,
> To muster for the fight,
> With pride to show their own true worth

> For what they know is right.
> Not for the glory of the fray
> They bare the shining steel,
> Only that justice hold the sway
> They set their hands and seal.[61]

A poet for the *Fifth Glo'ster Gazette* entitled his contribution 'Peace':

> And they know peace – though thunders loud and long
> The cannon's roar on battle fields storm-tossed
> Who faithful stand to fight against the wrong,
> Giving their all unheeding of the cost,
> The higher peace, the changeless peace of God.[62]

None of these poems mentioned Brooke by name, but the linguistic and thematic echoes speak to the development – and acceptance – of a common means for describing the war dead that his poetry and image advanced and helped to make ubiquitous.

*

'England's Poet-Soldier' found his way into other literary forms composed on various fronts as well. In January 1917, the *Liverpool Echo* published a letter written by Charles Lister prior to his own death at Gallipoli. 'From the battlefield', he described Brooke's grave:

> At Scyros we had a blow in the loss of Rupert Brooke ... He died of blood poisoning, and we buried him in a grove of olives, tucked deep in a rocky ravine under Mount Paphlee ... There was no doubt as to his fate; he died within twenty-four hours of the ill[ness] making itself manifest ... The grave is under an olive-tree that bends over it like a weeping angel. A sad end to such dazzling purity of mind and work, clean cut, classical, and unaffected all the time like his face, unfurrowed

or lined by cares. And the eaglet had begun to beat his wings and soar. Perhaps the Island of Achilles is in some respects a suitable resting-place for those bound for the plains of Troy.[63]

In April 1917, another soldier, Captain Fred Pepys Cockerell, sent a letter to Mary Brooke containing photographs of the gravesite and a description of 'a wild olive, the reward, for the soldier, of winning the race; and five paces away a bay-tree for the poet'.[64] Here was another spontaneous example of how the language and images associated with the Brooke myth continued to appeal to, and be drawn on, by soldiers throughout the war.

After first serving as a stretcher-bearer, Andrew Stewart Fox became a lieutenant with the 6th North Staffordshire Regiment in April 1915. He carried on a correspondence with his family throughout his period of service. On 12 October 1915, he wrote to his sister Iris that 'I should like the copy of Rupert Brooke you promised me above many things – when the "proceeds" arrive' (he had sent her money from his officer's paycheque to purchase the volume). Fox wondered if she was aware of the poem containing the lines '"If I should die, think only this of me"'. He then went on to conflate 'The Old Vicarage, Grantchester' with 'The Soldier', pointing out 'in the same poem' fragments, including, '"Oh there the chestnuts, summer through … Across the moon at Grantchester"'. He had been to the upper river whilst a student at Cambridge and 'some of the happiest afternoons and evenings of my life have been spent there'. In combining the two images Fox drew an implicit connection between his 'happiest memories' and his current situation; this was probably of some comfort to him as well as to his family back home. He had become aware of Brooke's poetry via an unspecified newspaper: 'Don't think I have read the book – it was only a review – & I copied out one or two pieces that I liked'.[65] The discussion of Brooke constituted the last entry of Fox's journal. He was killed four days later. Someone, most likely his sister, added a postscript, concluding with a typed copy of 'The Soldier'. This poem, and 'Grantchester', provided a link between England and France, and upon Fox's death offered a framework for private grief and remembrance.

Another soldier who recorded in a diary – more publicly than Fox – about what Brooke and his poetry meant to his fellow men in arms, and to the broader ideals of the war, was General Sir Ian Hamilton, the career soldier who had served in the Boer Wars, and later with the British Indian Army in Manchuria. In the months and years following the failed Dardanelles campaign, after which, in October 2015, he was recalled to London, for all intensive purposes ending his military career, Hamilton spent a fair amount of time explaining and contextualising his long service to the nation. This culminated with the publication of his *Gallipoli Diary* in 1920. In the months following the younger poet-soldier's death, the landings also became the specific military action most associated with Brooke: sailing 'for the Dardanelles' on the romantic voyage ending in his death and burial 'at Lemnos',[66] the false but often reprinted site of Brooke's famous grave.

Hamilton had been moved by Brooke's death in 1915, and charmed by the idea of such an overtly literary youth emerging as the ideal of the English officer. Hamilton's letter to Marsh of 23 April expressed his 'admiration for his intellect … which lost nothing as so many admirations do by contact with his personality and appearance'. He wished that he had convinced Brooke to join his staff, whatever fate had in store for the young man: 'whether it could have made a difference, I can't say, but at least I could have told you something'.[67] Hamilton was sufficiently impressed by Brooke to carry on his discussion and support of his life and image through to the 1919 dedication ceremony for the Rugby School Chapel, which housed the memorial plaque to the poet-soldier. Hamilton provided the eulogy, with *The Times* article describing the event under the headline, 'Sir Ian Hamilton on the Poet's Charm'.[68]

In his *Gallipoli Diary* Hamilton later recorded another epitaph to the young poet-soldier:

Rupert Brooke is dead … Death grins at my elbow. I cannot get him out of my thoughts. He is fed up with the old and sick – only the flower of the flock will serve him now, for God has started a celestial spring cleaning, and our star is to be scrubbed bright with the blood of our bravest and our best.[69]

In this passage Hamilton might have been sentimentalising about one particular figure, but it is difficult not to read the entry as a prophecy whose fulfilment on a larger scale was solemnly anticipated. Praising the gallant behaviour of the soldiers under his command was, for Hamilton, simultaneously genuine and self-serving, as was his alignment with Brooke. 'I have seen famous and brilliant figures in my day, but never one so thrilling, so vital as that of our hero'.[70] Brooke remained a hero for Hamilton throughout the war, an example of the type of young officer – many of whom lost their lives at Gallipoli – whom Hamilton wished publicly to recognise and support as a means of personal and public rehabilitation.

*

These examples offer some testimony to how Brooke was received; as with other reading constituencies, they are examples that can but should not necessarily be taken as offering overwhelming evidence of Brooke's general popularity with the soldiers. It is not clear how far his reputation spread throughout the full body of serviceman – bridging class, race, and nationality – but there is some evidence that this did occur. It is true that much of what transpired at the front is difficult to access, or to generalise about, even with – and perhaps because of – the myriad number of personal sources constantly being made available. It is only partly possible to interrogate or recreate actual conversations between soldiers, either arising from the arrival of a volume of poetry, or an article in a newspaper, unless they are recorded in some accessible format for posterity.

By example, in October 1915, Graves wrote to Marsh of a platoon officer, Arthur Parry, who 'quite spontaneously' began to discuss with him: 'Samuel Butler & Richard Middleton thence to Rupert Brooke and Denis Browne who was one of his intimates at Cambridge'.[71] It might be expected that friends of a common background, all acquaintances of Brooke, would discuss him and his poetry in the wake of his death, and Graves would want Marsh, who worked so hard to maintain Brooke's reputation, to be comforted by the idea of his popularity at the front. Still, Graves' recording of 'quite spontaneously' is telling.

The conditions that allowed for the spread of the ideal of the poet-soldier in England were, to a large extent, replicated at the front: the infrastructure that allowed for the spread of ideas, the ubiquity of the language of service, the idealisation of the exclusive brotherhood of the military unit, the emphasis on a shared dialogue between individuals, and the collective desire to recognise the sacrifices of fellow soldiers. In December 1915, the *Daily Mirror* published this report about the troops at the front:

> Would you like to know what they talk about in the trenches? It isn't the war. A friend of mine just got back from the front and told me that he and a dozen of his company embarked on a long discussion the other night as to who was the finest of our more recent poets. Most of them, I believe, voted for Rupert Brooke. And all day long these men had been under shellfire![72]

The values associated with Brooke and his poetry: ideals of honour, brotherhood, self-sacrifice, bravery, and particularly the calm acceptance of death, informed the general image of the poet-soldier and, by extension, his fellow brothers in arms. Whether or not these reflected actual experiences was another matter, and to an extent beside the point; people read about such exchanges, at home and at the front, and believed that the conversations were taking place 'spontaneously' between soldiers. Such images fed the public imagination. The notion of soldiers pontificating over the nobility of poetry under fire was a more comforting and culturally affirming conception of the war than many available alternatives. Brooke, whose fame owed itself to the consensus viewpoint that the volunteer fighting in defence of the nation should be valued above all else, aided in this process of common definition and reassurance by invoking ideals shared by soldiers and civilians and keeping the two parts of the whole familiar to one another.

The canonical works by war poets and novelists published in the late 1920s were much more conscious of divisions, contributing to historians 'advocating the existence of an unbridgeable gap'[73] between the ideals of the soldiers and those of the home front. In this conception, the front was one world, home was another, and the soldier was by virtue of his situation and sacrifices an exclusive member of the former. During the war, the relationship between the two was more porous. The constant stream of information travelled in two directions through postcards, letters, and newspapers. The home front defined soldiers even as soldiers (and idealisations of the men in arms) influenced the civilian view of the war.

15

Careful Critics

lthough the balance was grossly skewed in favour of praise,
even during the war reactions to the popular, abstracted ideal
of Brooke as 'England's Poet-Soldier' and 'the laureate of the
war he never really saw'[1] were not universally positive. It was almost
impossible, at least in public, to criticise him personally. He had fallen
out with a number of individuals in the years and months preceding
the war, particularly in Bloomsbury circles. But when he died, most
who had known him personally, or in a professional, literary capacity,
were genuinely sorry: everyone, whatever stance they took on the war,
read his death as tragic.

Still, as Brooke's very public death gave way to an even greater
public fashioning of his posthumous reputation, some took it upon
themselves to voice their scepticism. Reacting as much to the process
through which his memory was sanctified as to the sheer number of
people who felt empowered to join in the defining and distilling of his
life's worth, Cambridge friends first began to push back against the
myth as early as May 1915. Over the course of the war, a broader coali-
tion of critics called into question his authorial reputation, even as they
were careful to acknowledge his personal sacrifice.

*

Ironically, even as he introduced Brooke to a wider reading public, Dean Inge was one of the first to offer up a tentative criticism of elements of 'The Soldier' in 1915. His religious reading of the poem stressed that it did not go far enough in achieving a self-surrender, wherein the individual completely relinquished his body to reward the soul. There could be no holding back, no overt attachment to material and physical delights, because this was both the ideal inspired by Christ and the behaviour required in wartime.[2]

Charles Sorley had similar reservations about the poet-soldier's philosophical and stylistic approach to the War Sonnets. He appreciated Brooke's technical abilities as a poet, but took issue with the 'sentimental attitude' of the poems and what he viewed as their insularity and self-satisfaction: 'They', the soldiers of 'The Dead', had not given up 'anything of that list he gives in one sonnet: but … the essence of these things had been endangered by circumstances over which he had no control, and he must fight to recapture them'.[3] For Sorley, earlier works – including in particular *Poems* – were much more deserving of attention. He acknowledged the sad loss of a fellow poet-soldier, but he disliked how the War Sonnets – and Brooke – were portrayed in the press:[4] 'I saw Rupert Brooke's death in the *Morning Post*. The *Morning Post* is now loud in his praises because he has conformed to their stupid axiom of literary criticism that the only stuff of poetry is violent physical experience, by dying on active service'.[5]

In some ways Gilbert Murray's often quoted prediction that 'I cannot help thinking that Rupert Brooke will probably live in fame as an almost mythic figure'[6] had also sounded a note of caution. Murray was personally familiar with Brooke, and was fond of him; he had some misgivings about him being reduced to a stock metaphor for patriotic sacrifice, even as he was pleased that his sacrifice and poetry were now appreciated by such a wide audience. These readers appreciated the mass outpourings of grief and critical praise, otherwise 'we would have missed Rupert Brooke's triumphant war sonnets and Julian Grenfell's enraptured vindication of the soldier's vocation.[7] Yet the identification – in this example as expressed by the *Morning Post* – of Brooke's work and life as 'triumphant' was exactly what critics like E. J. Dent and John Sheppard, who published their critiques of the fervent obituaries in the *Cambridge Review* and the *Cambridge Magazine* in May 1915, found so disturbing, but they had to walk a careful line.

The dissenters objected to what was occurring as a result of the syndication of obituaries: the complete subsuming of Brooke the man by the poet-soldier of the War Sonnets. Sheppard criticised the process by which the death of an actual complex, living and breathing human being became a kind of balm for strangers when he wrote, 'Though it is not easy, we owe it to him not to comfort ourselves by letting our thoughts dwell on a mythical being who was not Rupert, and whose loss is therefore the easier to bear.'[8] Harold Monro objected to his being brought 'to the poster grade. "He did his duty. Will You [*sic*] do yours?" is hardly the moral to be drawn'. Monro wanted the focus brought back to Brooke's earlier poetry, which he argued was actually 'the repudiation of sentimentality'. Brooke was a poet first, he argued, and he should not be 'advertised' as a soldier in aid of the recruiting officer.[9] This line of criticism was similar to the tone Ezra Pound assumed when he considered writing something to 'defend' Brooke the poet from Brooke the myth.[10]

*

The extent to which the war cast a shadow over all public poetry and prose was something that all writers dealt with during the conflict. In 1914, Pound, then living in London, considered writing a poem about the burning of Louvain, but decided against it, considering the subject improper for an American and a civilian.[11] W. B. Yeats expressed a similar opinion in his poem 'A Reason for Keeping Silent',[12] with the lines, 'I think it better that at times like these / We poets keep our mouths shut'.[13] His concerns about civilian poets weighing in on the war combined with his distaste for the fashion for mobilising literature to create temporal canons expressed through literary compilations. In 1916, Yeats wrote to Harriet Monroe, editor of the influential review *Poetry*, about the vogue for 'greatest hits' publications that Brooke was now very much a part of: 'I detest anthologies. It means being paraded before the public with a lot of people to whom one hasn't been introduced'.[14]

During the war in England it was, however, incredibly difficult to create a kind of parallel literary culture separate from the one in which the conflict so predominated. After writing a satire of Brooke in the war issue of *Blast* in 1915, Pound learned of his early death, and tried to point out that his poetic parody was nothing personal. He felt a professional duty to identify the 'jeune poète' with his 'style Victorienne';[15] the critique was simply a 'complaint against literary method ... written months before'. He sensed the potential backlash in the small literary community of London, in which Edward Marsh, for one, as well as Henry James remained prominent figures. In April 1915, when the laudatory obituary reigned supreme, even a critique of Brooke's style could be taken in the wrong way, and Pound was sensitive to potential charges of bad taste. As much as he might wish to ignore the war as a topic, and the special circumstances it created for public discourses on literature, Pound found himself like everyone else, 'writing war poetry whether he wanted to or not'.[16]

T. S. Eliot's engagement with Brooke as a literary figure was, like Pound's, less constrained by personal considerations or cultural investment than some other careful critics of the Brooke myth. Like Pound, he could view Brooke from a critical distance, and from the point of view of a semi-outsider. But he still had to contend with the potential limitations imposed by the reigning literary establishment, and with the general discourse that influenced all that was written about the war. In June 1915, Pound wrote to Eliot's father, explaining the situation. While 'No one in London cares a hang what is written in America' as 'London likes discovering her own gods', if a literary man is 'doing the fine thing and the rare thing, London is the only possible place to exist'.[17] Eliot was invested in English society and literature, but as such had to contend with established figures, many whom he viewed as literary forefathers,[18] but who were also public proponents of the Brooke myth and his poetry during the war. Henry James, to name but one example, in *Letters from America*, characterised Brooke as a thoroughly English phenomenon and example of a pure, 'young English poetic possibility and faculty'.[19] Thus he found himself 'as on a darkling plain', surrounded by Georgian poets who were writing, as he said, a poetry that 'belongs to the sensibility of the ordinary sensitive person'.[20]

*

Eliot's poetry was on occasion placed in closer proximity to Brooke than he may have liked. After reprinting, in tribute, three of Brooke's War Sonnets in April,[21] in June 1915, Harriet Monroe published an article in *Poetry*, praising Brooke's abilities as a poet but bemoaning how the 'arts have taught that war is beautiful' through repetition of the ideals of 'the glory of heroic life'.[22] Eliot's poem 'The Love Song of J. Alfred Prufrock' appeared on the pages immediately preceding Monroe's review, and following Arthur Davison Ficke's poem 'To Rupert Brooke', describing the 'Beautiful lover of beauty!'[23] Eliot was literally surrounded by tributes to poet-soldiers.[24] This implicit juxtaposition of the two poets illustrates the muddled nature of Anglophone literature and criticism during the war. Eliot identified Brooke as part of a movement largely counter to what he was trying to achieve in his verse and prose: he objected to Brooke's Romanticism, categorising him with Swinburne, labelling their assessments of Elizabethan predecessors and their role in modern English poetry and prose as 'useful … though misleading'.[25]

When it came to a publicly curated ideal of Brooke, Eliot was no reactionary snob bemoaning the influence of popular culture. He praised authentic expression, wherever it originated, insofar as he could refigure it to serve his critical philosophy,[26] as in his 1923 memorial essay for the singer Marie Lloyd. In this essay, he lamented the decline of music halls and the rise of the cinema, which, like other forms of mass culture, produced passive as opposed to genuinely creative audiences. Their disappearance reduced the 'aesthetic production' of the working class, required to counter 'bourgeois incapacity for self-representation'.[27] Modern forms of communication allowing for the easy transmission of ideas were useful, but not if they resulted in a largely apathetic, uniformed public, a state viewed by many as a negative by-product of the rise in daily newspapers and periodicals promoting and repeating, day in and day out, the views of an established, but not necessarily exceptional, literary elite.

Some readers outside of these circles did actively engage in criticism of Brooke's poetry and myth, even to the point of being inspired to create their own implicit and explicit tributes. Most resorted to a kind of literary ventriloquism, recycling inherited language and subject, thereby excluding themselves from the true creative process. 'Middlebrow' writers exemplified this, particularly in their demonstrated hostility to modernist influence, and in their persistent pursuit of the ideals of 'development, progress and moral perfectibility'.[28] Eliot, for one, condemned this middlebrow voice. In 1917, he constructed an imaginary letter to the Editor of the *Egoist* (i.e. himself) responding to his dismissal of Brooke from the 1917 literary scene. 'Helen B. Trundlett' of 'Batton, Kent' wrote to express her view that:

> Brooke's early poems exhibit a youthful exuberance of passion, and an occasional coarseness of utterance, which offended finer tastes; but these were but dross which, as his last sonnets show, was purged away (if I may be permitted this word) in the fire of the Great Ordeal which is proving the well-spring of a Renaissance of English poetry.[29]

This sketch reveals how closely Eliot followed literary debates: note his satire of Trundlett's distaste for deploying the phrase 'purged away', a direct reference to public reactions to Brooke's 'A Channel Passage', with its description of seasickness, a subject unfit for the lofty poetic genre.[30] The correspondent was also aware of this poem and the minor controversy that ensued: she did 'pride herself' in keeping 'abreast of the times in literature'. Eliot's parody mocked not only such a character's self-congratulation, but also the unimaginative way that she fitted Brooke into the prefigured patriotic language of the times, praising – in capital letters – the opportunity for the 'Great Ordeal' to forge a 'Renaissance of English poetry'.[31] Yet letters like Trundlett's were being reprinted in the popular press as literary critique, and praised as expressions of cultural sensitivity and superiority.

Eliot disapproved of popular literary taste as defined by a false elite, the 'so-called cultivated and civilised class' that were often simply following sales as opposed to identifying real talent and innovation: 'It is assumed that poetry only pays if it is bought by thousands of people one has never heard of'.[32] Brooke was the definition of such a poet, having been crowned a public success largely on the strength of five sonnets, whereas audiences for Eliot's work developed more slowly, working hard to unpick layers of complexity. His publication in the 'little reviews' allowed for the deferral of the consumption elements associated with publishing 'into the future, to transform it into investment'. This followed the principle of art as 'news that stays news' as opposed to work that was merely temporal, reactionary, easy, or obvious.[33]

*

Over the course of the war the writer Virginia Woolf increasingly found the language and imagery – conflating the biographical and the literary – associated with Brooke and the ideal of the poet-soldier difficult to reconcile with her memories of the man. She had been a close friend of Brooke's until he fell out with Lytton Strachey, Harold Lamb, and the 'Bloomsbury' set in 1911; they had played together as children. As a young woman, she had spent a week at Grantchester with Brooke at a point when they were both in some psychological distress: they passed the time discussing and refining their poetry and prose.[34]

The sensitive, highly attuned Woolf, more capable than many writers and critics of understanding and expressing the shock that had engulfed English culture as the scale and nature of the war became clearer, and of recognising the depth of public mourning, did not attack Brooke's popular image as overtly or immediately as some. There were personal relationships to consider: the attempts by some Cambridge friends in 1915 to question the emerging public portrait of Brooke ended up upsetting his mother, who read any critique as a personal attack on her son.[35] To an extent, Mary Brooke's influence meant that Marsh constructed his 1918 'Memoir' to Brooke as ultimately 'uncritical of its subject as a man of literature'.[36] This resonated with the close London literary community. In her review of Marsh's tribute for the *Times Literary Supplement* in August 1918, Woolf attempted to address paradoxes presented in Brooke's popular reputation, and to gauge the possibility of reasserting certain 'truths' about the poet and his works, as 'Few people trouble to know much about his poetry – but everyone takes an intelligent interest in his death'.[37]

Privately, she was critical of Marsh's management of their friend's posthumous literary reputation, describing the 'Memoir' as 'disgraceful soppy sentimental rhapsody'.[38] Woolf's intention was to avoid 'summing up' Brooke in the way that had so many obituaries and articles. Her approach drew on her developing technique of creating a literary 'collage … conveying tones and moods'[39] that better expressed deeper psychological states, breaking with the Victorian 'official' biographical tradition – 'conventional, patriarchal, impersonal, censorious, and censored' – exemplified by the likes of the *Dictionary of National Biography*.[40]

She was already on record as raising objections to the manner in which the particulars of his life were so easily recast by obituarists and reviewers, for instance taking issue with his being used as a quasi-Christian symbol, buried in 'a grove of olives, tucked deep in a rocky ravine',[41] identifying him instead as 'consciously and defiantly pagan'.[42] Woolf felt that much of what she read about Brooke was, 'false', 'exploitative', and 'vulgar', furthering a war that she 'read' as a 'preposterous masculine fiction'.[43] She was offended by the many who moved so swiftly publicly to align their names with Brooke, not in order to honour his memory or express genuine grief at the disastrous loss not only of her former friend but of so many other young men and women, but to accrue political, economic, and cultural capital. These were 'the false gods of the popular factor, the charlatans, the panders, the crafty and unscrupulous flatterers of mob-sentimentality, who betray their consciences daily for the little unsavoury power'.[44] This was glib patriotism dressed up as literary critique.

In the *Times Literary Supplement*, she was conscious of balancing these views with her appreciation for Brooke as a person and as a poet of verses that went beyond the War Sonnets. She drew attention to his careful attention to his craft: 'You felt that to him literature was not dead nor of the past, but a thing now in process of construction by people many of whom were his friends; and that knowledge, skill, and, above all, unceasing hard work were required of those who attempt to make it'. For her, personally, 'to imagine him entombed, however nobly and fitly, apart from our interests and passions, still seems impossibly incongruous with what we remember of his inquisitive eagerness about life'.[45]

This review was to an extent 'sardonic',[46] but only a limited number of the public would have read the piece in that way in 1918: it seemed positive enough, although Marsh and others probably understood it as an attack. As much as he had wanted the 'Memoir' to be something that balanced both critical literary reflection with personal tribute and biography, Marsh had ultimately remained committed to his tribute from 1915 to 1918 because 'Rupert is a famous poet and his life will be read critically by all sorts of people all the world over, both now and long afterwards'.[47] Brooke was now the possession of the readership. Despite Woolf's intention, which she summarised to Bruce Richmond, editor of the *Times Literary Supplement* in 1918, to 'explain Rupert to the public',[48] achieving a 'critical notoriety'[49] on the pages of literary journals like the *Egoist* and even the *Times Literary Supplement* was one thing, but addressing and altering the tastes and needs of a readership beleaguered by war and constantly bombarded with the language of patriotism, who found in the figure of the poet-soldier consolation and inspiration, was something beyond the capacity of any one concerned – and reserved – reviewer.

Woolf was at least partially influenced by their once-friendly relationship when reviewing Brooke the poet. Hoping to avoid a repeat of the 1915 Cambridge situation, almost as soon as the review was published, Woolf wrote directly to Brooke's mother that 'he was a wonderful friend', and admitted to her that she had 'rather hoped that you would not see my review, as I felt that I had not been able to say what I wanted to say about Rupert'.[50] While other critics with less at stake might publish more polemic and controversial assessments of the poet-soldier, Woolf was more circumspect. In 1916, Alec W. G. Randall published an article on 'Poetry and Patriotism' in the *Egoist* that lambasted, in particular, *The Times* role in shaping the literary critical landscape of the war:

> Some misguided people, I believe, still hold that war is a good thing for arts, even this machine-made, absolutely unromantic war has not convinced them of the contrary. They may still be found writing in *The Times* letters full of panegyric nonsense on young heroes such as Rupert Brooke, whose death was a far greater poem than his life.[51]

Woolf would probably never have written anything so overtly dismissive of the actual young man she had known and been fond of, nor is it likely that such writing as Randall desired would be published in the *Times Literary Supplement*, which throughout the war continued to feel the need to promote the establishment ideal of 'England's Poet-Soldier', the parable of this particular young hero. Since Woolf's review could be read as a critique of the 'panegyric' as opposed to a negative reflection on Brooke as a literary figure, it did not represent an overt break with previous positions. In 1918, it was still the prerogative of the mainstream literary press to publish expressly positive assessments of Brooke's contribution to English literary culture, even if on some occasions these contained criticism of the consumerist and potentially vulgarising practices associated with the popular myth.

*

Careful critics of Brooke and the established literary structures and rhetoric that worked to create the ideal of the poet-soldier were careful not to go too far in their 'iconoclasm'.[52] These emerging modernists consistently demonstrated public respect for those risking their lives for the nation, even as they were uneasy about the way in which popular war culture – aided by many established literary figures – played with authorial reputations, and mixed literature with politics and some-times glib patriotism. In 1922, Eliot reviewed *An Anthology of Modern Verse* in the *National Review Français* (Methuen, the publishers of the volume, had published Eliot's *The Sacred Wood: Essays on Poetry and Criticism* in 1920). The new *Anthology* contained poems by Brooke. In his review, Eliot made it clear that while he acknowledged the existence and popularity of the 'War Poets' – from whom Brooke had emerged as the representative figure by virtue of the fact that popular taste had fused ideals about the beauty of the man and his sacrifice with his poetry – he was not interested in them, either stylistically or topically.[53]

For the duration, these critics were pushing against an increasingly heavy door, so established was Brooke as the poet-soldier of the war: the solitary island grave, peaceful and serene, shielded by a hovering pride in the individual and collective sacrifice of the war dead, 'honour's call' and the 'quenchless brightness of a patriot fire'[54] were simply too much to counter. At the same time as Dent and Sheppard were voicing their reservations about how Brooke was being portrayed by many, Arthur Quiller Couch, Professor of English Literature at Cambridge, in a lecture covered in the *Cambridge Magazine* – the same publication that published their careful critiques – posed the rhetorical question: 'Where in our time was a youth more Hellenic, eminent in all they could claim or the Fates grudge?'[55]

In the end, one of the most effective critical commentaries of the myth of the poet-soldier was provided by the artist Duncan Grant. In 1915, he created the abstract oil and collage portrait, *In Memoriam: Rupert Brooke*. This is a portrayal very much in revolt against the tendency of historical portraiture to encourage the viewer to discover something specific about the past 'or about acts of portrayal', be they 'individual or collective; and the tendency is ... to extrapolate the collective from the individual'.[56] The portrait of Brooke was intentionally 'tiny, private, and ... inscrutable to all but to a small group sympathetic to modern art',[57] designed as much to confuse the uninformed viewer as to offer a critique of the tendency to transpose personal expectations and sentiments onto the blank canvas of the poet-soldier. Embedded in the painting is a shard of glass, which at some angles reflects back the viewer's own image. Perhaps this is too literal a reading of the work, but it seems to say that, within all this turmoil, when one looks at Brooke, at least for a moment, one sees not the man or even his component physical or philosophical parts, but whatever one wants to see ... but, then again, perhaps one sees nothing at all.

16

Export

Rupert Brook's reputation during the war worked on the principle that the poet-soldier fitted within a cultural and literary continuum, and a common English heritage. This could be read as intensely nationalist or even localist in expression, but in practice those promoting the ideals associated with the poet-soldier did so in a manner designed to appeal to broad audiences. The nature of Brooke's reputation, and the near universal allure of the ideals associated with the myth that emerged during the war, made him relatively easy to 'sell' – literally and figuratively – to would-be patrons, critics, and readers abroad.

He was already recognised by figures with international reputations, from Emile Verhaeren to Henry James. In 1916, Edith Wharton chose to include Brooke's poem 'The Dance, A Song' in her *Book of the Homeless*, which was designed to raise money for hostels for Belgian refugees.[1] This was not a war poem, but instead conjured up memories of a dusky pre-war world: 'Following where your feet have gone, / Stirs dust of old dreams there'. It appeared on page four of the volume, well ahead of more established figures including Maurice Barrès, John Galsworthy, Edmund Gosse, Thomas Hardy, General Joffre, and Henry James. Theodore Roosevelt, furious at United States neutrality in the war, provided the Introduction to the volume, including the following lines, which attacked the apathy of many who ignored the 'cause of humanity': 'Nothing that can now be done by the civilized world, even if the neutral nations of the civilized world should at last wake up to the performance of the duty they have so shamefully failed to perform, can undo the dreadful wrong of which these unhappy children, these old men and women, have been the victims'.[2] Wherever he was introduced, and in whatever context, Brooke was offered as one he had given his all in a common cause.

*

The manner in which different national presses chose to report on Rupert Brooke as 'England's Poet-Soldier' responded to particular local contexts; however, the language deployed, and the themes identified, remained largely consistent with their English counterparts. The exporting of Brooke relied on existing infrastructure that supported the sharing of information between individuals and governments, which became even more important in times of war as the belligerent nations worked to influence international opinion.

From the perspective of Wellington House, which coordinated official British propaganda, Imperial unity was, to a relative degree, taken for granted, whereas US neutrality was something that required direct attention.[3] Articles such as one that appeared in Canada in *Everywoman's Weekly* under the headlines 'Seven Sons for King and Country' and 'No Need of Conscription Here'[4] reinforced the belief in a unity of philosophy and purpose. The department did act in logistical support of communication infrastructures, utilising connections with steamship companies such as the White Star and Orient Lines, the Australasian United Steam Navigation Company and the Canadian Pacific Railway Company to provide newspapers and pamphlets to journalists, religious leaders, clubs, writers, and publishers in Canada, South Africa, Australia, and New Zealand.[5]

Generally speaking, coverage of Brooke's death and his poetry in the various national presses testified to his abstracted, seemingly universal appeal, reinforcing local and national narratives about the war dead. This was largely the case in Scotland and Wales, whose geographical and, to an extent, cultural proximity to England contributed to the acceptance of Brooke as "'our poet" … the utterance of the youth of our generation'.[6] Canadian reactions to the poet-soldier and his poetry adopted a similar tone. In the introduction to the Toronto edition of Brooke's *Collected Poems*, George Edward Woodberry, like the reviewer for the *Aberdeen Free Press*, accepted the premise so often professed by English newspapers of the 'Greek lyricism'[7] evident in Brooke's poetry, death, and ultimate burial on the 'steep summit of a Greek island of infinite grace'.[8] The *Scotsman* concurred, imaging Brooke as 'slain by the arrows of Apollo'.[9] Margaret Lavington, in her biographical note for the Canadian edition, ended by reasserting themes already introduced and syndicated in the various obituaries and articles published in the English press in 1915 and 1916:

> And then came 1914; and his [Brooke's] passion for life had suddenly to face the thought of voluntary death. But there was no struggle; for instantly the passion for life became one with the will to die – and now it has become death itself. But first Rupert Brooke had told the world once more how the passion for beautiful life may reach its highest passion and most radiant beauty when it is the determination to die.[10]

The *Glasgow Herald* also used Brooke to argue that the soldiers of Great Britain gave up their lives 'in more honest warfare' than their enemy counterparts.[11] Not only in England, but in the nations across the Empire, soldiers like Brooke were identified as representative of 'peace-loving men forced into action by the aggressor'.[12]

*

Reception of the Brooke myth in Australia was somewhat less consistently in line with those in evidence in England. General Sir Ian Hamilton for one was very concerned about Australian press coverage of the Gallipoli campaign, in particular reports alluding to unsavoury relations between British and Australian commanders and troops.[13] His professional as well as his sentimental sympathies centred on preserving Imperial military unity.[14] With public opinion coalescing around the nationalist Anzac myth,[15] Australian poets like Leon Gellert appealed more directly to Antipodean readers than Brooke. The poet-soldier's reputation as a volunteer and an exemplar of the war dead still resonated, even as some expressed scepticism of 'English critics', who 'do not risk their reputations on anything living'. One reviewer for the Sydney *Bulletin* sympathised with the poet as the subject of posthumous myth-making: 'A writer becomes a great poet only after his post-mortem. And a dead poet is not at all likely to dispute the critic-coroner's findings. So Rupert Brooke is quite safe – and the critics can say what they like over his dead body'. He went on to explain the nature of the poet's and poems' appeal, stating that 'His poems have a special claim on England, where poetic reputations are made by their continual Englishness ... England he [Brooke] loved most of all; but he loved many other, though mostly English, things'.[16] This review continued to work within the context of a growing Australian nationalism, and in so doing avoided complete acceptance of the Brooke myth in exchange for a more particular ideal, and an assertion of Australian, as opposed to Imperial, patriotism.

That said, the myths were not mutually incompatible. The Anzac ideal was built on a 'sense of national identity ... courage and self-reliance, athleticism, fierce loyalty to mates, relaxed discipline, egalitarianism, dry humour and a wild streak – ingredients which make formidable soldiers'.[17] None of these qualities ran directly counter to those stressed in the English version of the idealised poet-soldier and in the War Sonnets, particularly in their celebrations of comradeship and physical beauty. In the end, even the more caustic *Bulletin* critic surmised that in the 'beautiful work' exhibited in *1914 and Other Poems*, 'The promise is indubitably there; but, dying the death he desired, he left behind a reputation begun'.[18] A post-war review of the *Collected Poems* with Marsh's 1918 'Memoir' was less reserved, praising Brooke's poetry and prose as 'so alive with his own eager, elusive, fascinating personality, that reading of it helps to bring us closer to knowledge of himself'. The 'five noble sonnets', stressing similar virtues to those propagated about Australian volunteers, provided the basis for his deserved 'fame'.[19]

*

Reactions to 'England's Poet-Soldier' in the 'highly symbolic world of Irish politics'[20] had the potential to be even more hostile. In May 1915, the Unionist *Irish Times* published Brooke's obituary in a varied article reporting 'fierce fighting round Ypres and the successful invasion of Gallipoli'. It went on to record the sacrifices of the French poet Charles Péguy and, representing England, Brooke, 'the most sincere and accomplished poet of his generation'. The writer proceeded to present Brooke as a would-be socialist hero, a poet-soldier who 'would be the last to make any distinction of sacrifice', and a representative of what all modern Irishmen should strive to be:

> Rich and poor, learned and simple, skilled in long practice of the soldier's art or newly called to the Colours, the men of our splendid Army are giving their all – their strength, their loves, their lives – to their country's service and their country's need. The reward on earth of those who have fallen will be the enduring pride and gratitude of the men and women whom they died to save. So long as Ireland lasts oblivion will not touch the Irishmen who sleep in Flanders and Gallipoli.[21]

Here appeared strains of what would later appear in debates about Irish conscription and what Lloyd George termed the 'equity of sacrifice'.[22]

Any idealised unity was, in reality, fragile, as the surprise Easter uprising of 1916 to an extent proved.[23] However, in 1915 – and beyond, despite what later Republican narratives of the period would come to suggest – recognition and commemoration of the Irish war dead was still possible and indeed welcome by the families who sent sons off to fight and die. Volunteers like the poet Thomas Kettle expressed a more moderate political position, stressing allegiance to an internationalist cause:[24] it is revealing of the uncertain attitude towards Britain that Brooke's Irish obituary included discussion of the sacrifices of French poets, the dead of Ypres and Gallipoli, and all Irish soldiers. The obituary ended with a plaintive question: 'May not the stricken fathers, mothers, and wives of this island to-day find comfort in the thought that the fate which has bereaved them has enriched the land of love – that through their loss, there are corners of foreign fields that are forever Ireland?'[25]

Later in the war such a question might not have been posed in such a way. The persistent and draconian treatment of the Irish by the nervous, exhausted, and increasingly repressive Parliament in London 'may have mobilized more Irish people politically than the Gaelic League or the Irish Parliamentary Party or Sinn Féin or the IRB ever dreamt of'.[26] Conscription efforts in 1918 further exacerbated tensions, alienating many potential Loyalist volunteers desperately required to replace troops depleted by the St Michael offensive.[27] Later in the war, for many patriotic Irish readers, 'England's Poet-Soldier' had been superseded by other poet-soldier martyrs like Patrick Pearse, who, like Brooke, became the object of numerous tribute poems and a fair amount of coverage in newspapers, periodicals, and pamphlets advocating the Republican cause, not only in Ireland but in the United States as well.[28]

*

The English poet John Masefield provides an example of a literary figure officially dispatched to the United States by Wellington House to report on popular opinion who, in turn, took the opportunity to discuss Brooke and his poetry. Masefield had been a personal friend of Brooke's, and had offered him general encouragement throughout his career. He had been equally impressed by his ready enlistment. In December 1914, Brooke wrote to Cathleen Nesbitt, 'I had a letter from Masefield, saying he was proud to know me, because I'd done a fine thing. It gave me a queer thrill'.[29] In New Haven in February 1916, Masefield was asked to read his own poem 'August 1914'. Upon reaching the line dealing with the sacrifice 'Which love of England prompted and made good', Masefield reportedly was 'overcome with emotion. He asked to be excused for not finishing the verse, and went on to read another of his poems.' Discussion immediately preceding the request had centred on his personal admiration for Brooke as a soldier and as a poet.[30]

This event occurred at the end of a tour of parts of the United States, beginning in Boston in early January. As he travelled across New England he observed and assessed attempts by German universities to offer exchanges designed to foster alliances, and the general feeling that 'the infamy of the invasion of Belgium put all of the rest out of accounts'.[31] The southern United States he also found quite Anglophile; he passed the time discussing plans for the allotment of Rhodes scholarships as a means to furthering brotherhood between the two nations, and countering enemy advances.[32] He reported back to London on the more mixed reactions to the war and the idea of direct military intervention that he observed as he travelled further west, to cities like Minneapolis, Milwaukee, and Chicago. His recommended that a 'constant stream of carefully selected literature should be sent from England to the most prominent men in the different departments of activity in America', which was very much in line with Charles Masterman's policy that 'literature should be personal and discriminating, and should be directed rather towards furnishing the recipient with the material on which he could form his own judgements',[33] thus avoiding appearing too didactic or interfering.

Brooke as the poet-soldier was just the sort of appealing representative of English youth capable of gently drawing people towards a more Anglo-centric view of the war. On the same evening as the poetry reading in New Haven, Masefield also accepted an interview with a reporter from the local *Evening Post*, an event that was then reported on and partially reprinted in the Scottish newspaper the *Dundee Advertiser*. When conversation turned to Brooke, Masefield offered the opinion that, had he lived, he 'would have stood the highest and have done the best work'. Masefield had, however, 'always felt that he would not live … there was something in his face that always made me feel that he would not live'. Brooke was noble and talented; he was the culmination of a romantic type, and he was destined to die, as Masefield asserted, in a manner 'Which love of England prompted and made good'.[34] In June of the same year, Yale University awarded Brooke the Henry Howland Memorial Prize; another English poet, Walter de la Mare, travelled over for the ceremony. The full notice for the award, as reported in *The Times*, read: 'On an isle in the Aegean under olives by the sounding sea lies buried a young Englishman, poet and soldier, dead on the way to Gallipoli. To Rupert Brooke, the patriot poet, the Howland Prize is this year given'.[35] The ideals associated with the poet-soldier translated easily, passing from London to New Haven, and back again.

*

As in Great Britain and the Empire, in the United States, various types of publications weighed in on Brooke and his poetry. *Vanity Fair* published a substantial spread on Brooke including photographs, with complete copies of the War Sonnets in January 1916.[36] *The Dial*, a periodical that 'mediated a tradition' between literary and popular magazines,[37] published an anonymous poem, 'To Rupert Brooke', in 1918. And, as in England, newspapers reported not only on the military, political, and economic mobilisations occurring abroad, but on cultural mobilisations as well.

The East Coast newspapers in particular gloried in the idea of shared English identity, aided by the proximate Anglophile academic and print cultures. This area Masefield characterised as 'The Brain of

America' and the most pro-British.[38] The dominance of the region in cultural affairs predicted a relative uniformity in how the poet-soldier was portrayed across the country. Many editors as well as their readers, fascinated by the spectre of a grand European war played on an international, Imperial scale as much as they were shocked by the violence of it, agreed with Ralph Waldo Emerson's view of the nation's literary and philosophic inheritance: 'The American has arrived at the old mansion-house and finds himself among uncles, aunts and grand-sires. The picture on the chimney-tiles of his nursery were pictures of these people'.[39] Having derived a sense of pride in the sister-nation's defence not only of territory but also of a culture 'in which England is contrasted with the Kaiserland',[40] Brooke's poetry and 'Remarkable Personality'[41] confirmed theories that were already largely set. For Henry James, writing about Brooke as the 'poet of to-day':

> What it first and foremost really comes to, I think, is the fact that at an hour when the civilised peoples are on exhibition, quite finally and sharply on show, to each other and to the world, as they absolutely never in all their long history have been before, the English tradition (both of amenity and of energy, I naturally mean) should have flowered at once in a specimen so beautifully producible.[42]

Much of what was written about the war from 1914 to 1918, regardless of political association, aligned with James's presentation of the close relationship between the two nations, and many Americans, reading articles travelling largely unchanged across increasingly internationalised syndication networks, recognised the affinities.

Yet millions of German Americans, for example, would take issue with Emerson's characterisation of the extended family of the nation, let alone with the idea that this should translate into cultural, material, political, and eventually military support for the Entente. The nation of immigrants was by no means completely convinced of the superiority of the Anglophile position. Elite intellectual culture on the coasts in particular might display its allegiance and sympathy to an English reading of the war, but there was no political or cultural uniformity.

Editors as well as British officials also had to contend with, for example, particularly strong Irish dissent, particularly following the Easter Rebellion in April 1916. Masefield noted this, characterising the Irish-American lobby as, 'Damn disloyal … They are very clever and very bitter and in some states the Irish vote is enormously strong'.[43] In addition, the experience of the American Civil War was not a distant memory, particularly, Masefield noted, in the South.[44] One veteran summed up this line of argument: 'My experience in the Civil War has saddened all my life … As I love my country I feel it is my sacred duty to keep the stalwart young men of today out of a barbarous war 3,500 miles away, in which we have no vital interest'.[45]

It followed that a large portion of the public required persuasion. Pro-intervention newspapers worked incrementally to convince their readerships that this course was of 'vital interest' to the nation, laying the groundwork for the declaration of war in April 1917. Using a supposedly apolitical, literary figure like Brooke, whose sacrifice was universally acclaimed, to make a broader case for support of England and the Allies was, in the particular political and cultural climate of the United States, in many cases more effective than other more direct lines of argument. The sort of language associated with the myth of the poet-soldier, reliant on ideals of honour in war as a means of instilling brotherhood and national unity, appealed to multiple reading – and political – constituencies.

Once war was declared, these same newspapers stoked patriotic enthusiasm and promoted identification with the Allies, encouraged by the example of the newly appointed head of the Committee on Public Information, the ex-reporter George Creel, who utilised every means at his disposal to convince the public that 'intervention in the European war was not at variance with America's tradition but was an affirmation of it'.[46] Creel, Masterman's more extreme counterpart in the United States, characterised his role as a 'plain publicity proposition, a vast enterprise in salesmanship, the world's greatest adventure in advertising'.[47]

Nuanced, gentle propaganda was, however, often more persuasive. Blatant attempts to mobilise culture in the name of patriotism were often unsuccessful. Pittsburgh, in a part of the Midwest heavily settled by German immigrants and considered by many interested observers, including Masefield, to be highly suspect in its sympathies, provided a case in point. Mirroring the 'All-English and No-German' concerts in Great Britain in the spring of 1915 as an act of 'patriotic symbolism', the city decided to ban the music of Ludwig van Beethoven.[48] Unsurprisingly, as in England,[49] the result was poor audience turnout and general disapproval from the established critics and public alike. More subtle, positive appeals of the kind made in the name of the poet-soldier were more successful.

*

Articles printed in the United States during the war reinforced the specific language and ideals associated with Brooke's poetry and sacrifice as they were first introduced by established literary figures in England. Many quoted Winston Churchill's 'glowing and sincere article' promoting the idea that the 'five sonnets have been called the finest utterances in English poetry concerning the war' and, more than this, 'the supreme utterance of English patriotism'. Reprinting H. W. Nevinson's obituary, the *Globe and Commercial Advertiser* also testified to the editor having first met Brooke and being struck by his 'browny-gold hair and blue eyes', which appeared 'almost ludicrously beautiful'.[50] The *New York Sun* reprised Gilbert Murray's opinion of the longevity of the myth, which 'so typified the ideal radiance of youth and poetry'.[51] Newspapers reported on the near-hysteria of the English press and reading public's reaction to the death of the poet-soldier. The *Globe and Commercial Advertiser* wrote, 'Small wonder that all England was aroused to a frenzy of grief', comparing the emergence of a kind of Brooke cult to reactions to the death of Edith Cavell. In the case of the poet-soldier this was considered to be justifiable, as he possessed a 'story ... so romantic and distressing that one is likely to become a little sentimental about him'.[52]

Hybrid obituaries and review articles appeared with the publication of each new Brooke volume: *1914 and Other Poems* in 1915; the *Collected Poems* published by the John Lane Company in 1916 (which corresponded to the British *Selected Poems* of 1917); *Letters from America*, published with Henry James's Preface in 1916; and Edward Marsh's *Rupert Brooke: A Memoir*, published in 1918, as well as the small run of Brooke's script *Lithuania: A Drama in One Act*, distributed by the small firm of Stewart Kidd in Cincinnati in 1915 coinciding with the run at Chicago's Little Theatre. The last introduced a new facet of Brooke to the mid-western public, and in reviews this evidence of his diversity as a poet, prose writer, and playwright testified to his reputation as a versatile 'literary genius'.[53]

Critical reception and promotion of each new piece of Brooke's poetry or prose did not limit itself solely to the title discussed. Articles also used the space provided to advertise forthcoming volumes, stoking public anticipation for the next work of genius. In its review of 'Rupert Brooke, Introduced by Henry James', the *New York Sun* began with the lines 'If I should die ...', making direct reference to *1914 and Other Poems*. The review also alluded to Marsh 'preparing a memoir', and advised its readers that 'of the young patriot's writings there remain for publication a book on John Webster and a one act play in prose'. Each new publication reinforced the previous and subsequent volumes' appeal, adding to the myth of the poet-soldier, inherited from England and continually employed as evidence of the cultural affinity that existed between the two nations.

Reviewers in the United States made a point of drawing readers' attention to Brooke's pre-war travels and observations about the nation. Incorrectly, one article stated that the material published in *Letters from America* was said to have been found as a 'notebook from which he planned to evolve a more ambitious volume'.[54] As a result, the 'bubbling humour of semi-adolescence combined with the genuine kindness and intelligence' subsumed the overall 'immature' quality of their 'bookification': the reviewer stressed that the editing had occurred posthumously.[55] These *Letters* allowed the reader to gain a greater insight into the poet-soldier, to 'see, through eyes not critical, what sort of a traveller he was'.[56] The 'Spirit of Youth in Letters of Brooke'[57] justified any limitations in Brooke's style or thematic range, just as patriotism informed the War Sonnets. The poignant 'short course' of his life enabled him to become the 'singer in his romantic embodi-ment'[58] of the war generation as the 'tragedy'[59] played out around him.

The figure of Brooke thus made more tangible the ideals informing the war to readers in the United States, allowing established cultural voices to draw direct links between the 'spirit' of the two nations:

> He has gone where he knows us and our vision better than he ever would during his lifetime here, and he knows now that sacred to us as the fields of England were to him are our fair coasts, or expectant cities, the trails our heroic pioneers trod, the battlefields where they fought for freedom and the peaceful places where the freedom has been realised.[60]

Arthur Guy Empey, in his 1917 book *'Over the Top' by An American Soldier Who Went*, advanced a similar image of the soldier defending European battlefields as his own, seeing in the trenches 'the emblem of "the land of the free and the home of the brave" beside them, doing its bit in this great war of civilization'.[61] Like Brooke's poetry and the derived ideal of the poet-soldier, this helped to create culturally consis-tent, appealing, and comfortable war icons and narratives.

*

Of all American newspapers, the *New York Times* provided the most substantial coverage of 'England's Poet-Soldier'. This began in 1915 and carried on until the end of the war. For the newspaper, he became a standard emblem of the war's heroism. He was, as one headline argued, the supreme example of 'A Genius Whom the War Made and Killed',[62] and through his poetry and reputation provided evidence of idealised 'loyalty and sacrifice'. Brooke offered the living an opportunity to stop and appreciate fundamental principles in an increasingly modern world, where 'recollection too often impairs efficiency', even as many endeavoured 'to forget, not to remember'.[63]

Reacting against this, the New York Times worked to keep the memory of Brooke front and centre for its readers. In 1917, it published an article under the headline 'War Letter of Rupert Brooke Comes To Light', containing 'Vivid Descriptions of the Evacuation of Antwerp and English Camp Life Written by Famous Poet to a Friend in America'.[64] Even this small discovery of writing attributed to the poet-soldier, traditionally a point of interest only for a biographer or scholar, became a full-length article, forming part of the record of a war that the United States had only recently formally entered into, but had had three years to anticipate, imagine, frame, and define.

Alongside articles detailing and expanding upon the Brooke myth, the paper provided a bevy of advertisements for his volumes, overtaking any single English newspaper, including The Times.[65] The advertisement for the Collected Poems of Rupert Brooke employed, again, Murray's 'mythical figure' quote from the Cambridge Magazine, specifically attributing it to the Professor and the University. This edition, published in early November 1915, also included a profile photograph of Brooke, on this occasion pictured in an open white shirt and black jacket, looking away from the camera.[66] This was also the photograph included as the frontispiece to the American edition of Collected Poems, and made Brooke's often-described beauty tangible to the readership. Later advertisements retained Murray's quote but did not include the photograph,[67] presumably to curtail costs. The blurb for Letters from America again managed to condense the most publicised points about Brooke's style: the letters were 'delightful first impressions' revealing the 'power and beauty' of the work of the 'English poet who was killed in the European war just as his works ... were everywhere becoming recognised'. Advertisements in December 1915 promoted first the *Collected Poems*[68] and later Marsh's *Memoir*[69] as gifts, directing readers to 'Give These Books'.[70]

Competing publishing houses such as the Houghton Mifflin Company helped to keep Brooke's name in the *New York Times*, publishing anthologies boasting 'Rupert Brooke' as a contributor to *A Treasury of War Poetry* alongside the likes of Rudyard Kipling and Robert Bridges. This volume placed British poets together with American ones, working side by side to pen the 'poems of the world war'.[71] These notices were accompanied by the review listings with titles such as 'Noteworthy Fiction and Works of Varied Interest This Month',[72] 'Five Hundred Leading Books',[73] and 'One Hundred Leading Books',[74] all promoting the Brooke myth in its short form. As in Great Britain, these notices worked in tandem with longer articles and obituaries, laying out the key tropes of the poet-soldier's famed life and work: 'The John Lane Company announces for early publication "The Collected Poems of Rupert Brooke", the gifted young English poet whose recent death while serving in the Aegean Sea ended a promising career'.[75] The 'Year in Books on the War' listed war publications by nation, with Brooke representing England; his name was at the top of the 'Poetry' section.[76]

Together these articles and advertisements pressed the idea that Brooke was the war's most universally recognised and feted poet. In the United States, as in England, Brooke was promoted as the poet-soldier celebrity of the war. In November 1917, the *New York Times* reported that 'The heroes of the present war are commemorated by ambulances' in aid of the Italian army. The eclectic list of names included Albert of Belgium, Marshal Joffre, Edith Cavell, Alan Seeger (who, as the American reincarnation of the poet-soldier, had two ambulances bearing his name), Woodrow Wilson, Abraham Lincoln, Byron, Shelley, Keats, Browning, Dante, and Rupert Brooke.[77]

*

In the United States, cultural exchange continued in the form of the genre most associated with 'England's Poet-Soldier'. In American newspapers and collected volumes, as in British ones, readers responded to Brooke's death with tribute poems. One published in the *Minne-apolis Journal* in the autumn of 1916 wondered '… if the flowers in Grantchester / Came up reluctantly this year …' and went on to consider whether 'the England that he loved / The England that had borne him "made aware"' would pause for a moment to commemorate him.[78] Another example, this by Arthur Davison Ficke, appeared in a collection entitled *An April Elegy*, in 1917, looking back to Brooke's visit to America in 1913, stressing a kind of physical and cultural prox-imity. Ficke had also published 'To Rupert Brooke' in *Poetry* magazine in June 1915. That tribute called attention to the tragedy of 'this age's sacrifice' of artists, including Brooke, who was 'Not of the age, but of all time a light'. It focused on Brooke's particular beauty, conjured up 'from my memory almost smooth away / The picture of your known and mortal face'.[79] It describes a scene where Brooke reads aloud to a group 'High above the city's giant roar'; the effect of the poet's voice is of 'exquisite tendrils twining to the heart's core'. The poem goes on to record the reactions of Maurice Browne, an American chronicler of Brooke.[80] Responding to the reading in Chicago, Browne is described by Ficke as 'a wreck of joy' who 'like a boy / Blushed suddenly, and looked at us, and smiled'. The impression of the beauty as much as the poetry lingered, so that when this group of poets learns of Brooke's death, 'All the conjecture we had felt before / Flashed into torch-flame, and at last we knew':[81] he had fulfilled his romantic destiny.

A poem by Caroline Russell Bispham published in the *New York Times* managed to condense almost all of the themes of the various obituaries, articles, and tributes down to a few lines of verse. It dwelt on Brooke as 'dowered with genius, beauty, power' in the 'flower of life', and returned to the theme of his being an 'adopted son of Greece'. Moving easily from classical to Christian religious sacrifice, the ode appeared under the title 'Chosen of God', opening with the lines: 'God let His hand and look / Rest on a soul and called it Rupert Brooke.' The 'Scholar and poet' becomes the 'Soldier, at the last': 'He took a sword and laid aside his pen, / Merging his life with the fighting men'. In dying in this predestined yet noble manner, 'God gave thee thy release', ensuring that the poet-solider played 'thy perfect part'.[82]

The *Dial*, the 'little review' cited as one of the bastions of 'high Modernist' culture in which 'the principal masterpieces of the Anglo-American avant-garde would first be published',[83] included 'To Rupert Brooke' in its March 1918 issue. The poem, written in 1916 but only published in March 1918, focuses on physical delights: 'Lips are kissing and limbs are clinging, / Breast to breast in a silence singing / Of unforgotten and fadeless things', with the 'Laughter and tears and the beat of wings'[84] echoing Brooke's 'laughter, learnt of friends; and gentleness' from 'The Soldier'. In 'To Rupert Brooke', the chorus of friends transforms into a flock of birds, and Brooke's 'English heaven',[85] becomes a 'far-off heaven' even as 'There is no glory gone from the air; / Nothing is less'. As in 'The Soldier' and 'The Dead', the body dissipates into a precious dust: 'You are dead and dust on your island shore. / A little dust are the lips where / Laughter and song and kisses were'. What lingers is the impression of the mythical being and, to some extent, his anticipated and now secured fame wherein 'a myriad lovers shout your name, / Rupert! Rupert! Across the earth'. The poem closes with an exultant homage to Brooke's life and death:

> And I give you glory, and I am glad
> For the life you had and the death you had,
> For the heaven you knew and the hell you knew,
> And the dust and the dayspring which were you.[86]

The triumph, once again, is the poet-soldier's, even – or especially – in death.

Tribute poems in the United States, as had their British counterparts, saw verses become public statements about aesthetics as well as the idealism of the period. All of this occurred within a particular context: for the first half of the war, American readers observed it from a distance. While opinions about the virtues of intervention and abstention differed, when it came to Brooke, coverage was consistently appreciative. Whether or not they were intended as political statements, the continuous publication of articles testifying to the alignment of the two literary cultures around the universal ideals of honour and sacrifice played a role in creating a more receptive audience for the nation's eventual declaration of war, and in turn influenced how the war dead would be presented in the United States, as in England, from 1917.

*

The idea that Rupert Brooke was 'one of the very few poets who has by his brilliant sonnets risen to the present crisis'[87] might have originated in England in 1915, but it proved saleable internationally as well. Not only the War Sonnets, but the ideal of the poet-soldier – and the themes that fed into it – proved extraordinarily resilient throughout the war as they spread and took hold within different reading communities. They passed almost completely intact around the world, securing a growing audience for the poetry and the language of sacrifice associated with the young, beautiful, tragically articulate war poet.

Conclusion

Landscapes are culture before they are nature; constructs of
the imagination projected onto wood and water and rock ...
But it should also be acknowledged that once a certain idea
of landscape, a myth, a vision, establishes itself in an actual
place, it has a peculiar way of muddling categories, of making
metaphors more real than their referents; of becoming, in fact,
part of the scenery.

> Simon Schama, *Landscape and Memory* (1995), p. 61

B rooke's emergence as the national poet from 1915 to 1918
was not accidental. His personal approach towards writing
poetry in a time of war, born of a period of self-mobilisation,
crystallised in the months leading up to his death during which time
he positioned himself – to the extent that he could control his own
circumstances – to become 'England's Poet-Soldier'. Throughout his
short life, he also maintained and expanded an influential web of
acquaintances. For these literary and political patrons and champions,
Brooke's accessible poetry and timely if tragic death allowed them to

place him before the reading public, almost ready-made, cast in the role of the perfectly self-surrendering fulfilment of his own poetic vision.[1] They did so in the obituaries of April and May 1915, which in turn were syndicated, recast, and expanded upon for new audiences in a variety of publications and formats throughout the war. The opportunistic way in which Brooke was promoted does not, however, negate the genuine grief – felt to varying degrees depending on the proximity to the man as opposed to the figure – expressed at the death of an individual who was in many cases a friend or protégé as well as a saleable patriotic entity. As Henry James midway through the war observed: 'His place is now very high & very safe – even though one walks round and round it with the aching soreness of having to take the monument for the man.'[2]

The language and discourse that settled on and around the poet-soldier fixed him as a standard for the war readership, including other would-be writers and poet-soldiers, who read his poems and the myriad articles and advertisements, reacted to their language and sentiments, and in some cases were inspired to compose their own variations on a theme. They also played a role in ensuring that during the war the ever-renewing appeal of the self-sacrificing young poet-soldier was not limited to one medium, nor simply to English lovers of verse: it floated freely across national borders and literary genres, shifting to serve the needs of various audiences. As cultural capital, the myth became a viable form of national promotion – of gentle propaganda – quietly but relentlessly permeating the rhetoric about the war in allied and neutral nations as much as it provided orientation and consolation to the home public.

Political and commercial networks, as much as literary ones, played a central role in the process of canonisation. Whether embracing the ideal of the poet-soldier or reacting to varying degrees against it, as some critics did, the ubiquity of the Brooke myth made it difficult to undermine set ideals about his celebrity once they were established. Readers will notice that this account of Rupert Brooke in the First World War does not attempt to assess the War Sonnets with the aim of

RCB/Ph/311. Photograph (photographer and date unknown) of a man
kneeling at the west end of Rupert Brooke's grave, possibly laying a wreath.

arguing that they are either 'good' or 'bad' poetry, or – given the very
real evidence of the war's carnage that confronted many readers over
the course of the war – to moralise about whether or not it was right
that they – and he – became a touchstone. Instead, this book is an
attempt to assess and understand a particular cult figure in the context
that created him. And it tries to collate and consider the language,
people, and institutions that encouraged them – and him – to be read
in the way that they were.

During the war, the Brooke myth allowed influential individuals
as well as private citizens to construct linguistic memorials to the
fallen, and to do so within a commonly recognised literary tradition
that elevated poetic discourse above the quotidian realities of a very
disturbing war. People required parables that helped them to explain

what was happening, and why. Even after the war, when alternative language with an altogether different register and purpose arose to describe the great disaster, when 'the doctrine of equality of sacrifice could be turned against deference,'[3] many still turned to Brooke to commemorate the war dead. In his 1929 memoir, *The Weary Road*, Charles Douie characterised Brooke as one of the 'remnants' of the period capable of acting as a 'spokesman' for the silent armies of the dead, one of the few with sufficient 'literary gifts to tell their story with justice and truth.'[4]

Much of the language that created the ideal of the poet-soldier may appear bombastic, repetitious, and clichéd to the 'modern' reader. During the war, belief in the beauty and value of self-sacrifice and the fantasy of a pure death in war virtually drowned out any potential dissent, at least for the duration, and in practice well beyond 1918. In the end, 'repetition … can make bad ideas seem extraordinarily clever, because listeners don't think too hard when they hear pretty words. They often just assume the words are true.'[5] The processes through which individuals and societies recast inherited forms in order to render violence familiar and manageable remain present, relevant, and troubling, and are likely to remain so for the foreseeable future.

Notes

Notes to the Introduction

1   King's College, Cambridge holds the archive for Rupert Chawner Brooke [hereafter abbreviated as RCB]. RCB Xc/16, Arthur Asquith to Violet Asquith, 23 April 1915. The account is derived from this letter and descriptions from Denis Browne sent to Mary Brooke: RCB Xc/8, 24 April 1915 and Xc/9, 29 April 1915, and from Denis Browne to Edward Marsh, Xc/10, 25 April 1915.

2   RCB Xc/6, Major John Churchill to Winston Churchill, undated letter.

3   RCB Xc/12, extracts from Sir Ian Hamilton's diary, April 1915. Also quoted in Christopher Hassall, *Rupert Brooke: A Biography* (1964), p. 510.

4   RCB Xc/21, Rupert Brooke, sketch maps of Scyros, April 1915.

5   RCB Xc/16: Arthur Asquith to Violet Asquith, 23 April 1915.

6   RCB Xc/15: Arthur Asquith to Edward Marsh, 25 April 1915.

7   Rupert Brooke, 'The Soldier', *1914 and Other Poems* (1915).

8   RCB Xf/11, sales figures to 31 December 1920 (see Table 1).

9   *Westminster Gazette*, 1 May 1915.

10 *Cambridge Magazine*, 8 May 2015.

11 Max Saunders, *Self Impression: Life-Writing, Autobiografiction, and the Forms of Modern Literature* (2010), p. 440.

12 Henry James to Marsh, 6 June 1915, in Philip Horne, ed., *Henry James: A Life in Letters* (1999), p. 548.

13 Pat Barker, *Toby's Room* (2012), p. 191.

14 Brooke, 'The Soldier', *1914 and Other Poems*.

15 Edmund Blunden, *Undertones of War* (1928), p. xii.

16   Hassall's *Rupert Brooke* remains the ultimate source for biographical
     detail, although it obscures some aspects of his life and character that were
     considered to be controversial at the time of its publication. Both Nigel
     Jones's *Rupert Brooke: Life, Death and Myth* (1999) and Paul Delaney's
     Fatal Glamour: The Life of Rupert Brooke (2015) provide further details, as
     do a series of edited collections devoted to correspondence with friends
     that supplement the already substantial *Letters of Rupert Brooke* (1968)
     edited by his then literary executor, Geoffrey Keynes [hereafter abbrevi-
     ated as LORB].
17   William St Clair, *The Reading Nation in the Romantic Period* (2004), p. 1.
18   My italics.

Notes to Chapter 1: Youth

1   Hassall, *Brooke*, p. 21.
2   J. A. Mangan, 'Social Darwinism and Upper-class Education in Late
     Victorian and Edwardian England', in J. A. Mangan and James Walvin,
     eds., *Manliness and Morality: Middle-class Masculinity in Britain and
     America, 1800–1940* (1987), p. 151.
3   Brooke to Dudley Ward, July 1908, *LORB*, p. 135.
4   Paul Delaney, *The Neo-Pagans: Friendship and Love in the Rupert Brooke
     Circle* (1987), pp. 77–80.
5   RCB P/1, *School Field Magazine*, Vol. 1, No. 1 (24 April 1899).
6   RCB Xa/2, R. Butler to William Parker Brooke, undated letter.
7   Brooke, 'The Path of Dreams', in Keynes, *Rupert Brooke: The Poetical
     Works* (1946).
8   'Evening', ibid.
9   'III. Dead', *1914 and Other Poems*.
10   'I. Peace', ibid.
11   Brooke, quoted in Hynes, *The Edwardian Turn of Mind* (1968), p. 146.
12   'The Bastille', in Keynes, *Poetical Works*.
13   RCB Xa/1, School Report, Rugby, 1906.
14   Brooke to Keynes, 19 August 1906, *LORB*, p. 60.
15   Delaney, *The Neo-Pagans*, pp. 31–32.
16   Brooke to Lytton Strachey, September 1906, quoted ibid., pp. 68–69.
17   Brooke to Erica Cotterill, January 1907, *LORB*, p. 75.

Notes to Chapter 2: The Idyll

1   RCB M/9, diary pages, April 1904.
2   Brooke to Erica Cotterill, January 1907, *LORB*, p. 75.

3   Brooke to Francis MacCunn, 17 January 1907, *LORB*, p. 76.

4   RCB M/11, lecture notes taken at the Fabian Summer School, Llanbedr, Harlech, 1907/8.

5   RCB P/6, papers read on 14 May 1910 and 3 December 1909 respectively.

6   Brooke to Mary Brooke, 25 May 1908, *LORB*, p. 129.

7   Rupert Brooke, 'The Old Vicarage, Grantchester', *Collected Poems with a Memoir by Edward Marsh* (1918).

8   Hassall, *Brooke*, p. 216.

9   RCB P/11, Rupert Brooke, 'Democracy and the Arts', typescript, 24 November 1910.

10   Hassall, *Brooke*, p. 374.

11   Brooke, 'The Old Vicarage, Grantchester, *Collected Poems*.

12   Brooke to Katherine 'Ca' Cox, 26 January 1912, *LORB*, p. 355.

13   Delaney, *The Neo-Pagans*, p. 110.

14   RCB L/1, Brooke to 'My dear', undated letter [1914].

15   Rupert Brooke to Cox, January 1912, *LORB*, p. 349.

16   Brooke to Cox, 26 January 1912, *LORB*, p. 355.

17   Brooke, 'Love'.

18   RCB Xb/1, Edward Marsh's annotated review of *Poems* (1911), published in *Poetry Review*, April 1912.

19   *Daily Chronicle*, 9 April 1912.

20   Brooke, 'The Old Vicarage, Grantchester', *Georgian Poetry 1911–1912* (1912).

21   RCB M/19.2, Rupert Brooke, diary fragments, 24 April 1912.

22   'The Old Vicarage, Grantchester', *Georgian Poetry*.

23   Marsh, 'Preparatory Note', *Georgian Poetry, 1911–1912* (1912).

24   'The Old Vicarage, Grantchester'; 'Dust'; 'The Fish'; 'Town and Country'; and 'Dining-room Tea'.

25   Brooke to Keynes, August 1907, *LORB*, p. 99.

26   Brooke to Harold Monro, October 1913, *LORB*, p. 520.

27   Brooke, 'Clouds', *Collected Poems*.

28   Brooke, *Letters from America* (1916), pp. 59–60.

29   Ibid., p. 62.

30   Ibid., p. 68.

31   Ibid., p. 83.

32   Ibid., pp. 145–46.

33   Ibid., p. 159.

34   Ibid., p. 181.

35   Brooke to Mary Brooke, 15 December 1913, *LORB*, p. 545.

36   Brooke to Marsh, 7 March 1913, *LORB*, p. 564.

Notes to Chapter 3: Self-mobilisation

1   RCB L/8/28b, Marsh to Brooke, 10 August 1914.
2   Brooke to Catherine Nesbitt, 12 August 1914, *LORB*, p. 607.
3   Siegfried Sassoon, *Memoirs of a Fox-Hunting Man* (1928), p. 227.
4   Brooke, 'I. Peace', *1914 and Other Poems*.
5   RCB/5/L/3, Brooke to Jacques Raverat, 1 August 1914.
6   Niall Ferguson, *The Pity of War* (1998), p. 184.
7   Brooke to Eileen Wellesley, 1 August 1914, *LORB*, p. 603.
8   Brooke to Marsh, 7 March 1913, *LORB*, p. 564.
9   RCB 5/L/11, Brooke to Marsh, 1 August 1914.
10 New York Public Library, Berg Collection, The Papers of T. E. Hulme, T. E. Hulme to Edward Marsh, undated letter [spring 1915].
11 RCB 5/L/3, Brooke to Jacques Raverat, 6 August 1914.
12 The first mention of the poems occurs in a letter to Marsh on 24 August 1914, quoted in Christopher Hassall, *Edward Marsh: Patron of the Arts* (1959), p. 294.
13 Kieth Hale, ed., *Friends and Apostles: The Correspondence of Rupert Brooke and James Strachey, 1905–1914* (1998), p. 261.
14 Brooke to Rosalind Murray, 20 November 1914, *LORB*, p. 634.
15 Duncan Wilson, *Gilbert Murray, OM, 1866–1957* (1987), pp. 70–71.
16 Gilbert Murray, 'How Can War Ever Be Right?', *Oxford Pamphlets* (1914), p. 3.
17 Garrett Mattingly, *Renaissance Diplomacy* (1955), p. 129.
18 Murray, 'How Can War Ever Be Right?', p. 4.
19 Ibid., p. 18.
20 See John Horn and Alan Kramer, *German Atrocities 1914: A History of Denial* (2001) for the definitive account of international reporting on the behaviour of the German army in Belgium in 1914.
21 Murray, 'How Can War Ever Be Right?', pp. 14–15.
22 Ibid., p. 21.
23 Ibid., p. 18.
24 Ibid., p. 24.
25 Brooke, 'An Unusual Young Man', in *Letters from America*, p. 215.
26 Ibid., p. 217.
27 Ibid., p. 218.
28 Ibid., p. 219.
29 Ibid., p. 222.
30 Ibid., p. 219.
31 Ibid., p. 220.
32 RCB V/1/f.16.
33 Brooke, 'An Unusual Young Man', in *Letters from America*, p. 221.
34 Ibid., p. 222.

35 Murray, 'How Can War Ever Be Right?', p. 24.
36 Brooke, 'I. Peace', *1914 and Other Poems*.
37 'III. The Dead', ibid.
38 'II. Safety', ibid.

Notes to Chapter 4: Enlistment

1   Adrian Gregory, 'British "War Enthusiasm" in 1914: A Reassessment', in Gail Braybon, ed., *Evidence, History and the Great War: Historians and the Impact of 1914–1918* (2003), p. 81.
2   RCB 5/L/3, Brooke to Jacques Raverat, 24 September 1914.
3   RCB 5/L/9, Brooke to Eileen Wellesley, 19 August 1915.
4   As Stephen Greenblatt writes about *Utopia* and another self-fashioning Englishman, Thomas More: 'the fantasy of self-annihilation may be indulged in playfully without real loss'. Greenblatt, *Renaissance Self-Fashioning from More to Shakespeare* (1980), p. 54.
5   Quoted in Hassall, *Brooke*, p. 457.
6   Gervas Huxley, *Both Hands: An Autobiography* (1970), p. 52.
7   Brooke, 'V. The Soldier', *1914 and Other Poems*. My italics.
8   RCB 5/L/11, Brooke to Edward Dent, 5 November 1914.
9   Issac Rosenberg, 'On Receiving News of the War', in Jean Liddiard, ed., *Isaac Rosenberg: Selected Poems and Letters* (2003), p. 61.
10 RCB Xa/10, 'Application for Appointment to a Commission', 12 September 1914.
11 RCB L/1, Brooke to Wellesley, 15–17 August 1914.
12 RCB 5/L/3, Brooke to Jacques Raverat, 24 September 1914.
13 Brooke to Andrew Gow, 22 August 1914, quoted in Hassall, *Brooke*, p. 460.
14 Ibid., p. 462.
15 RCB Xa/10. Marsh notes this on the envelope to the commission now in the archives at King's, explaining, 'He sent it to use, but they had given him the commission on my recommendation, so it wasn't wanted'.
16 Leonard Sellers, The Hood Battalion, Royal Naval Division: Antwerp, Gallipoli, France 1914–1918 (1995), p. 139.
17 RCB 5/L/5, Brooke to Cox, 16 December 1914.
18 RCB 5/L/5, Brooke to Cox, December 1914.
19 RCB 5/L/7, Brooke to Mary Brooke, 12 November 1914.
20 Hassall, *Brooke*, p. 472.
21 Ibid., p. 473.
22 RCB 5/L/7, Brooke to Mary Brooke, 13 November 1914.
23 Hassall, *Brooke*, p. 473.
24 RCB 5/L/5, Brooke to Cox, 30 November 1914.

25   RCB 5/L/3, Brooke to Jacques Raverat, 24 September 1914.
26   RCB 5/L/11, Brooke to Rosalind Murray, 20 November 1914.
27   RCB L/1, Brooke to 'My dear', September 1914.
28   RCB 5/L/11, Brooke to Dent, 2 November 1914.
29   RCB 5/L/3, Brooke to Jacques Raverat, 24 September 1914.
30   RCB 5/L/3, Brooke to Jacques Raverat, 6 August 1914.
31   RCB 5/L/5, Brooke to Cox, 5 November 1914.
32   RCB 5/L/8, Brooke to John Drinkwater, 15 January 1915.
33   Brooke, 'I. Peace', *1914 and Other Poems.*
34   Brooke to Rosalind Murray, 20 November 1914, *LORB*, p. 634.
35   RCB 4/P/20, Brooke, 'Mr. Ripe', in 'Notebook, March–April 1915'.

Notes to Chapter 5: War and Waiting

1   RCB 5/L/7, Brooke to Mary Brooke, 22 February 1915.
2   Hassall, *Brooke*, p. 462.
3   Leonard Smith, *The Embattled Self: French Soldiers' Testimony of the Great War* (2007), p. 43.
4   Hew Strachan, *The First World War: To Arms, Volume 1* (2001), p. 201.
5   Sellers, *Hood Battalion*, pp. 19–24.
6   Imperial War Museum Archive Centre [hereafter abbreviated as IWMAC] 06/49/1, John Baylis, ed., 'Antwerp Diary of H. P. Baylis', p. 41.
7   The casualties from the operation amounted to 5 killed, 64 wounded, and 2,040 missing. Sellers, *Hood Battalion*, p. 26.
8   Robin Prior, *Churchill's World Crisis as History* (1983), pp. 27–28.
9   Winston Churchill, quoted in Douglas Jarrold, *The Royal Naval Division* (1923), p. 327.
10   Jay Winter, 'Introduction: Henri Barbusse and the Birth of the Moral Witness', in Henri Barbusse, *Under Fire* (2003), p. viii.
11   RCB 5/L/11, Brooke to Rosalind Murray, 20 November 1914.
12   RCB 6/M/19, Brooke, Diary, 5–9 October 1914.
13   While some poets began drafts of their work on the front lines, Robert Graves, Siegfried Sassoon, Charles Sorley, and Wilfred Owen, to name just a few, all completed their poems either on leave or from the rear. Rosenberg, who, as a private, was afforded very limited leave, sent home his poems on scraps of paper caked in mud.
14   RCB 5/L/3, Brooke to Gwen Raverat, October 1914.
15   RCB 5/L/1, Brooke to Rosaline Murray, 20 November 1914.
16   IWMAC 06/49/1, Baylis, 'Antwerp Diary', p. 37.
17   RCB 5/L/1, Drinkwater to Brooke, 1 January 1915.
18   James Strachey to Lytton Strachey, 15 October 1915, quoted in Hale, *Friends and Apostles*, pp. 281–82.

19 RCB 5/L/1, Brooke to Rosalind Murray, 20 November 1914.

20 Brooke to Nesbitt, 17 October 1914, *LORB*, p. 624.

21 Wellington House distributed Murray's pamphlets in multiple languages throughout the war. His contribution to the war effort in this semi-official capacity includes 'Ethical Problems of the War' and 'How Can War Ever Be Right?' in 1915, and 'The Impressions of Scandinavia in War Time' and 'The United States and the War' in 1916. IWMAC 114/560, 525.69. Appendix, 'Schedule of Literature', *Schedule of Literature for Wellington House, 1916*.

22 RCB 5/L/5, Brooke to Cox, 16 December 1914.

23 RCB 5/L/3, Brooke to Jacques Raverat, 6 August 1914.

24 RCB 6/M/24, Brooke, Anson Battalion Notebook, October–November 1914.

25 RCB 5/L/5, Brooke to Cox, 30 November 1914.

26 RCB 5/L/5, Brooke to Cox, 21 October 1914.

27 RCB 5/L/5, Brooke To Cox, 22 January 1915.

28 Sellers, *Hood Battalion*, p. 40.

29 Delaney, *The Neo-Pagans*, pp. 84–85.

30 RCB 5/L/7, Brooke to Mary Brooke, 15 September 1914.

31 RCB 5/l/5, Brooke to Cox, 27 November 1914.

32 RCB 5/L/7, Brooke to Mary Brooke, 24 October 1914.

33 RCB 5/L/7, Brooke to Mary Brooke, October–December 1914.

34 Hassall, *Brooke*, p. 475.

35 RCB 5/L/7, Brooke to Mary Brooke, November 11 1914.

36 Jay Winter, 'The Practices of Metropolitan Life in Wartime', in Jay Winter and Jean-Louis Robert, eds., *Capital Cities at War: Paris, London, Berlin 1914–1919, Volume 2: A Cultural History* (2007), pp. 2–3.

37 RCB 5/L/5, Brooke to Cox, 28 October 1914.

38 Brooke to Andrew Gow, 22 August 1914, quoted in Hassall, *Brooke*, p. 460.

39 RCB 5/L/9, Brooke to Wellesley, 19 August 1915.

40 RCB 5/L/11, Brooke to E. J. Dent, 5 November 1914.

41 RCB 5/L/1, Brooke to Rosalind Murray, 20 November 1914.

42 Brooke to G. Lowes Dickinson, 28 October 1914, *LORB*, p. 627.

43 RCB 5/L/11, Brooke to Dent, 5 November 1914.

44 RCB 5/L/3, Brooke to Gwen Raverat, 10 October 1914.

45 RCB 5/L/7, Brooke to Mary Brooke, 3 November 1914.

46 Hassall, *Brooke*, p. 469.

47 RCB 5/L/11, Brooke to Murray, 20 November 1914.

48 RCB 5/L/11, Brooke to Dent, 5 November 1914.

49 RCB 5/L/11, Brooke to Rosalind Murray, 20 November 1914.

50 RCB 5/L/5, Brooke to Cox, 10 January 1915.

51 Simon Schama, *Landscape and Memory* (1995), p. 450.

Notes to Chapter 6: The War Sonnets

1   Keynes, Preface, *Poetical Works*, pp. 7–8.
2   The three sonnets most heavily referred to and quoted from during the war were: 'I. Peace'; 'III. The Dead' (reference above); 'V. The Soldier'. The alternative version of 'IV. The Dead', alongside 'II. Safety', which are both grouped together as a series of five, were composed well before the outbreak of war, and hence belong to Brooke's pre-war body of work. As far as I have found, they were never cited in newspaper articles during the war. However, Brooke did place them together in *New Numbers*, perhaps for the practical purposes of needing more poems for that publication, and because they seemed indicative of sentiments similar to the three composed in response to the war, thereby forming a bridge between his own 'peace' and 'war' mentalities. This is not something that he expressed directly in his letters, but it seems a likely explanation.
3   Santanu Das, *Touch and Intimacy in First World War Literature* (2005), p. 43.
4   RCB 5/L/9, Brooke to Wellesley, 19 August 1914.
5   RCB 6/M/25, Brooke, Notebook, November–December 1914.
6   Including Dean Ralph Inge and Charles Sorley, to name two. See Chapters 8 and 15 respectively for further discussion of critical reactions to Brooke's War Sonnets.
7   Jon Stallworthy, 'Rupert Brooke', in Tim Cross, ed., *The Lost Voices of World War I* (1998), p. 54.
8   Hassall, *Brooke*, p. 472.
9   One need only call to mind any twentieth- or twenty-first-century war film to affirm how culturally prevalent the ideal of unit camaraderie has become in Western society.
10 Brooke, 'I. Peace', *1914 and Other Poems*.
11 'III. The Dead', ibid.
12 RCB/5/L/5, Brooke to Raverat, 21 December 1914.
13 See C. M. Bowra, *Poetry and Politics, 1900–1960* (1966).
14 Most often mentioned are *The Times* and the *Nation*, as well as the literary journal *Land and Water*.
15 Delaney, *The Neo-Pagans*, p. 84. Brooke's allowance of £150 per annum, added to his freelance earnings and officer's pay, was more than the vast majority British soldiers were capable of earning in 1914–15. However, given the wealthy individuals that he regularly associated with, it becomes easier to understand how Brooke's concerns over his relative social and financial position might at least have been in his mind when he wrote the War Sonnets.
16 RCB 5/L/1, Frank Sidgwick to Brooke, 24 October 1914.

17 RCB 4/P/20, Brooke, Notebook, 'Fragment'.
18 Charles Péguy (1873–1914) was shot in the forehead near Villeroy, Seine-et-Marne on September 1914, the day before the beginning of the Battle of the Marne.
19 RCB 5/L/11, Brooke to Dent, 5 November 1914.
20 Denis E. Showalter, 'Manoeuvre Warfare', in Strachan, ed., *The Oxford Illustrated History of the First World War* (1998), p. 43.
21 Overall British losses in the First World War were also low compared with her allies and enemies, and the nation mobilised fewer man. See Dan Todman, *The Great War, Myth and Memory* (2005), p. 45.
22 Brooke to Drinkwater, quoted in Hassall, *Brooke*, pp. 480–81.
23 Edmund Wilson, 'Hemingway: Gauge of Morale', *Eight Essays* (1954), p. 97. Examples of this ideal abound, from Lord Byron in England – and beyond – to Marat in revolutionary France.
24 Brooke, 'Clouds', in Keynes, *Poetical Works*.
25 Timothy Rogers, *Rupert Brooke: A Reassessment* (1971), p. 8. Rogers also suggest that it is possible that contemporary leaders, specifically in the *Morning Post*, may have offered some inspiration for the War Sonnets, possibly even providing some of their expressions.
26 RCB 1/V/22, Notebook, 'Fragment', January 1915. Brooke was friendly with both Arthur and Violet Asquith, and as a result spent bits of his leave from camp in London at the home of the prime minister.
27 Brooke, 'II. Safety', *1914 and Other Poems* (1915).
28 'III. The Dead', ibid.
29 'V. The Soldier', ibid.
30 Hassall, *Brooke*, p. 484.
31 RCB 5/L/9, Brooke to Nesbitt, 7 August 1914.
32 This is discussed in greater depth in Part II.
33 For an assessment of Byron's national and international appeals, as well as how politics intertwined with poetry in his writing, see Paul Stock, *The Shelly–Byron Circle and the Idea of Europe* (2010).
34 Smith, *Embattled Self*, p. 10.
35 Rosa Marie Bracco, *Merchants of Hope: British Middlebrow Writers and the First World War* (1993), p. 12.
36 Hynes, *A War Imagined: The First World War and English Culture* (1990), p. 47.
37 RCB 5/L/1, Wilfrid Gibson to Brooke, 13 January 1915.
38 RCB 5/L/1, John Masefield to Brooke, 11 February 1915.
39 See RCB 5/L/1, Drinkwater to Brooke, January 1915.
40 Brooke, 'III. The Dead', *1914 and Other Poems*.
41 'V. The Soldier', ibid.
42 Elizabeth Vandiver, 'Early Poets of the First World War', in Das, ed., *The Cambridge Companion to the Poetry of the First World War* (2013), p. 76.

43   Brooke to Sybil Pye, 21 March 1915, quoted in Hale, *Friends and Apostles*, p. 282.

Notes to Chapter 7: Transport

1   RCB 5/L/3, Brooke to Raverat, 8 March 1915.
2   Violet Asquith to Rupert Brooke, 12 March 1915, in Mark Pottle, ed., *Champion Redoubtable: The Diary and Letters of Violet Bonham Carter, 1914–1945* (1998), p. 32.
3   RCB 5/3, Brooke to Jacques Raverat, 8 March 1915.
4   RCB 4/P/20, Brooke, Notebook, November 1914–February 1915.
5   RCB 5/L/5, Brooke to Cox, 8 March 1915.
6   RCB 5/L/3, Brooke to Jacques Raverat, 8 March 1915.
7   Sellers, *Hood Battalion*, p. 57.
8   RCB 5/L/7, Brooke to Mary Brooke, 15 April 1915.
9   RCB 1/V/13, Brooke, Notebook, March–April 1915, p. 18.
10   Brooke, 'Fragment', in Keynes, *The Poetical Works*.
11   Das, Touch and Intimacy, p. 94.
12   RCB 5/L/5, Brooke to Cox, 8 March 1915.
13   RCB 5/L/3, Brooke to Raverat, 8 March 1915.
14   RCB 5/L/5, Brooke to Cox, 1 March 1915.
15   RCB 5/L/7, Brooke to Mary Brooke, 22 February, 1915.
16   RCB 5/L/3, Brooke to Raverat, 1 August 1914.
17   RCB 1/V/13, Brooke, Notebook, March–April 1915, p. 8.
18   Stallworthy, 'Brooke', p. 54.
19   RCB 1/V/13, Brooke, Notebook, March–April 1915, p. 5.
20   Brooke, 'V. The Soldier', *1914 and Other Poems*.
21   Edmund Blunden, *Undertones of War* (1928), p. xi.
22   Hassall, *Brooke*, p. 487.
23   RCB 5/L/5, Brooke to Cox, 10 March 1915.
24   Smith, *Embattled Self*, pp. 62–63.
25   RCB 5/L/5, Brooke to Cox, 19–24 March 1915.
26   RCB 5/L/3, Brooke to Raverat, 8 March 1915.
27   RCB 5/L/3, Brooke to Raverat, 21 December 1914.
28   Brooke to Violet Asquith, 9 April 1915, in Pottle, *Champion*, p. 37.
29   Brooke to Sybil Pye, 21 March 1915, quoted in Hale, *Friends and Apostles*, p. 282.

Notes to Chapter 8: Patriotic Poetry

1   Louis Oppenheim, Poster, 'Wir Barbaren!', in Gerhard Hirschfeld, Gerd Krumeich, Irina Renz, and Markus Pöhlman, eds., *Enzyklopädie Erster Weltkrieg* (2003), p. 371.

2   *Nation* (New York), June 1915.

3   Peter Buitenhuis, *The Great War of Words: British, American and Canadian Propaganda and Fiction, 1914–1933* (1987), p. 12.

4   Collected in *Letters and Diary of Alan Seeger* (1917). See also Alisa Miller, 'An American soldier-poet': Alan Seeger and war culture in the United States, 1914–1918', *First World War Studies* 1:1 (2010), pp. 15–33.

5   *New Republic*, 22 May 1915.

6   See Ted Bogacz, 'A Tyranny of Words', *Journal of Modern History* 58 (1986), pp. 643–68.

7   Rudyard Kipling, 'The Battle of Jutland', *Daily Telegraph*, 19–31 October 1916.

8   Hynes, *War Imagined*, p. 110.

9   Michael Saunders and Philip Taylor, *British Propaganda during the First World War, 1914–1918* (1982), p. 31.

10 The House of Lords, The Papers of David Lloyd George [hereafter abbreviated as LG] C/3/7/5F, F. E. Smith to David Lloyd George, 9 September 1914.

11 George Creel, quoted in Stanley Coben, *Reform, War and Reaction: 1912–1932* (1972), p. 92.

12 Troy R. E. Paddock, Introduction, in Troy R. E. Paddock, ed., *A Call to Arms: Propaganda, Public Opinion, and Newspapers in the Great War* (2004), p. 3.

13 LG C/11/3/44, Ivor P. Nicholson to Lloyd George, 31 March 1915.

14 Winter, 'Popular Culture in Wartime Britain', in Aviel Roshwald and Richard Stites, eds., *European Culture in Wartime Britain: The Arts, Entertainment, and Propaganda, 1914–1918* (1999), p. 347.

15 Hynes, *Edwardian Turn*, p. 71.

16 Olive Anderson, *A Liberal State: English Politics and Economics during the Crimean War* (1967), p. 71.

17 *Sheffield Daily Telegram*, 24 November 1915.

18 Geoffrey Dawson officially changed his surname from 'Robinson' to 'Dawson' in 1920. For the purposes in consistency of citations, particularly those dealing with his personal papers, he is referred to as 'Dawson' throughout this book.

19 Dawson to 'Fraser', 23 June 1915, The Bodleian Library, Oxford, Modern Papers, The Papers of Geoffrey Dawson [hereafter abbreviated as GD] 65:5–6.

20 GD 66.62–8, Dawson, 'Memorandum', 30 May 1916.

21 GD 65.14–15, Dawson to 'Fraser', 6 July 1915.

22 John Evelyn Wrench, *Geoffrey Dawson and Our Times* (1955), p. 109.

23 *The Times*, 20 May 1915.

24 Bowra, *Poetry and Politics*, pp. 14–15.

25 Paul Fussell, *The Great War and Modern Memory* (2000), pp. 25–26.

26 Edmund Blunden, *Thomas Hardy* (1941), p. 141.

27 Gregory, 'A Clash of Cultures: The British Press and the Opening of the Great War', in *A Call to Arms: Propaganda, Public Opinion and Newspapers in the Great War* (2004), p. 31.

28 *The Times*, 23 November 1914.

29 Fussell, *Great War*, p. 21.

30 GD 64.13, Dawson to Lord Northcliffe, 23 February 1914.

31 *The Times*, 3 September 1914.

32 *Times Literary Supplement*, 3 September 1914.

33 Bracco, *Merchants*, p. 6.

34 Historian have recently reconsidered the extent to which religious institutions were mobilised during the war concluding that religion was 'far more important to individuals in wartime Britain than is generally believed'. See Gregory, *The Last Great War: British Society and the First World War* (2008), p. 183

35 Hassall, *Marsh*, p. 321.

36 RCB Xb/2, Dean William Ralph Inge, 'Why the dead shall live', March/April 1915.

37 Patrick Porter, 'Slaughter or Sacrifice? The Religious Rhetoric of Blood Sacrifice in the British and German Armies, 1914–1918', University of Oxford, DPhil. thesis, 2005, pp. 217–18.

38 *The Times*, 19 November 1915.

39 RBC Xb/2, Ralph Inge to Mary Brooke.

40 *Christian World Pulpit*, 17 November 1915.

41 *The Times*, 5 April 1915.

Notes to Chapter 9: Public Death

1 RCB 9/Xc, Diary of General Sir Ian Hamilton, 23 April 1915.

2 Armando Petrucci, *Writing the Dead: Death and Writing Strategies in the Western Tradition* (1998), p. xvii.

3 John Stevenson, *British Society 1914–1945* (1984), p. 43.

4 See John Wolf, *Great Deaths: Grieving, Religion and Nationhood in Victorian and Edwardian Britain* (2000) and Pat Jalland, *Death in the Victorian Family* (1996) for extended discussions of death practices in relation to public and private culture in the years leading up to the First World War.

5   Masterman to Vaughan Nash, 16 December 1915, University of Birmingham, Special Collections, The Papers of C. F. G. Masterman [hereafter abbreviated as CFGM] 6/2/22.

6   CFGM 6/6/4/1, Wilfrid Meynell to Masterman, 18 January 1917.

7   See Winter, *Sites of Memory, Sites of Mourning: The Great War in European Cultural History* (1995) for the fullest account of this period.

8   Mark Connelly, *The Great War, Memory and Ritual Commemoration in the City and East London* (2002), p. 31.

9   *The Times*, 6 January 1915.

10 In addition to critical obituaries, Eliot would later dedicate *Prufrock and other Observations* (1917) to the poet Jean Verdenal, like Brooke, 'mort aux Dardanelles'.

11 Marysa Demoor, 'From Epitaph to Obituary: The Death Politics of T. S. Eliot and Ezra Pound', *Biography* 28 (2005), p. 257.

12 T. S. Eliot, 'Poems by Alan Seeger', *Egoist* 4 (1917), p. 172.

13 William Haley, 'Rest in Prose: The Art of the Obituary', *American Scholar* 46 (1977), p. 209.

14 *The Times*, 6 January 1915.

15 *Globe*, 24 April 1915.

16 *Pall Mall Gazette*, 24 April 1915.

17 *Globe*, 24 April 1915.

18 *Pall Mall Gazette*, 24 April 1915.

19 Keith Hale contends that Marsh in fact wrote the obituary. See Hale, *Friends and Apostles*, p. 271. While any evidence of Marsh's marking is missing from *The Times* original, it is likely that he contributed significantly to the drafting. Hassall, friend to Marsh and biographer of both Marsh and Brooke, more specifically claims that Marsh contributed the final two lines of the second section of the obituary: 'He died before he had fulfilled ... life full of promise joyfully laid down', although this is not justified by *The Times* proofs, which attribute the section to Arthur Clutton-Brock. Regardless, Hassall considers Churchill's contribution as pre-eminent, stating that 'Marsh's few sentences were only a preface to a valediction published over the initials of the First Lord of the Admiralty'. Hassall, *Brooke*, p. 515.

20 Clutton-Brock was a leader writer for *The Times* and general essayist from 1908 to 1924.

21 A. Clutton-Brock, 'Sweden and the Anglo-Russian Alliance' (1915); IWM 114/560, 525.69, Appendix, 'Schedule of Literature', *Second Report on the Work Conducted for the Government at Wellington House*.

22 Asquith to Venetia Stanley, quoted in Martin Gilbert, *Winston S. Churchill, Volume 3, 1914–1916* (1971), p. 130.

23 David Stevenson, *Cataclysm: The First World War as Political Tragedy* (2004), pp. 164–65.

24   RCB Xc/1, Telegram, Admiralty to V. A. Mudros (John Churchill), 23 April 1915.

25   RCB Xc/6, John Churchill to Winston Churchill, 24 April 1915.

26   RCB Xc/17, Telegram, General Sir Ian Hamilton to Marsh, 23 April 1915.

27   Brooke to Mary Brooke, 5 April 1915, *LORB*, p. 675.

28   Brooke to Marsh, April 1915, *LORB*, p. 680.

29   *The Times*, 26 April 1915.

30   Jan Rüger, 'Entertainments', in Winter and Robert, *Capital Cities, Volume 2*, p. 109.

31   *The Times*, 26 April 1915.

32   This became a marked feature of some post-war literature and of political discourses around hierarchies of sacrifice and general disillusionment. See, for instance, George Mosse, *Fallen Soldiers: Reshaping the Memory of the World Wars* (1990); Fussell, *Great War*; and Robert Gerwarth, *The Vanquished: Why the First World War Failed to End* (2016).

33   *The Times*, 26 April 1915.

34   Brooke, 'III. The Dead', *1914 and Other Poems*.

35   'The Soldier', ibid.

36   Bogacz, 'Tyranny', p. 643.

37   See Pierre Nora, *Realms of Memory: The Construction of the French Past* (1992).

38   *The Times*, 26 April 1915.

39   *Globe*, 27 April 1915.

40   *The Times*, 17 June 1915.

41   *The Times*, 25 November 1915.

42   *The Times*, 6 May 1915.

43   See Winter, *Sites of Memory* and Gavin Stamp, *The Memorial to the Missing of the Somme* (2006) to name but two sources that present an in-depth assessment of post-war memorialisation practices.

44   *The Times*, 26 April 1915.

45   RCB Xd/19, Mary Brooke, clippings album.

46   RCB V-21, Marsh, 'Note' to *1914 and Other Poems*.

Notes to Chapter 10: Syndication

1   *Sketch*, 12 May 1915.

2   *The Times*, 26 April 1915.

3   *Sketch*, 12 May 1915.

4   Connelly, *Great War*, p. 25.

5   *Sketch*, 12 May 1915.

6   Erez Manela, *The Wilsonian Moment: Self-determination and the International Origins of Anticolonial Nationalism* (2007), pp. 45–53.

7   Paris, *Images*, p. 82.
8   This had a longer history beyond the First World War. See Jonathan Marwil, *Visiting Modern War in Risorgimento Italy* (2010) and in particular, pp. 77–96.
9   Vanessa R. Schwartz, *Spectacular Realities: Early Mass Culture in fin-de-siècle Paris* (1998), p. 2.
10 Winter, 'Popular Culture', pp. 347–48.
11 Jane Potter, 'For Country, Conscience and Commerce: Publishers and Publishing, 1914–1918', in Mary Hammond and Shafquart Towhead, eds., *Publishing in the First World War: Essays in Book History* (2007), p. 11.
12 *Book Monthly*, Autumn 1915.
13 *Westminster Gazette*, 1 May 1915.
14 *Echo*, 26 April 1915.
15 *Northampton Mercury*, 1 May 1915.
16 *Daily Citizen*, 27 April 1915.
17 *Nation*, 1 May 1915.
18 *Daily News*, 29 April 1915.
19 *Nation*, 1 May 1915.
20 H. A. Cocks, '"Sporty" Girls and "Artistic" Boys: Friendship, Illicit Sex, and the British "Companionship" Advertisement, 1913–1928', *Journal of the History of Sexuality* 11 (2002), p. 458. Cocks asserts that the increased discussion of sexuality in newspapers had its limits, as revealed by the June 1921 trial of the *Link* for helping to facilitate connections between a group of homosexual males through a series of 'companionship' advertisements. The terminology used by the offenders included phrases such as 'Oxonian … 26'; 'brilliant, courteous, humorous … future novelist, in love with beauty … and masculine', *Link* (September 1920), p. 9, quoted in Cocks, '"Sporty" Girls', p. 459.
21 *Birmingham Gazette*, 27 April 1915.
22 *Globe*, 24 April 1915.
23 *The Times*, 26 April 1915.
24 *Globe*, 24 April 1915.
25 *Daily News*, 27 April 1915.
26 *Daily Sketch*, 28 April 1915.
27 *Nation*, 1 May 1915.
28 *Sunderland Echo*, 27 April 1915.
29 *Daily Telegraph*, 27 April 1915.
30 *Birmingham Gazette*, 4 May 1915.
31 *Sketch*, 12 May 1915.
32 *Sunderland Echo*, 27 April 1915.
33 *Pall Mall Gazette*, 24 April 1915.

34   Paul Fussell has written about the standardisation of language during the war, particularly between the front and the home front. See Fussell, *Great War*, pp. 184–85.

35   Hynes, *War Imagined*, p. 110.

36   *Free Thinker*, 16 May 1915.

37   *Sketch*, 12 May 1915.

38   Hassall, *Brooke*, p. 503.

39   *The Times*, 26 April 1915.

40   *Star*, 26 April 1915.

41   *Sheffield Daily Telegraph*, 24 November 1915.

42   *The Times*, 5 April 1915. This was the article covering Inge's Easter sermon at St Paul's, reporting that the Dean 'ventured to think' that the young writer would 'take rank with our great poets'.

43   Connelly, *Great War*, p. 25.

44   *Bookman*, July 1915.

45   *Pall Mall Gazette*, 7 July 1915.

46   *Bristol*, 10 July 1915.

47   *Aberdeen Free Press*, 28 September 1915.

48   Examples include *The Times*, 5 April 1915; *Sunderland Echo*, 27 April 1915; *Daily Telegraph*, 27 April 1915; *Saturday Westminster Gazette*, 8 May 1915; *Birmingham Gazette*, 4 May 1915; *Scotsman*, 1 May 1915; *Dewsbury Reporter*, 1 May 1915.

49   Mary Brooke, left alone in Rugby following the loss of a husband and two sons to illness, and one son to injuries sustained in battle, did immediately involve herself in his literary estate.

50   Hassall, *Marsh*, p. 441.

51   IWMAC, Papers relating to Rupert Brooke Mis. 230.328, Alfred Brooke to Mary Brooke, undated letter [May 1915].

52   *Daily Sketch*, 25 June 1915.

53   *Rugby Observer*, 18 June 1915.

54   IWMAC, 88/52/1, Captain Sir George N. Clark, ed., Narrative of the First Battalion, The Post Office Rifles, 8th Battalion, The London Regiment in France and Flanders 1915–1918.

55   *Millgate Monthly*, December 1915.

Notes to Chapter 11: Image

1   *The Times*, 6 August 1915.

2   *Bookman*, Special Christmas Number, 1917.

3   Michael Paris, Warrior Nation: Images of War in British Popular Culture, 1850–2000 (2000), p. 82.

4   *The Times*, 7 May 1915.

5   *Punch*, 30 June 1915.

6   *1914 and Other Poems* was already in its sixth impression.

7   *The Times*, 9 August 1915.

8   Explored in Benedict Anderson, *Imagined Communities: Reflections on the Origin and Spread of Nationalism* (1991).

9   *Land and Water*, 30 December 1915.

10 John Ireland, *The Soldier* [musical score] (1917).

11 *Musical Opinion*, October 1918.

12 *Bookman*, Special Christmas Number, 1917.

13 See James Fox, 'British Art and the First World War, 1914–1919', *Art History* 36.4 (September 2013), 810–33 for a discussion of different forms of portraiture during the war.

14 The few informal images of Brooke in uniform to survive would probably not have been deemed professional enough to be included in published volumes.

15 Alan Kramer, *Dynamic of Destruction: Culture and Mass Killing in the First World War* (2007), p. 2.

16 *Nation*, 1 May 1915.

17 *Daily Sketch*, 28 April 1915.

18 *Globe*, 24 April 1915.

19 *Birmingham Mail*, 26 April 1915.

20 *Pall Mall Gazette*, 24 April 1915.

21 *Times Literary Supplement*, 8 August 1918.

22 Joanna Bourke, *Dismembering the Male: Men's Bodies, Britain and the Great War* (1996), p. 221. This study offers a full and fascinating history of the unresolved cultural history of the war's legacy of disfigurement.

23 Writing about the almost irresistible urge to capture and examine the physiognomies of fellow humans for how and where they fit into their particular worlds, and ours, particularly after they have died, in his essay from 1931, Walter Benjamin concluded that, 'Whether people come from the Left or the Right, they will have to get used to being inspected for signs of provenance. And they in turn will have to scrutinize others'. See Walter Benjamin, 'Small History of Photography', in Walter Benjamin, *On Photography*, Esther Leslie, transl., ed. (2015), p. 87.

24 Brooke to Nesbitt, April 1913, *LORB*, p. 447.

25 RCB Xg/10, Emery Walker to Mary Brooke, 26 March 1917.

26 RCB Xg/9, Walker to Marsh, 14 November 1919.

27 *Amateur Photographed and Photographic News*, 10 May 1915.

28 Hassall, *Brooke*, p. 447.

29 *The Times*, 26 April 1915.

30 Hassall, *Brooke*, p. 390.

31 *New Statesman*, 2 December 1916.

32   Woollacott, '"Khaki fever" and its control: gender, class, age and sexual morality on the British home front in the First World War', *Journal of Contemporary History* 29 (1994), p. 328.

33   Ibid., p. 325.

34   *Globe*, 27 April 1915.

35   James to Marsh, 6 June 1915, in Horne, *Henry James*, p. 548.

36   *Nation*, 1 May 1915.

37   *Country Life*, 8 April 1916.

38   See Delaney, *The Neo-Pagans*, pp. 77–80 for discussion of Brooke's fully articulated encounter with Hugh Russell-Smith.

39   RCB Pr/4, Souvenir of the Royal Naval Division.

40   *The Times*, February 19, 1917.

41   *Land and Water*, 23 August 1917, p. 20.

42   Helen McCartney, *Citizen Soldiers: The Liverpool Territorials in the First World War* (2005), p. 9.

43   *Nation*, 26 June 1915.

44   Alex Pots, '"Constable Country" between the Wars', in Raphael Samuel, ed., *Patriotism: The Making and Unmaking of British National Identity, Volume 3: National Fictions* (1989), p. 165.

45   Brooke, 'I. Peace', *1914 and Other Poems*.

46   'III. The Dead', ibid.

47   'V. The Soldier', ibid.

48   'III. The Dead', ibid.

49   *Glasgow Citizen*, 22 July 1915.

50   *Public Opinion*, 30 April 1915.

51   See *Star*, 5 September 1920; *Manchester Guardian*, 5 September 1928; *Graphic*, 29 September 1928.

52   *Sphere*, 22 January 1916.

53   RCB Xc23, Captain Fred Pepys Cockerell to Sidgwick & Jackson, 14 April 1917.

54   'Le Premier Mort des Dardanelles', *Mercure de France* 131.454 (May 1917), pp. 27–29.

55   The run of this publication was limited to 300 copies per nation.

56   IWMAC 94/2723, Vincent O'Sullivan, transl., *Rupert Brooke's Death and Burial* (1917).

57   Schama, *Landscape and Memory*, p. 15.

58   RCB Xg/10, Walker to Mary Brooke, 26 March 1917.

59   The initial agreement set royalties at 25 per cent of profits, reduced to 20 per cent in September 1916. RCB Xg/9, Sidgwick to Marsh, 26 September 1916.

60   RCB Xg/9, Sidgwick to Marsh, 11 November 1919.

61   RCB Xg/9, Walker to Marsh, 14 November 1914.

62 *The Times*, 9 August 1915.
63 RCB Xg/9, Sidgwick to Marsh, 29 September 1916.
64 RCB Xf/11, Sales figures to 31 December 1920.

Notes to Chapter 12: Patrons

1   RCB Xg/9, Sidgwick to Marsh, 30 September 1915.
2   Brooke to Marsh, 9 March 1915, *LORB*, p. 669. This is the letter in which Brooke set out his intentions vis-à-vis his literary estate.
3   RCB Xg/9, Lascelles Abercrombie to Marsh, 2 April 1917.
4   RCB Xg/9, Abercrombie and Fuller & Son, Ltd., Figures for Tax Purposes, included in a letter to Marsh, 29 November 1920.
5   Further examples include numerous poems such as Abercrombie's, 'R.B'. and Wilfred Gibson's 'Gone', which were sent to *The Times* and the *Nation* respectively in May 1915, and John Drinkwater's article for the *Sphere* on 27 April 1918. Drinkwater and Abercrombie were both quoted in Joyce Kilmer's review of *Collected Poems* for the *New York Times* on 12 September 1915, and de la Mare and Gibson both contributed general articles on verse mentioning Brooke in the same newspaper on 17 December 1916 and 14 January 1917 respectively.
6   Hassall, *Marsh*, p. 391.
7   This was 'printed for the author' by the Chiswick Press, and given a short run of 115 copies.
8   John Drinkwater, *Rupert Brooke: An Essay* (1916), p. 2.
9   RCB Xg/9, Gibson to Marsh, 1 April 1917.
10 Robert Wohl, *The Generation of 1914* (1979), p. 5.
11 Coulson Kernahan, 'Preface', *The Experiences of a Recruiting Officer: True Pictures of Splendid Patriotism* (1915).
12 Marsh to Brown, 4 June 1915, quoted in Hassall, *Marsh*, p. 347.
13 Kernahan, 'Preface', *Experiences*.
14 As outlined, for example, in RCB 5/L/5, Brooke to Cox, 21 October 1914.
15 CFGM 6/2/6, Lord Durham to Herbert Asquith, 26 October 1914.
16 LG C/3/16/13, Churchill to Lloyd George, undated letter [September 1914].
17 LG D/18/1/2, Thomas Marlow to Lloyd George, 25 May 1915.
18 *The Times*, 26 October 1916.
19 *Contemporary Review*, December 1915.
20 *Daily News and Leader*, 28 April 1915.
21 *The Times*, 19 November 1915.
22 *The Times*, 26 October 1916.
23 *The Times*, 8 November 1918.
24 *Cambridge Magazine*, 1 May 1915.

25 *Public Opinion*, 7 May 1915.

26 *Cambridge Magazine*, 1 May 1915.

27 *Contemporary Review*, December 1915.

28 *New Witness*, 13 May 1915.

29 *Sketch*, 12 May 1915.

30 *Contemporary Review*, December 1915.

31 *Free Thinker*, 16 May 1915.

32 *Morning Post*, 20 January 1916.

33 RCB Ag/1, Edmund Goss to Marsh, April 1915.

34 *Daily News and Leader*, 28 April 1915.

35 *Cambridge Magazine*, 1 May 1915.

36 Edward Thomas, 'Rupert Brooke', *English Review*, June 1915, p. 328.

37 Ibid., p. 325.

38 *Daily Chronicle*, 18 June 1915.

39 Thomas, 'England', *English Review*, April 1915, p. 99.

40 Thomas, 'Rupert Brooke', *English Review*, June 1915, p. 328.

41 *Cambridge Magazine*, 1 May 1915.

42 Hermione Lee, *Edith Wharton* (2007), p. 484.

43 *Contemporary Review*, December 1915.

44 Emile Verhaeren, 'Rupert Brooke: Poète et Soldat', in *Les Ailes rouge de la guerre* (1916), p. 167.

45 Verhaeren, 'Ceux de Liège', ibid., p. 25.

46 Verhaeren, 'Rupert Brooke', ibid., p. 169.

47 Ibid., p. 171.

48 *The Times*, 29 November 1916.

49 Verhaeren, 'Rupert Brooke', *Les Ailes*, p. 171.

50 *The Times*, 29 November 1916.

51 *Glasgow News*, 17 February 1916.

52 *Daily Chronicle*, 8 March 1916.

53 *Liverpool Courier*, 8 March 1916.

54 *Sunday Chronicle* (Manchester), 12 March 1916.

55 Ibid.

56 James to Marsh, 6 June 1915, in Horne, *Henry James*, p. 548–49.

57 James, 'Preface', in Brooke, *Letters from America*, p. 39.

58 Ibid., pp. 41–42.

59 Ibid., p. 42.

60 *Liverpool Post*, 8 March 1916.

61 *Daily Mail*, 1 March 1916.

62 *Daily News and Leader*, 8 March 1916.

63 *Sunday Times and Sunday Special*, 12 March 1916.

64 *Dundee Advertiser*, 9 March 1916.

65 *Punch*, 29 March 1916.

66 *Aberdeen Free Press*, 8 March 1916.

67 *Times Literary Supplement*, 9 February 1916.

68 *Manchester Guardian*, 8 March 1916.

69 *Philadelphia North American*, 5 February 1916.

70 *Christian Science Monitor*, 20 April 1916.

71 *New York Times*, 30 January 1916.

72 Ibid.

73 *Saturday Westminster Gazette*, 11 March 1916.

74 James to Marsh, undated letter, quoted in Hassall, *Marsh*, p. 357.

75 Marsh to Asquith, December 1915, ibid., p. 375.

76 Hassall, *Marsh*, p. 441.

77 Marsh to Mary Brooke, 10 May 1916, quoted in Hassall, *Marsh*, p. 391.

78 Mary Brooke to Marsh, May 1916, ibid., p. 387.

79 Marsh to Frank Sidgwick, quoted in Hassall, *Marsh*, p. 385.

80 Mary Brooke, Introductory note in *The Collected Poems of Rupert Brooke* (1918).

81 Marsh, 'Memoir', ibid., p. cxxiii.

82 Denis Brown to Marsh, June 1915, quoted ibid., p. clvi.

83 *Illustrated London News*, 19 October 1918.

84 *Cambridge Review*, 22 November 1918.

85 *Oxford Magazine*, 22 November 1918.

86 *Times Literary Supplement*, 8 August 1918. See Chapter 15 for further discussion of Woolf's reaction to the 'Memoir'.

87 Marsh to Mary Brooke, June 1917, quoted in Hassall, *Marsh*, p. 426.

88 *Town Topics*, 10 August 1918.

89 *Town Topics*, 31 August 1918.

90 *Town Topics*, 14 September 1918. The original letter from Marsh is dated 3 September 1918. RCB 13/Xg/3.

91 Hassall, *Marsh*, p. 439.

92 Verhaeren, 'Rupert Brooke', *Les Ailes*, p. 170.

Notes to Chapter 13: Readers

1 St Clair, *Reading Nation*, p. 1.

2 Ibid.

3 Derek Thomspon, *Hitmakers: How Things Become Popular* (2017), p. 240.

4 Nicoletta F. Gullace, *'The Blood of Our Sons': Men, Women and the Renegotiation of British Citizenship during the Great War* (2002), p. 54.

5 *Westminster Gazette*, 1 May 1915.

6 Vera Brittain, *Chronicle of Youth* (2000), p. 328.

7 Brittain's fiancé Roland Leighton was killed on 23 December 1915, friends Victor Richardson and Robert Thurlow on 9 June and 23 April 1917 respectively, and Edward Brittain on 15 June 1918.

8   Brittain, *Chronicle*, p. 206.

9   Ibid., p. 210.

10   Brittain later became a nurse, and as such confronted what this particular modern war did to men's bodies on a daily basis.

11   Woollacott, "'Khaki Fever'", p. 332.

12   Hynes, *Edwardian Turn*, p. 172.

13   Brooke, 'V. The Soldier', *1914 and Other Poems*.

14   S. Gertrude Ford, 'To the Memory of Rupert Brooke', *A Crown of Amaranth* (1915).

15   Brooke, 'V. The Soldier', *1914 and Other Poems*.

16   Ford, 'To the Memory of Rupert Brooke', *Crown of Amaranth*.

17   *Millgate Monthly*, December 1915.

18   *T.P'.s Weekly*, 1 April 1916.

19   *Oxford Magazine*, 11 May 1917.

20   *Glasgow Herald* in RCB Xg/21, Edward Marsh Clipping's Album.

21   *Reptorian*, December 1915.

22   Brooke, 'IV. The Dead', *1914 and Other Poems*.

23   'V. The Soldier', ibid.

24   *Westminster Gazette*, 12 October 1915.

25   *Nation*, 29 May 1915.

26   *Bookman*, 20 June 1915.

27   Ana Carden-Coyne's *Reconstructing the Body: Classicism, Modernism, and the First World War* (2009) touches on some ways classical ideals were mobilised during and after the war, particularly in aesthetic contexts.

28   *Nation*, 29 May 1915.

29   *Nation*, 1 May 1915.

30   *Westminster Gazette*, 1 May 1915.

31   *Nation*, 1 May 1915.

32   *Muscular Opinion*, October 1918.

33   *Bookman*, 20 June 1915.

34   *Rugby Observer*, 18 June 1915.

35   RCB Xf/4, Poem included with Lawrence Binyon to Mary Brooke, 31 March 1917.

36   Hassall, *Marsh*, p. 341.

37   RCB Xd/3, Robert Whitelaw to Mary Brooke, undated letter.

38   RCB 11/Xe/i, Sir Francis Elliot to Marsh, 13 June 1915.

39   RCB 11/Xe/2, Mary Brooke to Elliot, 2 May 1917.

40   Hassall, *Marsh*, p. 343.

41   RCB 11/Xe/2, E. B. Hoare to Elliot, 16 April 1917.

42   RCB 11/Xe/2, Elliot to Mary Brooke, 4 June 1917.

43   RCB Xd/3, Robert Whitelaw to Mary Brooke, undated letter.

Notes to Chapter 14: Poet-soldiers

1   St Clair, *Reading Nation*, p. 1.
2   Winter, *The Great War and the British People* (1985), p. 285.
3   Brooke, 'III. The Dead', *1914 and Other Poems*.
4   Hynes, *War Imagined*, pp. 109–10.
5   Nils Clausson, '"Perpetuating the language": romantic tradition, the genre function, and the origins of the trench lyric', *Journal of Modern Literature* 30 (2006), 107.
6   New York Public Library, The Papers of Robert Graves [hereafter abbreviated as RG], Graves to Marsh, 22 May 1915.
7   RG, Graves to Marsh, 26 July 1915.
8   RG, Graves to Siegfried Sassoon, 25 April 1917.
9   RG, Graves to Marsh, 24 February 1916.
10 See Chapter 15 for further discussion of Sorley vis-à-vis Brooke.
11 Graves to Marsh, undated letter [January 1916], quoted in Hassall, *Marsh*, p. 380.
12 New York Public Library, The Papers of Isaac Rosenberg [hereafter abbreviated as IR], Isaac Rosenberg to Marsh, undated letter [August 1916].
13 *Times Literary Supplement*, 11 April 1915.
14 Dan Todman's *The Great War, Myth and Memory* (2005) discusses the ubiquity of the mud of the trenches of the Western Front as the assumed leitmotif of active service, to the detriment of other fronts and experiences.
15 *Liverpool Courier*, 23 April 1915.
16 Thomas, 'England', *English Review*, April 1915, p. 89.
17 Wilfred Owen to Leslie Gunston, 25 July 1915, in Harold Owen and John Bell, eds., *The Collected Letters of Wilfred Owen* (Oxford, 1967), p. 349.
18 Thomas, 'England', *English Review*, April 1915, p. 889.
19 Ibid., p. 97.
20 Bourke, *Dismembering*, pp. 127–28.
21 Owen, quoted in Tim Kendall, *Modern English War Poetry* (2006), p. 48.
22 Max Egremont, *Siegfried Sassoon* (2005), p. 229.
23 Brooke, 'I. Peace', *1914 and Other Poems*.
24 James Scott Campbell, '"For you may touch them not": misogyny, homosexuality, and the ethics of passivity in First World War poetry', *English Literary History* 64 (1997), p. 824.
25 *Millgate Monthly*, December 1915.
26 RG, Graves to Marsh, 9 February 1916.
27 RG, Graves to Sassoon, 26 August 1918.
28 Sassoon, quoted in Robert Richman, 'In Search of Edward Thomas', *New Criterion* 1 (1982), p. 13.
29 IR, Rosenberg to Marsh, undated letter [1917].

30 Seeger, *Letters and Diary*, p. 127.

31 See Miller, 'An American poet-soldier' and Chapter 16 for further discussion of Brooke's reputation in the United States.

32 *Bookman*, Special Christmas Number, 1917.

33 Imogen Gassert, 'In a foreign field: what they really read in the trenches', *Times Literary Supplement*, 10 May 2007, pp. 17–19.

34 IWM 86/46/1, E. G. de Caux, ed., The Notes of a French Interpreter.

35 Hynes, 'Personal Narratives and Commemoration', in Jay Winter and Emmanuel Sivan, eds., *War and Remembrance in the Twentieth Century* (1999), p. 207.

36 See Shafquat Towheed and Edmund G. C. King, Introduction, in Shafquat Towheed and Edmund G. C. King, eds., *Reading and the First World War: Readers, Texts, Archives* (2015), 1–25.

37 RG, Graves to Sassoon, undated letter, May 1916.

38 RG, Graves to Marsh, 18 March 1916.

39 IR, Rosenberg to Marsh, undated letter [1918].

40 Roland Leighton to Brittain, 22 May 1915 in Alan Bishop and Mark Bostridge, eds., *Letters from a Lost Generation* (1999), p. 111.

41 Brittain to Leighton, 29 July 1915, ibid., p. 135.

42 Leighton to Brittain, 2 August 1915, ibid., p. 138.

43 The Australian War Memorial Archive Centre, Canberra, The Chauvel Papers PR00535 Box 2 Series 4/10, Chauvel to Lady Chauvel, 21 July 1917.

44 The Australian War Memorial Archive Centre, Canberra, The Chauvel Papers, HC PR00535 Box 2 Series 4/10, Chauvel to Lady Chauvel, 9 September 1917. Many thanks to Dr James Kitchen for providing me with this reference.

45 RG, Graves to Marsh, 9 February 1916.

46 IWM 07/12/1, Andrew Stewart Fox, *Testament: From the Letters and Diary of Andrew Stewart Fox 1914–15*, p. 50.

47 Cambridge University Library, The First World War: A Documentary Record, Trench Journal Collection [hereafter abbreviated as CTJ] microfiche 43.2, reel 1, WRA 492, *Fifth Glo'ster Gazette*, No. 14 (September 1916).

48 When he returned to England for good after being invalided out of the front lines, Graves observed that 'England looked strange to us returned soldiers. We could not understand the war-madness that ran wild everywhere, looking for a pseudo-military outlet. The civilians talked a foreign language; and it was newspaper language. I found serious conversation with my parents all but impossible'. This may be read as a product of the complex situation of being a soldier who had directly confronted the war and was now forced into a semi-civilian existence, as opposed to a soldier on the front line, likely to be more forgiving of those on the home front

who had limited access the war. Still, it is interesting to note that Graves, like Sassoon, ran hot and cold in his assessment of civilians. Furthermore, it is important to remember that this is a retrospective account of the period: later, in the post-war years, for some the distance between soldier and home front widened, at least in memory. Graves, *Goodbye to All That* (1929), p. 237.

49   RG, Graves to Marsh, 12 July 1917.

50   Graves to Marsh, undated letter [1918], quoted in Hassall, *Marsh*, p. 446.

51   RG, Graves to Sassoon, 26 August 1918.

52   Sassoon, 15 June 1917, quoted in Egremont, *Sassoon*, pp. 143–44.

53   Ibid., p. 193.

54   The extent to which merchants in Britain benefited from their advertisements, placed in trench journals edited at the front and printed at home, remains unclear. Regardless, the trench journals were never commercial enterprises on the scale of the large dailies run out of London. See Chapter 4 for further consideration of their importance to the Brooke myth.

55   'The Wipers Times or Salient News', 20 March 1916, *Wipers Times* (2006), p. 45.

56   IR, Rosenberg to Marsh, 28 March 1918.

57   IR, Rosenberg to Marsh, undated letter [autumn 1917].

58   CTJ microfiche 43.2, reel 1, WRA 458, *British Prisoners of War*, 1.9 (September 1918).

59   CTJ microfiche 43.2, reel 1, WRA 458, *British Prisoners of War*, 1.1 (January 1918).

60   CTJ microfiche 43.2, reel 1, WRA 487, *Gasper: The Unofficial Organ of the BEF*, 26 June 1916.

61   CTJ microfiche 43.2, reel 1, WRA 488, *Listening Post: 7th Canadian Infantry Battalion*, 29 October 1915.

62   CTJ microfiche 43.2, reel 1, WRA 494, *Fifth Glo'ster Gazette*, No. 24 (September 1918).

63   *Liverpool Echo*, 3 January 1917.

64   RCB Xc/23, Pepys Cockerell to Mary Brooke, 14 April 1917.

65   IWM 07/12/1, Fox, *Testament*, p. 64.

66   *The Times*, 26 April 1915.

67   RCB Dalton Bequest, General Sir Ian Hamilton to Edward Marsh, 23 April 1915.

68   *The Times*, 29 March 1919.

69   Hamilton, *Gallipoli Diary: Volume 1* (1920), p. 125.

70   Hassall, *Brooke*, p. 527.

71   RG, Graves to Marsh, undated letter [October 1915].

72   *Daily Mirror*, 20 December 1915.

73   McCartney, *Citizen Soldiers*, p. 103.

Notes to Chapter 15: Careful Critics

1   Hynes, *Edwardian Turn*, p. 358.
2   RCB Xb/2, Inge, 'Why the dead shall live'.
3   Charles Sorley to his mother, 28 April 1915, in Jean Moorcroft Wilson, ed., *The Collected Letters of Charles Hamilton Sorley* (1990), pp. 218–19.
4   Sorley, Diary, 2 March 1913, *Collected Letters*, pp. 47–48.
5   Sorley to his mother, 28 April 1915, in Wilson, *Collected Letters*, pp. 218–19.
6   *Cambridge Review*, 30 April 1915.
7   *Morning Post*, 29 November 1915.
8   *Cambridge Review*, 1 May 1915.
9   *Cambridge Magazine*, 22 May 1915.
10 See Demoor, 'From Epitaph to Obituary'. For a further discussion of the commercialisation of Brooke and his poetry, see Chapter 4.
11 James Longenbach, *Stone Cottage: Pound, Yeats and Modernism* (1988), p. 114.
12 Yeats revised and retitled the poem 'On Being Asked for a War Poem' in 1919.
13 W. B. Yeats, 'A Reason for Keeping Silent', in Edith Wharton, ed., *The Book of the Homeless* (1916).
14 Yeats, quoted in Roy F. Foster, *W. B. Yeats: A Life* (2003), pp. 552–53.
15 Ezra Pound, 'Our Contemporaries', *Blast* 2 (July 1915), p. 21. The full text of the poem reads:

    When the Tahitian princess
    Heard that he had decided,
    She rushed out into the sunlight and swarmed up a coconut palm tree,
    But he returned to this island
    And wrote 90 Petrarchan sonnets.

16 Longenbach, *Stone Cottage*, p. 115.
17 Ezra Pound to Henry Ware Eliot, 28 June 1915, in Valerie Eliot, ed., *The Letters of T. S. Eliot, Volume 1, 1898–1922* (1988), p. 99.
18 See Deemor, 'Epitaph', p. 8 for a discussion of Eliot's obituary of James.
19 James, 'Preface', *Letters from America*, p. 41.
20 Ronald Schuchard, *Eliot's Dark Angel: Intersections of Life and Art* (1999), p. 18.
21 'I. Peace'; 'III. The Dead'; and 'V. The Soldier', in Harriet Monroe, ed., *Poetry: A Magazine of Verse* 4:1 (April 1915), pp. 18–19.
22 Harriet Monroe, 'Comments and Reviews: The Death of Rupert Brooke', *Poetry*, 6:3 (June 1915), p. 138.
23 Aruthur Davison Ficke, 'To Rupert Brooke', *Poetry* 6:3 (June 1915), pp. 113–16.

24 See Eliot's 'Prufrock' on pages 130–35 in the same edition as Ficke's poem, and Monroe's review on pages 136–38.

25 Eliot, 'Elizabethan Literature', syllabus for the Southall Tutorial Class, University of London Extension Board, 1915, reprinted in Schuchard, *Eliot's Dark Angel*, pp. 48–49.

26 Barry Faulk, 'Modernism and the Popular: Eliot's Music Halls', in *Modernism / Modernity* 8 (2001), pp. 603–604.

27 Ibid., p. 606.

28 Bracco, *Merchants*, p. 12.

29 *The Letters of T. S. Eliot, Volume 1*, p. 236.

30 Sidgwick anticipated problems with the poem when it was published in *Poems* (1911), which caught the condemning eye of some reviewers, even though the overall reception of the volume was positive. Marsh wrote to Brooke in December that although he found the poem 'clever and amusing … there are some things too disgusting to write about, especially in one's own language'. Hassall, *Brooke*, pp. 293–94.

31 Eliot to the *Egoist*, December 1917; *The Letters of T. S. Eliot, Volume 1*, p. 211.

32 Eliot to the Editor of the *Athenaeum*, 27 February 1920, *Athenaeum* 4687, p. 285, quoted in *The Letters of T. S. Eliot, Volume 1*, p. 369.

33 Lawrence Rainey, *Institutions of Modernism: Literary Elites and Public Culture* (1998), p. 39.

34 Lee, *Virginia Woolf* (1996), p. 291.

35 Mary Brooke to Marsh, 21 May 1915, quoted in Hassall, *Marsh*, p. 342.

36 Hassall, *Marsh*, p. 445.

37 *Cambridge Magazine*, 22 May 1915.

38 Woolf, 18 July 1918, in Anne Olivier Bell, ed., *The Diary of Virginia Woolf, Volume 1: 1915–1918* (1977), p. 170.

39 Saunders, *Self Impression*, p. 440.

40 Ibid., pp. 438–39.

41 *Echo*, 3 January 1917.

42 *Times Literary Supplement*, 8 August 1918.

43 Lee, *Virginia Woolf*, pp. 338–39.

44 *Standard*, 10 March 1916.

45 *Times Literary Supplement*, 8 August 1918.

46 Lee, *Virginia Woolf*, p. 289.

47 Marsh to Mary Brooke, January 1917, quoted in Hassall, *Marsh*, p. 424.

48 Woolf, 18 July 1918, *Diary, Volume 1*, p. 170.

49 Schuchard, *Eliot's Dark Angel*, p. 199.

50 RCB Xf/10, Virginia Woolf to Mary Brooke, 21 May 1918.

51 Alec W. G. Randall, 'Poetry and Patriotism', *Egoist*, 1 February 1916, p. 26.

52 Hassall, *Marsh*, p. 443.

53 Eliot, 'Dans l'Angleterre', *National Review Français*, May 1922, p. 617.

54 RCB Xd/1, S. E. Birrell, 'The Lost Keys', 1915.
55 *Cambridge Magazine*, 30 October 1915.
56 Marcia Pointon, *Portrayal and the Search for Identity* (2013), p. 28.
57 Diane Dillon and Christopher Reed, 'Looking and difference in the abstract portraits, Charles Demuth and Duncan Grant', *Yale Journal of Criticism* 11 (1998), p. 43.

Notes to Chapter 16: Export

1   *The Book of the Homeless* would go on to raise approximately $9,500 for Wharton's Belgian hostels. See Lee, *Edith Wharton* (2007), p. 493.
2   Wharton, *The Book of the Homeless*, p. x.
3   See Michael Saunders and Philip Taylor, *British Propaganda during the First World War, 1914–1918* (1982) for the fullest account of official efforts to coordinate and share information about the war internationally.
4   *Everywoman's Weekly*, August 1917.
5   IWM 114/560, 525.69, Second Report on the Work Conducted for the Government at Wellington House 1915.
6   *Aberdeen Free Press*, 8 March 1916.
7   George Edward Woodberry, 'Introduction', *The Collected Poems of Rupert Brooke* (1916), p. viii.
8   *Aberdeen Free Press*, 8 March 1916.
9   *Scotsman* (Edinburgh), 1 January 1916.
10 Margaret Lavington, 'Biographical Note', in *Collected Poems* (Toronto, 1915), p. 168.
11 *Glasgow Herald*, 1 January 1916.
12 Suzanne Evans, *Mothers of Heroes, Mothers of Heroes: World War One and the Politics of Grief* (2007), p. 44.
13 LG/D/17/2/1, Hamilton to David Lloyd George, 6 November 1916.
14 Jenny Macleod, *Reconsidering Gallipoli* (2004), p. 32.
15 In addition to Macleod, see also Bill Gammage, *The Broken Years: Australian Soldiers in the Great War* (1974) and John Lack, ed., *Anzac Remembered: Selected Writing of K. S. Inglis* (1998) for further discussion of the development and evolution of the Anzac myth in the Australian experience and memory of the First World War.
16 *Bulletin* (Sydney), 30 December 1915.
17 Macleod, *Reconsidering*, p. 5.
18 *Bulletin* (Sydney), 30 December 1915.
19 *Register* (Adelaide), 29 January 1919.
20 Gregory, '"You might as well recruit Germans": British Public Opinion and the Decision to Conscript the Irish in 1918', in Adrian Gregory and

Senia Pašeta, eds., *Ireland and the Great War: A War to Unite Us All?* (2002), p. 128.

21 *Irish Times*, May 1915.

22 David Lloyd George, Speech to the Ministers and the War Cabinet, 6 April 1918, quoted in Gregory, "'You might as well recruit Germans'", p. 123.

23 Roy Foster's assessment of the Uprising argues that it cannot be presented as a popular uprising but the result of the somewhat improvised actions of a core group of men and women, even as much as grievances and ideals motivating these individuals were long-standing and broadly shared by many Irish Catholics and Protestants alike. The real consensus about the Uprising formed after the event, and later formed around narratives that were heavily edited. See Foster, *Vivid Faces: The Revolutionary Generation in Ireland, 1890–1923* (2015).

24 Senia Pašeta, 'Thomas Kettle: "An Irish Soldier in the Army of Europe?"', in Gregory and Pašeta, *Ireland and the Great War*, p. 9.

25 *Irish Times*, May 1915.

26 Foster, *Paddy & Mr. Punch: Connections in Irish and English History* (1992), p. 279.

27 Gregory, "'You might as well recruit Germans'", p. 128.

28 Seán Farrell Moran, *Patrick Pearse and the Politics of Redemption* (1994), p. 336.

29 Brooke to Nesbitt, 25 December 1914, *LORB*, p. 642.

30 *Dundee Advertiser*, 17 February 1916.

31 CFGM 32/2/7/1–2, Masefield to Masterman, 8 January 1916.

32 CFGM 32/2/7/1–2, Masefield to Masterman, 31 January 1916.

33 CFGM 32/2/7/1–2, 'Final Report', Masefield to Masterman, 15 February 1916.

34 *Dundee Advertiser*, 17 February 1916.

35 *The Times*, 22 June 1916.

36 *Vanity Fair*, January 1916.

37 Rainey, *Institutions*, p. 95.

38 CFGM 32/2/7/1–2, Masefield to Masterman, 8 January 1916.

39 Ralph Waldo Emerson, 'English Traits', in Carl Bode, ed., *The Portable Emerson* (1981), p. 416.

40 *Globe and Commercial Advertiser*, 20 November 1915.

41 *Philadelphia Public Ledger*, 12 October 1918.

42 James, 'Preface', *Letters from America*, pp. 13–14.

43 CFGM 32/2/7/1–2, Masefield to Masterman, 8 January 1916.

44 CFGM 32/2/7/1–2, Masefield to Masterman, 31 January 1916.

45 Quoted in David Kennedy, *Over Here: The First World War and American Society* (1980), p. 23.

46 Stephen Vaughn, *Holding Fast the Inner Lines: Democracy, Nationalism and the Committee for Public Information* (1980), pp. 83–84.
47 George Creel, quoted in Coben, *Reform*, p. 92.
48 Menand, *The Metaphysical Club*, p. 418.
49 Hynes, *War Imagined*, p. 76.
50 *Globe and Commercial Advertiser*, 20 November 1915.
51 *New York Sun*, 6 February 1916.
52 *Globe and Commercial Advertiser*, 20 November 1915.
53 *Philadelphia North American*, 5 February 1916.
54 *New York Sun*, 6 February 1916.
55 *Louisville Courier Journal*, 14 February 1916.
56 *New York Sun*, 6 February 1916.
57 *Springfield Union*, 6 February 1916.
58 *Louisville Courier Journal*, 14 February 1916.
59 *Philadelphia Public Ledger*, 12 October 1918.
60 *Chicago Daily Tribune*, 12 February 1916.
61 Arthur Guy Empey, *'Over the Top' by an American Who Went* (1917), pp. 279–80.
62 *New York Times*, 12 September 1915.
63 *New York Times*, 26 December 1915.
64 *New York Times*, 22 April 1917.
65 From 1914 to 1918, the *New York Times* published 79 articles, reviews, and, primarily, advertisements dealing with Brooke, whereas *The Times* published 28.
66 *New York Times*, 13 November 1915.
67 *New York Times*, 20 and 28 November 1915, to name two examples; others exist, and the image was presumably reprinted in other newspapers and trade journals.
68 *New York Times*, 12 December 1915.
69 *New York Times*, 6 October 1918.
70 *New York Times*, 12 December 1915.
71 *New York Times*, 21 October 1917.
72 *New York Times*, 3 October 1915.
73 *New York Times*, 21 October 1917.
74 *New York Times*, 13 October 1918.
75 *New York Times*, 3 October 1915.
76 *New York Times*, 28 November 1915.
77 *New York Times*, 11 November 1917.
78 *Minneapolis Journal*, 11 September 1916.
79 Ficke, 'To Rupert Brooke', in *Poetry* 6:3 (June 1915), p. 114.
80 Browne published *Recollections of Rupert Brooke* in Chicago in 1927.
81 Ficke, 'Portrait of Rupert Brooke', *An April Elegy* (1917).
82 *New York Times*, 4 February 1916.

83   Rainey, *Institutions*, p. 39.
84   *The Dial*, March 1918.
85   Brooke, 'V. The Soldier', *1914 and Other Poems*.
86   *The Dial*, March 1918.
87   *The Times*, 7 May 1915.

Notes to the Conclusion

1   *The Times, 26 April 1915.*
2   James to Marsh, 6 June 1916, in Horne, *Henry James*, p. 548.
3   King, *Memorials*, p. 197.
4   Douie, *The Weary Road*, p. 11.
5   Thompson, *Hit Makers*, p. 93.

Bibliography

Manuscript and Archival Sources

The Australian War Memorial Archive Centre, Canberra
The Chauvel Papers

The Bodleian Library, Oxford
The Papers of Geoffrey Dawson

Cambridge University Library
The First World War: A Documentary Record, Trench Journal Collection
The Anzac Book: written and illustrated in Gallipoli by the men of Anzac (London, 1916).
Anzac Bulletin, Nos 78, 80–95 (London, 1918).
The AOC Workshops Gazette, No. 30 (n.p., 1918).
The Barncroft Magazine. D-Company No. 14 Officer Cadet Battalion (Catterick, 1918).
The Brazier. 16th Battalion. The Canadian Scottish, No. 1 (Bailleul, 1916).
Breath o' The Heather (OC 236h Bn CEF, Nos 3 and 7 (Valcantier, 1917).
The British Prisoner of War, Vol. 1, Nos 1–12 (London, 1918).
Chronicles of the NZEF, Vols 1–5 (London, 1916–19).
Chronicles of the White Horse (Queen's Own, Royal West Kent), Nos 2 and 3 (n.p., 1917).

The Dead Horse Corner Gazette. Canadian BEF, Nos 1–3, 28 (London, 1915–16).

The Fifth Glo'ster Gazette, Nos 13–16, 18–25, 31 (Gloucester, 1916–19).

The Gasper. The unofficial organ of the BEF, Nos 10, 12–21, 38 (Salisbury, 1915–16).

The Gehenna Gazette: being the summer members of the Hades Herald, the (un) official organ of the Inns of Court OTC (Berkhamstead, 1917).

The Gnome, Nos 2–5 (Cairo, 1917).

The Golden Horseshoe. The Journal of the 37th Division, BEF (London, 1919).

The Iodine Chronicle … No. 1 Canadian Field Ambulance, No. 5 (France, 1916).

The Journal of the Anti-Aircraft Corps, Nos 2, 3, 26 (London, 1917).

The Lead Swinger. The Bivouac Journal of the 1/3 West Riding Field Ambulances, 3 Vols (Sheffield, 1915–19).

The Listening Post. 7th Canadian Infantry Battalion, Nos 1–4, 6–8, 12–16, 19–32 (France, 1915–18).

The Mudhook, with which is incorporated 'Dardanelles Dug-Out Gossip', The Journal of the 63rd (RN) Division, Vol. 1, Nos 1 and 2 (Boulogne, 1917).

Now and Then, being the official organ of No. 3 Canadian Field Ambulance, 1st Canadian Division, BEF, No. 1 (Yeovil, 1915).

Pulham Patrol,Vol. 1, Nos 4, 5, 9, 10 (Pulham, 1917–18).

The Queen's Own Gazette (Royal West Kent Regiment), Vol. 35, Nos 4–9 (Maidstone, 1916).

The Salient. Being a seasonable supplement to the 6 corps magazine (At the Front, France, Christmas 1915).

The Tenedos Times. A monthly journal of the Mediterranean destroyer flotilla during the early part of the war (London, 1917).

The Thistle. Scottish Women's Hospitals for Foreign Service Souvenir Book, Vols 1 and 2 (Glasgow, 1916–17).

Ultimus Magazine. D-Company 14th Officer Cadet Battalion (Catterick, 1918–19).

Harvard University, Houghton Library

The Papers of Alan Seeger

The House of Lords, Westminster, London

The Papers of David Lloyd George

Imperial War Museum, London

Baylis, John., ed., Antwerp Diary of H. P. Baylis, 06/49/1.

de Caux, E. G., ed., The Notes of a French Interpreter, 86/46/1.

Clark, Captain Sir George N., ed., Narrative of the First Battalion, The Post Office Rifles, 8th Battalion, The London Regiment in France and Flanders 1915–18, 88/52/1.

Fox, Andrew Stewart, Testament: From the Letters and Diary of Andrew Stewart Fox 1914–15, 07/12/1.

O'Sullivan, Vincent (transl.), *Rupert Brooke's Death and Burial* (New York and London, 1917), 94/2723.

Schedule of Literature for Wellington House, 1915–1916, 114/560, 525.69.

King's College, Cambridge, Archive Centre
The Papers of Rupert Chawner Brooke

New York Public Library, The Berg Collection
The Papers of Isaac Rosenberg
The Papers of Robert Graves
The Papers of T. E. Hulme

The Times Archive, London (proofs courtesy of Nicholas Mayes)

The University of Birmingham, Special Collections
The Papers of C. F. G. Masterman

Newspapers and Periodicals

Aberdeen Free Press
Amateur Photographed and Photographic News
Birkenhead News
Birmingham Gazette
Birmingham Mail
Bristol
Bulletin (Sydney)
Chicago Daily Tribune
Christian Science Monitor
Christian World Pulpit
Daily Chronicle
Daily Citizen
Daily Mail
Daily Mirror
Daily News
Daily News and Leader

Daily Sketch
Daily Telegraph
Dewsbury Reporter
Dundee Advertiser
Echo
Everywoman's Weekly
Free Thinker
Glasgow Citizen
Glasgow Herald
Glasgow News
Globe
Globe and Commercial Advertiser
Graphic
Illustrated London News
Irish Times
Liverpool Courier
Liverpool Echo
Liverpool Post
Louisville Courier Journal
Manchester Guardian
Minneapolis Journal
Morning Post
Morning Post (New York)
Muscular Opinion
Musical Opinion
Nation
New Witness
New York Sun
New York Times
Newcastle Daily Chronicle
Northampton Mercury
Pall Mall Gazette
Philadelphia North American
Philadelphia Public Ledger
Public Opinion
Punch
Register (Adelaide)
Reptorian
Rugby Observer
Scotsman
Sheffield Daily Telegraph
Sketch
Spectator

Sphere
Springfield Union
Standard
Star
Sunday Chronicle (Manchester)
Sunderland Echo
T.P.'s Weekly
The Times
Times Literary Supplement
Town Topics
Westminster Gazette

Journals, Magazines, and Periodicals

Athenaeum
Book Monthly
Bookman
Cambridge Magazine
Cambridge Review
Contemporary Review
Country Life
Dial
Egoist
English Review
Land and Water
Mercure de France
Millgate Monthly
National Review Français
New Republic
New Statesman
Oxford Magazine
Poetry: A Magazine of Verse
Poetry Review
Vanity Fair

Printed Primary Sources

Barker, Pat, *Toby's Room* (2012).
Baron, Alexander, *From the City, From the Plough* (2010 [1948]).
Bell, Anne Olivier, ed., *The Diary of Virginia Woolf, Volume 1: 1915–1918* (1977).

Bishop, Alan and Mark Bostridge, eds., *Letters from a Lost Generation* (1999).

Blunden, Edmund, *Undertones of War* (1928).

Brittain, Vera, *Chronicle of Youth* (2000).

Brooke, Rupert, *1914 and Other Poems* (1915).

——. *The Collected Poems with a Memoir by Edward Marsh* (1918).

——. *John Webster and the Elizabethan Drama* (1916).

——. *Letters from America* (1916).

——. *Poems* (1911).

——. *Selected Poems* (1917).

Browne, Maurice, *Recollections of Rupert Brooke* (1929).

Clutton-Brock, A., 'Sweden and the Anglo-Russian Alliance' (1915).

A Crown of Amaranth (1915).

Dawson, Geoffrey, *The Christian Year in 'The Times'* (1930).

de la Mare, Walter, *Rupert Brooke and the Intellectual Imagination* (1919).

Douie, Charles, *The Weary Road* (1929).

Eliot, T. S., 'A Note on War Poetry', in *London Calling* (1942).

——. 'Dans l'Angleterre', *National Review Français*, May 1922, p. 617.

Eliot, Valerie, ed., *The Letters of T. S. Eliot, Volume 1, 1898–1922* (1988).

Emerson, Ralph Waldo, 'English Traits', in Carl Bode, ed., *The Portable Emerson* (1981), pp. 395–518.

——. 'The Poet', in Carl Bode, ed., *The Portable Emerson* (1981), pp. 241–65.

Empey, Aruthur Guy, *'Over the Top' by an American Who Went* (1917).

The English Association, *Poems of To-day: An Anthology* (1916, 1917, 1920).

Ervine, St John G., *Changing Winds* (1917).

Fisher, H. A. L., *British Universities and the War: A Record and its Meaning* (1917).

Ford, Ford Maddox, *Parade's End* (1950).

Fowles, John, *The Magus* (1966).

Freud, Sigmund, *On Murder, Mourning and Melancholia* (2005).

Friedman, Melvin J. and Thomas L. Scott, eds., *The Letters of Ezra Pound to Margaret Anderson: The Little Review Correspondence* (1988).

Georgian Poetry, 1911–1912 (1912).

Graves, Robert, *Fairies and Fusiliers* (1917).

——. *Goodbye to All That* (1929).

Hale, Keith, ed., *Friends and Apostles: The Correspondence of Rupert Brooke and James Strachey, 1905–1914* (1998).

Hamilton, General Sir Ian, *Gallipoli Diary: Volume 1* (1920).

Horne, Philip, ed., *Henry James: A Life in Letters* (London, 1999).

Huxley, Gervas, *Both Hands: An Autobiography* (1970).

Ireland, John, *The Soldier* [musical score] (1917).

Jones, David, *In Parenthesis* (1937).

Kernahan, Coulson, *The Experiences of a Recruiting Officer: True Pictures of Splendid Patriotism* (1915).

Keynes, Geoffrey, ed., *The Letters of Rupert Brooke* (1968).

——. *Rupert Brooke: The Poetical Works* (1946).

Marsh, Edward, 'Memoir', in Marsh, ed., *Rupert Brooke: The Collected Poems* (1918).

Masefield, John, *Gallipoli* (1916).

Monroe, Harriet, 'Comments and Reviews: The Death of Rupert Brooke', *Poetry*, 6:3 (June 1915).

Murray, Gilbert, *Essays and Addresses* (1921).

——. 'How Can War Ever Be Right?', *Oxford Pamphlets* (1914).

Noakes, Vivian, *Voices of Silence: The Alternative Book of First World War Poetry* (2006).

The Office of *The Times*, *The History of 'The Times', Part I, Chapters I–XII, 1912–1920* (1952).

Owen, Harold and John Bell, eds., *The Collected Letters of Wilfred Owen* (1967).

Oxenham, John, *'All's Well!' Some Helpful Verse for these Dark Days of War* (1915).

——. *Bees in Amber: A Little Book of Thoughtful Verse* (1913).

——. *1914* (1916).

Pottle, Mark, ed., *Champion Redoubtable: The Diary and Letters of Violet Bonham Carter, 1914–1945* (1998).

Quiller-Couch, Arthur, ed., *The Oxford Book of Victorian Verse* (1912).

Rosenberg, Isaac, *Poems* (1920).

Russell, Bertrand, *The Autobiography of Bertrand Russell, Volume 2: 1914–1944* (1971).

Sassoon, Siegfried, *Memoirs of a Fox Hunting Man* (1928).

——. *Memoirs of an Infantry Officer* (1930).

——. *Old Huntsman and Other Poems* (1917).

Seeger, Alan, *Letters and Diary of Alan Seeger* (1917).

Stallworthy, Jon, ed., *The Oxford Book of War Poetry* (2003).

Thomas, Edward, *The Heart of England* (1906).

Tillyard, Aelfrida, ed., *Cambridge Poets, 1900–1913, An Anthology* (1913).

Vansittart, Peter, ed., *John Masefield's Letters from the Front* (1984).

Verhaeren, Emile, *Les Ailes rouge de la guerre* (1916).

Wharton, Edith, ed., *The Book of the Homeless* (1916).

Wilson, Jean Moorcroft, ed., *The Collected Letters of Charles Hamilton Sorley* (1990).

Wilson, W. N., *Rugby School Memorial Chapel* (1923).

The Wipers Times (2006).

Woolf, Virginia, *Jacob's Room* (1922).

——. 'Rupert Brooke', in Andrew McNiellie, ed., *The Essays of Virginia Woolf, Volume 2* (1987), pp. 277–83.

Yeats, W. B., ed., *The Oxford Book of Modern Verse* (Oxford, 1936).

Printed Secondary Texts

Amis, Kingsley, *Rudyard Kipling and his Work* (1975).

Anderson, Benedict, *Imagined Communities: Reflections on the Origin and Spread of Nationalism* (1991).

Anderson, Olive, *A Liberal State at War: English Politics and Economics during the Crimean War* (1967).

Ankersmit, Frank, *Historical Representation* (2001).

Audoin-Rouzeau, Stéphane, *Men at War, 1914–1918: National Sentiment and Trench Journalism in France during the First World War*, Helen McPhail, transl. (1992).

Audoin-Rouzeau, Stéphane and Annette Becker, *1914–1918: Understanding the Great War*, Catherine Temerson, transl. (2002).

Beaven, Brad, *Leisure, Citizenship and Working-Class Men* (2005).

Becker, Annette, *Apollinaire: une biographie de guerre* (2009).

Behlman, Lee, 'From Ancient to Victorian Cultural Studies: Assessing Foucault', *Victorian Poetry* 42 (2003), 559–69.

Benjamin, Walter, *On Photography*, Esther Leslie, tranls., ed. (2015).

Bergonzi, Bernard, *Heroes' Twilight: A Study of the Literature of the Great War* (1980).

Blanning, T. C. W and David Cannadine, eds., *History and the Media: Essays in Honour of Derek Beales* (1996).

Blunden, Edmund, *Thomas Hardy* (1941).

Bogacz, Ted, 'A Tyranny of Words', *Journal of Modern History* 58 (1986), pp. 643–68.

Bond, Brian, *The Unquiet Western Front: Britain's Role in Literature and History* (2002).

Bourdieu, Pierre, *Ce que parler veut dire: l'économie des exchange linguistique* (1982).

——. *The Logic of Practice*, Richard Nice, transl. (1990).

Bourke, Joanna, *Dismembering the Male: Men's Bodies, Britain and the Great War* (1996).

Bourne, John, *Britain and the Great War* (1989).

Bowra, C. M., *Poetry and Politics, 1900–1960* (1966).

Bracco, Rosa Marie, *Merchants of Hope: British Middlebrow Writers and the First World War, 1919–1939* (1993).

Bradbury, Malcolm, 'The Telling Life: Some Thoughts on Literary Biography', in Eric Homberger and John Charmley, eds., *The Troubled Face of Biography* (1988), 131–40.

Bradshaw, David, Laura Marcus and Rebeccca Roach, eds., *Moving Modernisms: Motion, Technology and Modernity* (2016).

Brett, Gary, *Nervous Liberals: Propaganda Anxieties from World War I to the Cold War* (1999).

Brockington, Grace, *Above the Battlefield: Modernism and the Peace Movement in Britain, 1900–1918* (2010).

Brown, Malcolm, *The Imperial War Museum Book of 1914: The Men Who Went to War* (2004).

Buitenhuis, Peter, *The Great War of Words: British, American and Canadian Propaganda and Fiction, 1914–1933* (1987).

Campbell, James Scott, "'For you may touch them not': Misogyny, Homosexuality, and the Ethics of Passivity in First World War Poetry', *English Literary History* 64 (1997), 823–42.

Cannadine, David, *Class in Britain* (1998).

——. ed., *History and the Media* (2004).

——. 'War and Death, Grief and Mourning in Modern Britain', in Joachim Whaley, ed., *Mirrors of Mortality: Studies in the Social History of Death* (1981), 187–242.

Capdevilla, Luc and Danièle Voldman, eds., *War Dead: Western Societies and the Casualties of War* (2006).

Carden-Coyne, Ana, *Reconstructing the Body: Classicism, Modernism, and the First World War* (2009).

Carrington, Charles, *Rudyard Kipling: His Life and Work* (1955).

Carsten, F. L., *War Against War: British and German Radical Movements during the First World War* (1982).

Cecil, Hugh, *The Flower of Battle* (1996).

Cecil, Hugh and Peter Liddle, eds., *Facing Armageddon: The First World War Experienced* (1996).

Clausson, Nils, "'Perpetuating the language': Romantic Tradition, the Genre Function, and the Origins of the Trench Lyric', *Journal of Modern Literature* 30 (2006), pp. 104–28.

Coben, Stanley, *Reform, War and Reaction: 1912–1932* (1972).

Cocks, H. A., "'Sporty' Girls and 'Artistic' Boys: Friendship, Illicit Sex, and the British 'Companionship' Advertisement, 1913–1928', *Journal of the History of Sexuality* 11 (2002), pp. 457–82.

Coker, Christopher, *Waging War without Warriors? The Changing Culture of Military Conflict* (2002).

Connelly, Mark, *The Great War, Memory and Ritual Commemoration in the City and East London* (2002).

Cork, Richard, *A Bitter Truth: Avant-garde Art and the First World War* (1994).

Cross, Tim, ed., *The Lost Voices of World War I* (1998).

Das, Santanu, ed., *The Cambridge Companion to the Poetry of the First World War* (2013).

——. *Race, Empire and First World War Writing* (2011).

——. *Touch and Intimacy in First World War Literature* (2005).

Davie, Donald, 'Poet: Patriot: Interpreter', in W. J. T. Mitchell, ed., *The Politics of Interpretation* (1983), 33–49.

DeBell, Diane, 'Strategies for Survival: Robert Graves, *Goodbye to All That*, and David Jones, *In Parenthesis*', in Holger Klein, ed., *The First World War in Fiction* (1972), 160–73.

Delaney, Paul, *Fatal Glamour: The Life of Rupert Brooke* (2015).

——. *The Neo-Pagans: Friendship and Love in the Rupert Brooke Circle* (1987).

Demoor, Marysa, 'From Epitaph to Obituary: The Death Politics of T. S. Eliot and Ezra Pound', *Biography* 28 (2005), pp. 255–75.

——. *Marketing the Author: Authorial Personae, Narrative Selves and Self Fashioning, 1880–1930* (2004).

Diani, Mario and Doug McAdams, eds., *Social Movements and Networks: Relational Approaches to Collective Action* (2003).

Dillon, Diane and Christopher Reed, 'Looking and Difference in the Abstract Portraits of Charles Demuth and Duncan Grant', *Yale Journal of Criticism* 11 (1998), pp. 39–51.

Douglas, Roy, *The Great War, 1914–1918: The Cartoonists' Vision* (1995).

Doyle, Barry M., 'Religion, Politics and Remembrance: A Free Church Community and its Great War Dead', in Martin Evans and Ken Lunn, ed., *War and Memory in the Twentieth Century* (1997), 222–38.

Edwards, Ruth Dudley, *Patrick Pearse: Triumph and Failure* (1979).

Egremont, Max, *Siegfried Sassoon* (2005).

Eksteins, Modris, *Rites of Spring: The Great War and the Birth of the Modern Age* (1990).

Evans, Suzanne, *Mothers of Heroes, Mothers of Martyrs: World War One and the Politics of Grief* (2007).

Faulk, Barry, 'Modernism and the Popular: Eliot's Music Halls', *Modernism / Modernity* 8 (2001), 602–21.

Ferguson. Niall, *The Pity of War* (1998).

Field, Frank, *British and French Writers of the First World War: Comparative Studies in Cultural History* (1991).

Foster, Roy, *Paddy & Mr. Punch: Connections in Irish and English History* (1992).

——. *Vivid Faces: The Revolutionary Generation in Ireland, 1890–1923* (2015).

——. *W. B. Yeats: A Life* (2003).

Freeden, Michael, *Liberalism Divided: A Study in British Political Thought 1914–1939* (1986).

Fuller, John G., *Troop Morale and Popular Culture in the British and Dominion Forces, 1914–1918* (1988).

Fussell, Paul, *The Great War and Modern Memory* (2000).

Gammage, Bill, *The Broken Years: Australian Soldiers in the Great War* (1974).

Gassert, Imogen, 'In a foreign field: what they really read in the trenches', *Times Literary Supplement*, 10 May 2007, pp. 17–19.

Gerwarth, Robert, *The Vanquished: Why the First World War Failed to End* (2016).

Gilbert, Martin, *Winston S. Churchill, Volume 3, 1914–1916* (1971).

Gilmour, David, *The Long Recessional: The Imperial Life of Rudyard Kipling* (2003).

Goebel, Stefan, *The Great War and Medieval Memory: War, Remembrance and Medievalism in Britain and Germany, 1914–1940* (2007).

——. *Medievalism in the Commemoration of the Great War in Britain and Germany, 1914–1939* (2001).

Greenblatt, Stephen, *Renaissance Self-Fashioning from More to Shakespeare* (2005).

Gregory, Adrian, 'British "War Enthusiasm" in 1914: A Reassessment', in Gail Braybon, ed., *Evidence, History and the Great War: Historians and the Impact of 1914–1918* (2003), 67–85.

——. 'A Clash of Cultures: The British Press and the Opening of the Great War', in Troy Paddock, ed., *A Call to Arms: Propaganda, Public Opinion, and Newspapers in the Great War* (2004), 15–49.

Gregory, Adrian and Senia Pašeta, eds., *Ireland and the Great War: A War to Unite Us All?* (2002).

——. *The Last Great War* (2008).

——. *The Silence of Memory: Armistice Day, 1919–1946* (1994).

Griggs, John, 'Nobility & War: The Unselfish Commitment', *Encounter* 74.2 (1990), 21–27.

Guhu, Ramachandra, *A Corner of a Foreign Field: The Indian History of a British Sport* (2002).

Gullace, Nicoletta, 'The Blood of Our Sons': Men, Women and the Renegotiation of British Citizenship during the Great War* (2002).

Haley, Sir William, 'Rest in Prose: The Art of the Obituary', *American Scholar* 46 (1977), 206–11.

Hammond, Mary, *Reading, Publishing and the Formation of Literary Taste in England, 1880–1914* (2006).

Hammond, Mary and Shafquart Towhead, eds., *Publishing in the First World War: Essays in Book History* (2007).

Harlen, David, 'Intellectual history and the death of the author', *American Historical Review* 94.3 (1989), pp. 581–609.

Hassall, Christopher, *Edward Marsh: Patron of the Arts* (1959).

——. *Rupert Brooke: A Biography* (1964).

Haste, Cate, *Keep the Home Fires Burning: Propaganda in the First World War* (1977).

Havighurst, Alfred F., *Radical Journalist: H. W. Massingham, 1860–1924* (1974).

Hibberd, Dominic, ed., *Strange Meetings: Poems by Harold Monro* (2003).

Higgens, Trumbell, *Winston Churchill and the Dardanelles* (1963).

Hirschfeld, Gerhard, Gerd Krumeich, Irina Renz and Markus Pohlmam, eds., *Enzyklopädie Erster Weltkrieg* (2003).

Hobsbawn, Eric J., *Nations and Nationalism since 1980: Programme, Myth and Reality* (1990).

Horne, John, ed., *State, Society and Mobilization in Europe during the First World War* (1997).

Horne, John and Alan Kramer, *German Atrocities 1914: A History of Denial* (2001).

Hynes, Samuel, *The Edwardian Turn of Mind* (1968).

——. 'Personal Narratives and Commemoration', in Jay Winter and Emmanuel Sivan, eds., *War and Remembrance in the Twentieth Century* (1999), 205–20.

——. *A War Imagined: The First World War and English Culture* (1990).

James, Robert R., *Gallipoli* (1965).

Jarrold, Douglas, *The Royal Naval Division* (1923).

Jaylland, Pat, *Death in the Victorian Family* (1996).

Jones, Max, *The Last Great Quest: Captain Scott's Antarctic Sacrifice* (2003).

Jones, Nigel, *Rupert Brooke: Life, Death & Myth* (1999).

Kendall, Tim, *Modern English War Poetry* (2006).

Kennedy, David, *Over Here: The First World War and American Society* (1980).

Kermode, Frank, *Poetry, Narrative and History* (1990).

Kershaw, Ian, *The Hitler Myth: Image and Reality in the Third Reich* (2001).

King, Alex, *Memorials of the Great War in Britain: The Symbolism and Politics of Remembrance* (1998).

Kitchen, James, *The British Imperial Army in the Middle East* (2015).

Kramer, Alan, *Dynamic of Destruction: Culture and Mass Killing in the First World War* (2007).

Lack, John, ed., *Anzac Remembered: Selected Writings of K. S. Inglis* (1998).

Lamont, Corliss, *Remembering John Masefield* (1971).

Laqueur, Thomas, 'Memory and Naming in the Great War', in John R. Gillis, ed., *Commemorations: The Politics of National Identity* (1994), 150–67.

Le Naour, Jean-Yves, *The Living Unknown Soldier: A Story of Grief and the Great War*, Penny Allen, transl. (2005).

Lee, Hermione, *Edith Wharton* (2007).

——. *Virginia Woolf* (1996).

Leed, Eric, *No Man's Land: Combat and Identity in Word War One* (1979).

Lehmann, John, *Rupert Brooke: His Life & Legend* (1980).

Leps, Marie-Christine, 'Critical Productions of Discourse: Angenot, Bahktin, Foucault', *Yale Journal of Criticism* 17 (2004), pp. 263–86.

Levenson, Michael, ed., *The Cambridge Companion to Modernism* (1999).

Lewis, Pericles, 'The Politics of Modernism', *Modern Fiction Studies* 46.4 (2000), pp. 959–65.

Liddiard, Jean, ed., *Isaac Rosenberg: Poetry Out of my Head and Heart* (2007).

——. *Isaac Rosenberg: Selected Poems and Letters* (2003).

Liddle, Peter H., *Gallipoli 1915: Pens, Pencils and Cameras at War* (1985).

Lloyd, David and Paul Thomas, *Culture and the State* (1998).

Lodge, David, 'Modernism, Antimodernism and Postmodernism', in Paul Keegan, ed., *Working with Structuralism* (1981), 3–16.

Longenbach, James, *Stone Cottage: Pound, Yeats and Modernism* (1988).

McAleer, Joseph, *Reading and Publishing in Britain, 1914–1950* (1992).

McCartney, Helen, *Citizen Soldiers: The Liverpool Territorials in the First World War* (2005).

Macleod, Jenny, 'General Sir Ian Hamilton and the Dardanelles Commission', *War in History* 8 (2001), pp. 418–41.

——. *Reconsidering Gallipoli* (2004).

McNicol, Jean, 'Something Rather Scandalous', *London Review of Books* 38: 20 (October 2016), pp. 19–22.

Manela, Erez, *The Wilsonian Moment: Self-Determination and the International Origins of Anti-Colonial Nationalism* (2003).

Mangan, J. A. and James Walvin, eds., *Manliness and Morality: Middle-class Masculinity in Britain and American, 1800–1940* (1987).

Marsland, Elizabeth, *A Nation's Cause: French, English and German Poetry of the First World War* (1991).

Marwick, Arthur, *The Deluge* (2006).

Marwill, Jonathan, *Visiting Modern War in Risorgimento Italy* (2010).

Mattingly, Garrett, *Renaissance Diplomacy* (1955).

Menand, Louis, *The Metaphysical Club* (2001).

Millard, Kenneth, *Edwardian Poetry* (1991).

Miller, Alisa, '"An American soldier-poet": Alan Seeger and war culture in the United States, 1914–1918', *First World War Studies* 1:1 (2010), pp. 15–33.

Money, David, 'Free Flattery or Servile Tribute? Oxford and Cambridge Commemorative Poetry in the Seventeenth and Eighteenth Centuries', in James Raven, ed., *Free Print and Non-Commercial Publishing since 1700* (2000), 48–66.

Moran, Seán Farrell, *Patrick Pearse and the Politics of Redemption* (1994).

Moriarty, Catherine, 'Private Grief and Public Remembrance: British First World War Memorials', in Martin Evans and Ken Lunn, ed., *War and Memory in the Twentieth Century* (1997), 125–42.

Mosley, Nicholas, *Julian Grenfell* (1999).

Mosse, George L., *Fallen Soldiers: Reshaping the Memory of the World Wars* (1990).

Nora, Pierre, *Realms of Memory: The Construction of the French Past* (1992).

Oliver, Lois, 'Chatterton', in Alexander Sturgis, Rupert Christiansen, Lois Oliver and Michael Wilson, eds., *Rebels and Martyrs: The Image of the Artist in the Nineteenth Century* (2006), 83–84.

Paddock, Troy, ed., *A Call to Arms: Propaganda, Public Opinion, and Newspapers in the Great War* (2004).

Pakenham, Thomas, *The Boer War* (1979).

Palmer, Svetlana and Sarah Walis, eds., *A War in Words* (2003).

Paris, Michael, *Warrior Nation: Images of War in British Popular Culture, 1850–2000* (2000).

Peel, Robin, *Apart from Modernism: Edith Wharton, Politics and Fiction before World War One* (2005).

Petrucci, Armando, *Writing the Dead: Death and Writing Strategies in the Western Tradition* (1998).

Pfaff, William, *The Bullet's Song: Romantic Violence and Utopia* (2004).

Pointon, Marcia, *Portrayal and the Search for Identity* (2013).

Porter, Patrick, 'Slaughter or Sacrifice? The Religious Rhetoric of Blood Sacrifice in the British and German Armies, 1914–1918', University of Oxford, DPhil. thesis, 2005.

Prior, Robin, *Churchill's World Crisis as History* (1983).

Rainey, Lawrence, *Institutions of Modernism: Literary Elites and Public Culture* (1998).

Reed, Christopher, *Bloomsbury Rooms: Modernism, Subculture and Domesticity* (2004).

Richman, Robert, 'In search of Edward Thomas', *New Criterion* 1 (1982), pp. 1–16.

Robert, Jean-Louis, 'The Image of the Profiteer', in Jay Winter and Jean Louis Robert, eds., *Capital Cities at War: Paris, London, Berlin 1914–1919, Volume 1* (1997), 104–32.

Rogers, Timothy, *Rupert Brooke: A Reassessment* (1971).

Rousso, Henry, *The Vichy Syndrome: History & Memory in France since 1944* (1991).

Rozario, Kevin, '"Delicious Horrors": Mass Culture, The Red Cross and the Appeal of Modern American Humanism', *American Quarterly* 55.3 (2003), pp. 417–55.

St Clair, William, *The Reading Nation in the Romantic Period* (2004).

Samuel, Raphael, ed., *Patriotism: The Making and Unmaking of British Identity, Volume 3: National Fictions* (1989).

Saunders, Max, *Self Impression: Life-Writing, Autobiografiction and the Forms of Modern Literature* (2010).

Saunders, Michael and Philip Taylor, *British Propaganda during the First World War, 1914–1918* (1982).

Schama, Simon, *Landscape and Memory* (1995).

Schuchard, Ronald, *Eliot's Dark Angel: Intersections of Life and Art* (1999).

Schwartz, Vanessa, *Spectacular Realities: Early Mass Culture in Fin-de-Siècle Paris* (1998).

Sellers, Leonard, *The Hood Battalion, Royal Naval Division: Antwerp, Gallipoli, France 1914–1918* (1995).

Sharp, Kevin, 'Representations and Negotiations: Texts, Images and Authority in Early Modern England' *Historical Journal* 42.3 (1999), pp. 853–81.

Sheehan, James. J., *Where Have All the Soldiers Gone? The Transformation of Modern Europe* (2008).

Sheffield, Gary P., *Forgotten Victory* (2001).

——. 'The Shadow of the Somme: The Influence of the First World War on British Soldiers' Perceptions and Behaviour in the Second World War', in Paul Addison and Angus Calder, eds., *Time to Kill: The Soldiers' Experience in the West, 1939–1945* (1997), 29–39.

Sherman, Daniel J., *The Construction of Memory in Interwar France* (1999).

Showalter, Denis E., 'Manoeuvre War', in Hew Strachan, ed., *The Oxford Illustrated History of the First World War* (1998), 39–53.

Sivan, Emmanuel and Jay Winter, *War and Remembrance in the Twentieth Century* (1999).

Smith, Leonard V., *The Embattled Self: French Soldiers Testimony of the Great War* (2007).

Stamp, Gavin, *The Memorial to the Missing of the Somme* (2006).

Stephen, Martin, *The Price of Pity: Poetry, History and Myth in the Great War* (1996).

Stevens, Paul, 'Pretending to be real: Stephen Greenblatt and the legacy of popular existentialism', *New Literary History* 33 (2002), 491–519.

Stevenson, David, *Cataclysm: The First World War as Political Tragedy* (2004).

Stevenson, John, *British Society 1914–1945* (1984).

Stock, Paul, *The Shelly-Byron Circle and the Idea of Europe* (London, 2010).

Strachan, Hew, *The First World War: To Arms, Volume 1* (Oxford, 2001).

Stromberg, Roland N., *Redemption by War: The Intellectuals and 1914* (1982).

Takács, Adám, 'Between theory & history: on the interdisciplinary practice in Michel Foucault's work', *Modern Language Notes* 119.4 (2004), pp. 869–84.

Thompson, Derek, *Hitmakers: How Things Become Popular* (2017).

Todman, Dan, *The Great War, Myth and Memory* (2005).

——. '"Sans peur et sans reproche": The Retirement, Death and Mourning of Sir Douglas Haig, 1918–1928', *Journal of Modern History* 67.4 (2003), pp. 1083–106.

Toews, John E., 'Intellectual history after the linguistic turn', *American Historical Review* 92.4 (1987), pp. 879–907.

Towheed, Shafquat and Edmund G. C. King, eds., *Reading and the First World War: Readers, Texts, Archives* (2015).

Vaughn, Stephen, *Holding Fast the Inner Lines: Democracy, Nationalism and the Committee for Public Information* (1980).

Waites, Bernard, *A Class Society at War: England 1914–1918* (1987).

Waller, Philip, *Writers, Readers and Reputations: Literary Life in Britain 1870–1918* (2006).

Walworth, Arthur, *Woodrow Wilson* (1965).

Watney, Simon, *The Art of Duncan Grant* (1998).

Waugh, Joan, '"Pageantry of Woe": The Funeral of Ulysses S. Grant', *Civil War History* 51.2 (2005), pp. 151–74.

Whalen, Robert W., *Bitter Wounds: German Victims of the Great War 1914–1939* (1984).

White, Hayden, *Metahistory* (1973).

Whittier-Ferguson, John, 'Stein in Time: History, Manuscripts and Memory', *Modernism / Modernity* 6.1 (1999), pp. 115–51.

Wilson, Duncan, *Gilbert Murray, OM, 1866–1957* (1987).

Wilson, Edmund, *Eight Essays* (1954).

Winter, Jay, *The Great War and the British People* (1985).

Winter, Jay and Jean-Louis Robert, eds., *Capital Cities at War: Paris, London, Berlin1914–1919, Volume 2: A Cultural History* (2007).

——. 'Introduction: Henri Barbusse and the Birth of the Moral Witness', in Henri Barbusse, *Under Fire* (2003), vii–xix.

——. 'Popular Culture in Wartime Britain', in Aviel Roshwald and Richard Stites, eds., *European Culture in Wartime Britain: The Arts, Entertainment and Propaganda, 1914–1918* (1999), 330–48.

——. *Remembering War: The Great War between Memory and History in the Twentieth Century* (2006).

——. *Sites of Memory, Sites of Mourning: The Great War in European Cultural History* (1995).

Wohl, Robert, *The Generation of 1914* (1979).

Wolf, John, *Great Deaths: Grieving, Religion and Nationhood in Victorian and Edwardian Britain* (2000).

Woollacott, Angela, '"Khaki fever" and its control: gender, class, age and sexual morality on the British home front in the First World War', *Journal of Contemporary History* 29 (1994), pp. 325–47.

Wrench, John Evelyn, *Geoffrey Dawson and Our Times* (1955).

Index

275